OVERNIGHT
FATHER

A Secret Relationship, Hidden Pregnancy,
and a Premature Baby that Built Character and
Changed the Narrative

NICHOLAS   J.   WEDLOW

Published by University of Moguls Publishing and Design

Cover design, editing, formatting, and layout by University of Moguls Publishing and Desi₢
www.universityofmoguls.com

ISBN-13: 978-1-7366581-1-6

For speaking engagements and bulk book orders:
Nicholas J. Wedlow
nicholasjwedlow@gmail.com

Website:
www.nicholasjwedlow.com

Instagram and Facebook:
@NicholasJWedlow
@UnfalteringFathers

Twitter:
@njwedlow

This memoir is presented to you by:
Unfaltering Fathers LLC

Disclaimer

This book is based on a true story. This is my recollection of events. Some text is copied verbatim from personal correspondences. Some characters' names have been changed, merged, and documents have been redacted to protect the innocent and the guilty.

I would like to thank the real-life members, characters, and all of their family members who are portrayed in this book. They all are fine, decent, and hardworking people. I recognize that their memories of the events described in this book may differ and may conflict with my own. This book was not created to hurt or tarnish the reputations of any of the characters involved or their family members. No harm is intended by the publishing and marketing of *Overnight Father*; its purpose is to inspire and educate.

TABLE OF CONTENTS

ABOUT THE AUTHOR

*N*icholas J. Wedlow serves as an active-duty member in the United States Air Force while simultaneously doubling as an author of educational non-fiction memoirs which is his true passion! He currently serves as an MQ-9 Instructor/Evaluator Sensor Operator with over 2,000 combat flying hours. While training new and upgrading flight crews to effectively employ Remotely Piloted Aircraft (RPA) combat tactics against national-level targets, he somehow finds the time to create inspirational novels. Nicholas has been a lifelong writer and began writing poems, short stories, and essays in elementary school. Nicholas is a graduate of Embry-Riddle Aeronautical University, where he earned a B.S. in Aeronautics with a Minor in Unmanned Aircraft Systems. During his educational journey, he was on the Dean's List on numerous occasions, inducted into the national honor society, and elected into the elite group of Who's Who Among Students in American Universities and Colleges. Nicholas is an 80s baby originally from Atlanta by way of Statesboro, Georgia, and proudly embraces his southern roots by creatively incorporating a "lil taste of the south" throughout his novels to engage and remind the reader that he hasn't forgotten where he came from.

As an entrepreneur, Nicholas is very goal-oriented, ambitious, and driven to succeed. These characteristics helped him win the 3rd place prize of $2K in the Air Force Army Exchange Services (AAFES) Proud to Serve Essay Contest, $4K as the team leader of a community service competition amongst many other military awards and achievements. As a husband and father of three, Nicholas has made a lifelong commitment to continuously pursuing self-improvement opportunities in hopes to increase his worth and provide better for his family. Nicholas aims to entertain, educate, and inspire his audience by sharing lessons learned from his personal experiences and providing keys for success. He wholeheartedly believes that adding value to the reader and providing them with content they can relate to and learn from should be the goal of every author! If you want to stay up to date with Nicholas's projects and release dates, please visit his website at **www.nicholasjwedlow.com**

PREFACE

This story took place in southeast Georgia, in a small town called Statesboro. Life in southeast Georgia is rural, abundant in fertile soil, filled with beautiful pine trees, cornfields, green pastures, and did I mention peaches?! My grandparents owned a farm in Metter, Georgia where my mother and her siblings used to pick cotton and tobacco as daily chores on their family farm. From the red clay to the Smokey Mountains, and the beautiful Savannah Riverwalk, there is so much to see and do in the gorgeous Peach State. However, not everything about Georgia is unicorns and fairies. Historically, as a confederate state, Georgia residents have always endured struggles with racism and inequality. My mother was in middle school during segregation, which means that I was just one generation removed from having to use a bathroom designated for negros only and just a few generations removed from being a slave. You'll find out later in the book why this information is applicable. My intentions for writing this book are twofold: First, I would like to share my journey as a teenage father who endured a grueling custody battle. Second, I would like to share some lessons learned and keys to success regarding custody battles in hopes that fathers in a similar situation can increase their chances of being successful in court. If I can get just one father to apply what they learned from this book in their pursuit of child custody, then I've accomplished my goal!

MISSION

Nicholas J. Wedlow is the CEO of Unfaltering Fathers LLC. The mission of Unfaltering Fathers is to connect, educate, and inspire fathers from all walks of life to continuously pursue time with and be role models for their children. Nicholas has created an acronym for the word F.A.T.H.E.R.S, "Families Always Thrive Having Essential Role-Models"; and our company stands behind this powerful phrase 100%! Fathers are considered as the cornerstone of the family unit and undertaking this huge responsibility shouldn't be taken lightly. Children are gentle impressionable beings and our future depends on them.

Raising a child requires mentorship, guidance, nurturing, encouragement, and a positive influence to ensure that the child's safety and success are manifested. Fatherhood is a very challenging yet rewarding privilege and we want nothing more than to promote and connect the men who excel at their fatherly duties. Our intent is to maintain an inclusive platform for our members to interact and engage with one another via social media, celebrate our victories as fathers, and build and encourage togetherness. As we strive to become better fathers and productive members of society, we can leverage each other as resources and increase our capabilities by sharing lessons learned. Please join us as we combine efforts and strive to empower fathers all over the world to be persistent, consistent, and UNFALTERING!

Follow us on Facebook **@UnfalteringFathers** and make sure you visit **unfalteringfathers.com** to purchase some merchandise and show your support. Thanks in advance.

DEDICATION

This book is dedicated to all my fathers out there! Specifically, the fathers who are experiencing difficulties spending time with their children. I feel your pain, bro! I hope this book can provide some inspiration and resources to assist you with your trials and tribulations regarding child custody and visitation. Please reach out to me if you need a helping hand or someone to vent to. Custody success stories like mine are few and far between. Additionally, stories like mine aren't being discussed or promoted on a mass scale like they should be. I want this book to change that narrative. When I went through my custody battle, I wasn't aware of the helpful resources that were available to me, so it made the process more difficult until I found them. I would hate for any more fathers to encounter the same hurdles I did, so I prepared this book as a blueprint for success. Please share my book with someone who can benefit from its contents, I'd greatly appreciate it.

Remember, if I can do it, so can you!

CHAPTER 1

MY CHILDHOOD FATHER FIGURES

"The quality of a father can be seen in the goals, dreams, and aspirations he sets not only for himself, but for his family."
—*Reed Markham*

So, there I was; cold, wet, crying uncontrollably, with a beautiful woman coddling and marveling over me. I later found out that woman was my mother Connie, and she had just given birth to me. From that day forward, she has been everything I've ever needed in a mother and more. This phenomenal day took place early in the morning on February 24, 1987, at Southwest Hospital and Medical Center in Atlanta, Georgia. At the time, my mother was still legally married but separated from Henry Wedlow Sr. aka "Big Henry" (may God rest his beautiful soul). Big Henry was a phenomenal man who went to great lengths to provide a fatherly figure for my older brother and me. Although Big Henry and Connie were separated, my brother and I were allowed to visit with him frequently during the summer and some major holidays. One of the fondest memories I have with Big Henry was watching him prepare and cook barbeque ribs that he would sell to anyone who approached his mobile rib shack. Those were the best ribs I've ever tasted in my life and still to this day I wish I had paid more attention to the process so that I could replicate them as an adult.

As a child, I used to hate having to spend my summer break sitting around his rib shack all day as my brother and I struggled to entertain ourselves. As a young kid, your focus is on fun and not on learning a unique skill like the process of making succulent barbeque ribs. I understand now that Big Henry was utilizing his skill to provide for my brother and me. Taking care of two young men for an entire summer requires a significant amount of income and since he had been recovering from a stroke, he was only relying on an innovative way to generate some revenue so that he could provide the essentials and entertainment during his summer visitations with us. These visitations would remain regular up until I was around the age of 12. This brings me to the perfect segue to discuss my truth.

What I'm about to reveal will be a shock to my closest family members, friends, and supporters—especially the Wedlow side of my family. I've been internally withholding this information in my heart and carrying this burden on my shoulders since I was a preteen. I hope that after revealing this information it gives me the opportunity to live comfortably and no longer internally struggle with this gut-wrenching truth and fear of not being accepted. Please understand that this is a very controversial topic and as I reveal this near and dear family secret, I would like you to realize that I am vulnerable and tired of living a lie. Venting about this will finally bring closure, act as an enormous weight being lifted off of my shoulders, and an opportunity to live freely and remove this mask I've been wearing for quite some time. In addition to healing from this wound, I humbly ask my Wedlow family to put themselves in my shoes and not pass judgement. I am praying that this information doesn't sever the relationship between myself and the Wedlow family with hopes to continue building on the bond we've fostered over the years. If not, I completely understand and there will be no love lost for you guys from me; but this book is regarding fatherhood and this experience is one of the many factors that helped mold me into the father I am today.

I remember this experience like it was yesterday. I was riding in the car with my mom, brother, and little sister. Everything seemed to be going perfectly fine and we were out taking advantage of what was a beautiful day. Then it happened. Out of the blue, my mother handed me a letter and told me to read it. The letter was addressed to me from a prison inmate named Lindsey. I was curious about why some random dude in jail would be sending me a letter and was instantly overcome by an eerie feeling about it. My intrigue didn't allow me to not open it and I trusted that it must have been important enough for my mother to prompt me to read it. I remember slowly opening the letter while my heart was pounding. As I began to read, the only words that jumped off the page were "… you are my only son." I immediately fell into a state of shock and confusion. "Mom, what is he talking about?" I asked. My mother got quiet. After a brief silence, she then verified that he was telling the truth. I couldn't believe my ears. For 12 years of my life, I was led to believe that Big Henry was my biological father and what I knew to be true came to a screeching halt upon opening that letter. Crushed, led astray, betrayed, fooled, and taken advantage of are just several terms that come to mind when I even begin to describe how I felt after I found out the truth!

A 12-year-old child, who was forced into the realization that he had been living a lie was just too much for me to fathom at the time. I remember thinking, *Why was this information withheld from me for so long?! Why would they even tell me at this point in time, so late in the game; it would have been easier to just let me continue believing the lie since I had grown comfortable with what I thought was the truth. Why hasn't my biological father made it a priority to develop a relationship with me until now?! How am I supposed to react to this?! Should I start treating my Wedlow family members differently now that I know we aren't blood relatives? Should I resent my mother? Should I try to develop a relationship with the Byrd family now that I know they are my true blood relatives? Should I continue keeping this a secret and act like nothing has changed even though I feel like a stranger around my own family members? How many of them knew the truth and assisted in withholding the information? Do I need to change my last name? How did I even end up with this last name?* After weeks of generating questions that I probably wouldn't get the answer to, it finally started making sense, I just didn't recognize the clues.

There was this lady at my church named aunt Faye. From what I understood at the time, she didn't have any blood relation to my mother's side of the family, but I still called her aunt Faye because that's what I knew her as. She was always so nice to me during church and every time I saw her, she gave me a dollar. I thought that was the nicest gesture ever, but I never questioned why her name was aunt Faye or why she would always give me money. It turns out that she and Lindsey are brother and sister, so unknowingly, I was addressing her as her proper title, and she was so nice to me because she knew the truth! I also never questioned why my brother's physical characteristics didn't look like mine but after realizing the truth, it made sense why we didn't look alike. As time went on, I found myself growing less and less interested in continuing the visitations with Big Henry because I felt like I didn't belong and was uncomfortable with the new truth I had to bear. Luckily, I was able to internalize my pain and continue the relationship with the Wedlow family without skipping a beat, but it took some time and maturing to do so.

Big Henry's visitations with us were limited to summers and holidays and deep down I knew he wanted to spend more time with us. Due to the failed relationship between him and my mother and the geographical separation, it proved to be difficult. Prior to knowing that he wasn't my biological father, I longed to spend more time with him as well. This was my first exposure to the limitations of child custody and visitation, and I knew that when I became an adult, I didn't want to experience being limited to certain times that I could visit my own children.

Now that I've lifted that huge burden off of my shoulders, I can provide more background on my experiences as a child with fatherhood. Around the age of 5, my mother remarried a man named Jeremy. Soon after their marriage, my mom, my brother Henry, and I lived together in a double-wide trailer as a family unit. Not much time had passed before my youngest sibling Claire was born and we promptly became a family of five. Initially, it was a huge adjustment period to go from experiencing life with a single mother for most of the childhood I could remember, to adjusting to having a new stepfather being the head of household. I commend Jeremy for his efforts to love, honor, and cherish my mother in addition to taking in two other young boys that weren't his biological children. This must have been a huge undertaking for him, but when you love someone, you are willing to do pretty much anything for them. Jeremy did a great job being the cornerstone of the family for us and was able to assist my mother in making ends meet and filling in the parental and financial gaps that she wasn't able to cover.

Throughout the process of getting to know Jeremy, I learned that he was adopted for one reason or another as a child and didn't maintain a strong relationship with his biological parents. I learned that the man who adopted him went by the name Brock. He was a great guy and spent some time as the County Commissioner for Bulloch County, Georgia. According to Jeremy, Brock was very strict and stern when it came to parenting. Some of the stories that he shared with us regarding some of the punishments he received from Brock were startling and traumatizing to process. I don't want to go too in depth because Brock passed away some time ago and I want him to be remembered for all of his great accomplishments; but I truly believe that the way Brock raised Jeremy shaped how he raised us.

Although Jeremy was a nice guy on the outside, he had a temper that not many people other than our small family would see. Jeremy was very intimidating when he became upset and was also strict and stern parentally. Primarily, my brother and I were held accountable more often than not for our mistakes, but my little sister could get away with murder and get nothing other than a stern talking to as punishment. There were two instances that stand out to me the most when I reflect on punishments that I've received which scarred me as a child.

One day, I was playing inside the house with a new BB gun that I had recently been gifted. Jeremy told me sternly, "Don't shoot that gun inside the house!" I remember my heart starting to pound after he spoke those words because the sound of his voice made me uneasy at times. In hindsight, I should have just put the BB gun down or taken it outside at that point because I knew as a young boy, I would easily succumb to the temptation of practicing my aim with the new toy and shooting the gun inside anyway. I decided to take a chance and avoid the temptation in hopes that I would be disciplined enough to not fire the gun inside the house.

Obviously, that didn't last long. "Nick! Come here!" Jeremy yelled after hearing the BB gun discharge a round. Knees shaking, I slowly walked towards him timidly like a newborn deer. When I got close enough to him, he snatched the BB gun from me and gently said, "Turn around. Didn't I tell you not to shoot this gun in the house?" Jeremy said with extreme frustration. "Yes," I whimpered. Next thing I knew, I heard a loud crack and felt a blunt force across my back simultaneously that instantly propelled me to the floor! As I struggled to get my wind back, I instantly began crying before I was even physically able to make a sound or generate tears. As I tried to process what had just happened, I could hear him yelling in the background but couldn't make out what he was saying due to the immense pain and attempts to regain my composure. At that moment, I didn't understand Jeremy's intent but now that I'm older, I realize that guns are not toys and he was just trying to make his point.

I remember thinking to myself, *Did he just strike me across the back with a BB Gun?!* Mind you, this gun was constructed of wood and metal and wasn't some flimsy object. After the process of elimination, I realized that was exactly what just happened! This elevated my fear of being around him and I struggled to come to terms with whether or not the severity of punishment for that mistake was justified. Over time, I began to believe that maybe I deserved it. I struggled with whether or not I should tell my mother about the incident, but I decided against it because I feared that if she confronted him, he would get angry with her and I didn't want to risk getting her hurt as well. I never saw him become abusive with her, but I also didn't want to be the reason it started. I decided to bottle it up and pretend like it never happened, although I resented him for it for quite some time. This was the first of several punishments that scarred me. There were numerous times where I would get spankings in between those scarring incidents but only the most severe ones remained with me throughout my childhood and adulthood.

A similar traumatic experience took place not too long after the first incident regarding unjustified punishment. This event took place at the same household we were living in which let me know in memory that they weren't too far apart. We lived in a very rural area in small-town Georgia more commonly referred to as "the country". We had to take several dirt roads through a thick wooded area just to access our double-wide trailer which would get so muddy and flooded from the rain that we couldn't get home at times.

On this particular day, we were cleaning up the front yard after a bad wind storm the day prior displaced a generous number of branches from the pine trees onto our lawn. It was a hot sunny day and Jeremy tasked my brother and me to pick up as many branches as we could and take them to the burn pile that we used to disintegrate items like leaves, pinecones, pine straw, and trash. After he provided us with his instructions, he left us in the front yard to work while he was back and forth between the back yard and inside the house taking care of other priorities on his list. I don't recall being provided with a time limit for us to complete the task, but it seemed like we were out there for hours. Young children typically don't have an attention span that allows them to be focused on a task for very long, especially when the task doesn't involve fun. I fell victim to this reality quickly as my brother and I worked diligently to accomplish this juggernaut of a chore. I would have much rather been riding my bike or playing with my friends.

Jeremy would periodically check on us as we were working, but for the majority of the time, we didn't have anyone overseeing us as we chipped away at cleaning up the mountain of limbs. At some point, I grew extremely bored with the task and saw no end in sight. I got distracted by my eagerness to have fun and began doing cartwheels and other flips. My timing couldn't have been any worse! Jeremy came out of the house and saw my legs in the air mid-rotation as I was completing another cartwheel. He immediately became enraged! "Nick, what the hell are you doing?!" he screamed with anger and confusion. I almost aborted mid rotation as I was completing the incriminating cartwheel that I was performing. I immediately felt like a deer staring at headlights when I heard his voice. Caught red-handed not working diligently, I tried to quickly think of a valid reason for being off-task but the fear of what was about to happen stifled my ability to produce any audible words and I could only mumble gibberish.

Disappointed with my actions and lack of response, he approached me very angrily. As he got closer, all I can remember is cowering into fetal position and bracing myself for the worst. As I slightly opened one eye to see what was coming my way, I saw him pick up one of the limbs from a pine tree near me. This was no small twig—it had to be between an inch and an inch and a half in thickness and approximately four to five feet long. Thinking to myself, *No not again… is he really about to do what I think he's about to do?!* Moments later, I heard and felt a loud chopping sound similar to an axe cutting through a tree stump! Unfortunately, there was no tree stump in sight, the only object available to suppress a blow like that was my lower back. Wincing in pain and fighting back the tears, I remember screaming out in a way similar to the slaves in the movie Roots when they were being struck with a whip. My brother stood there helpless and could only watch in sympathy. I rolled around on the ground crying and trying to manage the pain. As I struggled to open my eyes and face reality, I saw the pine tree limb he had just struck me with laying on the ground in two pieces.

During all the pain and agony, I thought to myself, *Did he really just hit me hard enough to break that branch as thick as it was?!* and *Man, my bones must be made of steel because as small as I am that branch broke pretty easily over my back!* Again, I elected not to tell my mother about this incident but in hindsight, I should have spoken up because coincidentally these types of situations only happened when she wasn't present. Traumatized by these two abusive situations, I learned to be more alert, attentive, and cooperative when Jeremy was around. I internalized my resentment towards him and forced myself to mature quickly and conform to his stern ways to avoid any more parental brutality.

As I grew older, my behavioral changes unintentionally strengthened our relationship. I noticed that my fear of his consequences assisted me with my behavior in and out of the classroom. As a student, I rarely made below a B+ on my report card and I was never suspended from school for behavioral issues. I easily could have been involved with the wrong crowds doing the wrong things, but I always considered what was waiting on me at home if I got in trouble and it helped with my decision-making process. Although I'm not justifying the extreme punishments I received as a child, I do appreciate the structure and discipline that my mother and Jeremy provided because it prevented me from steering off on the wrong path. Other than the traumatic experiences I briefly mentioned earlier, Jeremy was a great fatherly figure in my life, and he deserves a ton of praise!

I was heavily involved in sports throughout my entire childhood, primarily football. Throughout it all, Jeremy was right there in my corner every step of the way. At the time, I took it for granted but I now realize how valuable that type of support is for a child to have! Throughout my entire stint with middle and high school football, I can count on three fingers how many of my games Jeremy missed. As I was warming up before every game, it was a tradition to look into the stands and find my parents because it motivated me to play harder knowing that they were watching. They were always there whether or not the game was home or away. That was a phenomenal level of support from a stepfather! I wish I would have been mature enough to realize that despite the resentment I had towards my biological father for not being there, the father figure I longed for was right there in my corner supporting me in everything I did. He took me deep sea fishing, he had the "birds and the bees" talk with me, he taught me how to drive, how to do yard work, and provided enough structure in my life to keep me out of trouble. He taught me how to prioritize finishing my chores to eliminate any excuse that a parent may give a child when they want to go play with their friends. I could go on and on about the positive things Jeremy did for me as a father but by now I'm sure you get the point.

The intent behind sharing my experiences with abuse is to be transparent about one of the most important lessons he taught me. Throughout those experiences, I learned how NOT to punish my children. I couldn't imagine myself getting mad enough to punish my children in a way that I was punished as a child, and I believe the lessons I learned from Jeremy helped me to be a stern parent but gentle enough to make my children feel safe around me. The goal isn't to make Jeremy look like he was a terrible and abusive father, but I've never spoken about my experiences with child abuse until now. Ultimately, Jeremy stepped up to the plate as a father when I needed that void to be filled and I want to publicly thank him for everything he's done for me! Revealing how child abuse has shaped my style of parenting is therapeutic and speaking on it from a child's perspective may help the fathers reading this book adjust how they approach disciplining their children.

Jeremy was able to patch the wound that my biological father left on my heart by not being heavily involved with my life. However, I have always been curious as to why my biological father wasn't there for me. After reading the letter he wrote to me, he returned home from prison not too long afterwards. My mother supported my desire to begin a relationship with him and attempts to build a bond. Initially, I was excited because everyone said I am a split image of him, and I wanted to learn more about my true heritage.

Both of my grandmothers, Della and Thelma, lived in Metter, Georgia. Grandma Della is my mother's mother. She was the sweetest woman one could have ever known and made the best soul food in the south (God rest her beautiful soul). Thelma is Lindsey's mother and she only lived about ten minutes away from grandma Della's house. Grandma Thelma is another beautiful soul who is so sweet and nurturing every time I see her. It's bittersweet that grandma Thelma is my only living grandparent. As I was drafting this section of my book, I felt compelled to give her a call and let her know I was thinking of her and I told her I love and miss her dearly. She was very grateful to hear from me, excited to read my book, and told me that she is proud of me and congratulated me on recently being selected for Master Sergeant which is the pay grade of E-7 in the Air Force.

During the phone call, she mentioned that she wasn't feeling well and just taking it day by day. She also said, "I hope I get to see you guys again soon before I leave this world." Those words were difficult to process because it showed that she is acknowledging the reality that she may not have much longer to live and it's a difficult conversation to have with someone you love. Unfortunately, I live far away from Georgia at this time and don't get the opportunity to visit very often. After speaking with her, I am going to make it a priority to visit her and give her the roses she deserves while she can still smell them. If you are fortunate enough to still have living grandparents, I strongly recommend reaching out to them and showing them some appreciation while they are still here because it will mean the world to them!

As a child, my mother would regularly take us to visit with grandma Della every weekend. Some of my most cherished childhood memories took place at grandma Della's house. We would have routine Sunday dinners, jump on the trampoline, climb in the tree and play backyard football. Our aunts and uncles would always intervene while we were climbing the huge tree in grandma Della's yard to prevent us from getting hurt. They were also hesitant to let us play tackle football because they felt like we were being too rough. However, they were aware that boys will be boys and only slowed us down from our competitive activities despite their attempts to stop us completely. As I got older and learned who my biological father was, my mother supported my attempts to rekindle a relationship with him. Since grandma Thelma only lived ten minutes from grandma Della's house, it was convenient for Lindsey and me to briefly meet up and spend time together.

My older cousin Ashley "Tank" Donaldson (who's more like a brother to me) was old enough to drive and the majority of the time he was the one who would give me a ride to visit Lindsey at grandma Thelma's house. Initially, the excitement of meeting Lindsey was something to look forward to because he would always pull out a wad of cash and put some money in my pocket. He also had a cool personality and had a laid-back vibe that I could relate to (I guess that's where I got it from). These brief interactions with him on the weekends lasted for a few years and over time, I realized that although it was cool to see him, it didn't really meet my expectations of the type of interactions and quality time a father should be spending with his child. I was cool with meeting at grandma Thelma's house for a few minutes initially, but over time I expected it to evolve into him eventually coming to get me more often and doing father-son activities together. After all, my mother's house in Statesboro was only about fifteen minutes away from Metter and I'm sure if he wanted to take me to a football game or a theme park, it wouldn't take much effort to coordinate with my mother and make it happen.

I began to notice that the only time I would get to see him was when I initiated the effort to go visit him and quickly came to terms with him never reciprocating those efforts. Once I realized that Lindsey was content with those quick pop-up meetings at grandma Thelma's house, I started to lose faith in his desire to be the father that I hoped he would turn out to be. I had to manage my own expectations and force myself to be okay with how quickly our father-son relationship plateaued. I never expressed how disappointed I was in his lack of effort to be involved with my life, but I did enjoy the perk of him giving me cash when we did meet up. One day after meeting with him, Jeremy discovered that I had a pocket full of money. "Where did you get that money from?" Jeremy asked. "Lindsey gave it to me," I responded. My mother overheard the conversation and they both immediately got upset. At the time, I didn't understand why they were mad. After all, the way I saw it as a child was a father trying to help his kid out financially.

As an adult, I now understand why they got upset. Lindsey never paid my mother any child support. So, it was a slap in the face for my parents to foot the bill for every expense of mine without any help from my biological father. My parents seeing him give me money showed that he *did* have the ability to help out financially. He either chose not to or preferred to give the money directly to me. The mindset of a child with some cash in his pocket isn't mature enough to spend the money on things that he or she needs like clothing, shelter, school supplies. Most often, I used the money to buy myself some candy, a soda, and or some potato chips from the store. In hindsight, that money should have been given directly to my parents to offset the expenses they had to fork out for my wellbeing. I truly believe that Lindsey was only giving me cash every time he saw me to use as a carrot that he would dangle in my face to give me the impression that he truly cared about me. Meanwhile, behind the scenes, he wasn't paying child support or doing anything else to assist my parents with my upbringing.

When I entered high school, I began to take football very seriously. In fact, I was a standout running back who began to emerge as a star amongst my peers and surrounding counties. Lindsey was also a pretty good athlete in high school, and I figured that this would bring us closer together because fathers love to see their sons experience success in sports. Once Lindsey got word of my success, it was very coincidental that he became a lot more supportive of me. I'll never forget the day that I realized that he was never going to be the supportive father that I longed for him to be. I saw him one weekend and informed him that I had a home game the following Friday that I wanted him to attend. He acknowledged it and assured me that he would be there. I had a hell of a game that night! I had over one hundred yards rushing and scored three touchdowns. We were beating the opposing team so badly that they decided to take me out of the game late in the 3rd quarter and let the younger players get an opportunity to play. There was a large crowd at this particular game, and I remember scanning the crowd to try and find him because he told me that he would be there. I hoped to locate him in the crowd because I wanted to see his reaction after witnessing his son's awesome performance.

I wasn't able to find him during the game, but after the game was over, everyone in attendance was allowed onto the field to interact and celebrate with the players. After we celebrated briefly and the crowd started to dissipate, I saw him as I started to leave the field. He greeted me with a smile but before I could ask him if he saw me play, he told me that he wasn't able to make it to the game until the 4th quarter so he decided to hang out in the parking lot. I thought to myself, *How were you THIS late to my game when you only live 15 minutes away?* Although I was extremely disappointed that he had just missed one of my best performances, I pretended to not be phased by it and proceeded to have a cordial interaction with him. Deep down inside, I was hurt but I wasn't going to let it get me down because Jeremy, my mom, and the rest of the city saw every second! This is the only game of mine I recall Lindsey ever attending. To put this into perspective for you, I played football all four years of high school and we averaged about 13 games per season. Do the math on that and empathize with me for a moment. How is it possible for a father to miss that many opportunities to support their child in doing something that they love to do when he lived only 15 minutes away? I vowed to never let any of my children experience this feeling and I make every effort to attend any of my children's extracurricular activities.

Communication with Lindsey slowly became less and less as I became an adult. The many times he showed me that he wasn't consistently going to be involved in my life made me okay with the minimal communication and over time, I grew numb to the situation. However, Lindsey did make an attempt to stay connected with me via social media through Facebook. Initially, I was okay with staying connected through social media, but over time I grew uncomfortable with it based on how he interacted with the content I posted. My youngest child Prestigious had just taken his Pre-K pictures and I was so proud of his progress that I posted them on my Facebook page. Per usual, family and close friends commented with their gratitude and support underneath the post. Lindsey decided to include his support in the midst of everyone else, but he did it in a way that didn't sit well with me. Keep in mind, I am also connected on social media with a large amount of my Wedlow family members. At the time, I still had not been open about who my biological father was with the Wedlow side of the family and Lindsey's comments under my son's picture could have potentially revealed my secret prematurely.

My son's pictures were of him wearing a nice outfit holding some baseball gear. Lindsey commented under the picture saying, "Lil Lindsey ready to get at the world. Batters up!" He also commented again soon after saying, "Yeah he's a product of granddaddy Lindsey, great granddaddy JT, great great granddaddy Henley, and great great great granddaddy Tobe. #thatway." I immediately became upset after reading his comments for several reasons. The first and most obvious reason was because I didn't want the Wedlows to find out the truth via a comment on Facebook. Second, although we were separated from him geographically, he didn't make the effort to consistently stay in touch with myself or his grandchildren via phone call or text. It seemed as though he wanted to associate himself with my family's success publicly, but in private, he was nonexistent. Lastly, I didn't want him to give people the perception that he's been this phenomenal grandfather when in reality my children couldn't even pick him out of a lineup.

After regaining my composure, I responded to his comment with, "Why don't you get more involved in their life since you're so proud and make up for all the time you missed in my life... a Facebook comment doesn't make up for it... a call or text would be nice." I hoped by me prompting him to get more involved that he would begin to make an effort. Unfortunately, my comment got a negative reaction from him. He never responded to my comment and I haven't heard from him since. I wish he would have taken advantage of all the opportunities he's been given to rekindle a relationship with my family.

Recently, my nine-year-old daughter randomly asked me, "Daddy, who is your daddy?" This was one of the toughest questions I've been faced with answering for my children. I attempted to explain it the best I could, but it would have made it so much easier had he consistently made an effort to involve himself with my life so that my kids can put a name with a face. It saddens me that my daughter has noticed the lack of a biological father figure in my life and was curious enough to attempt getting closure. In lieu of my daughter asking about him, I decided to reach out to him and try to get some closure myself. Surprisingly, he answered the phone. We briefly spoke about his lack of involvement in my life and what I planned to say about him in this book. He gave me his support for the book and his word that he would try and be more involved with his grandchildren's lives. The lack of effort from my biological father was one of the most valuable lessons I learned regarding fatherhood and it molded the blueprint for becoming the relentless and unfaltering father I am today. The intent behind sharing my experiences as a child with the father figures I had in my life was to identify the defining moments that I believe motivated me to become the best version of myself as a father for my children. I took a piece (lesson learned) from each fatherly figure and used those experiences to ensure that my children don't have to go through similar struggles.

CHAPTER 2

HOW IT ALL
STARTED

*"Of all the titles I've been privileged to have,
'Dad' has always been the best."*
—Ken Norton

*G*rowing up in Statesboro, Georgia was blissful as a child. The southern hospitality was abundant, and my parents did a great job providing opportunities for me and my siblings. I was always drawn to athletics and I ended up developing a passion for football. By the time I was a sophomore, I was the starting running back for Statesboro High School back in 2002. During my sophomore season, I accumulated 1,300 yards rushing and 18 touchdowns in only 11 games. Of course, I couldn't have done it without my teammates, but my individual accomplishments increased my popularity in the community after I became a regular in the local newspaper. I began to realize that if I continued to excel, I had a bright future in sports post high school.

Historically, after football season ended, I would run track in the off season to increase my speed and endurance. Some of my football teammates chose to participate in cross country, basketball, soccer, etc., to stay active in the off season as well. For one reason or another, I decided to give baseball a shot after I completed a phenomenal football season as a sophomore. I was inspired by athletes like Bo Jackson and Deion Sanders who experienced success with multiple sports and their legacies influenced my decision the most. I have never played any organized baseball up until that point, but I relied on my athletic ability to provide an opportunity for me. Initially, I was nervous because I was embarking on new territory. I decided to invite Leroy, my best friend at the time, to tryout with me. Surprisingly, we both made the team! I know for a fact that I didn't make the team due to my baseball skillset because I was awful during tryouts. I honestly think the main reason we were both allowed to play was to add some diversity to the team because Leroy and I were the only Black athletes on the team.

Leroy and I were two of the least skilled players on the baseball team; so, we ended up spending a lot of the time in the dugout just spectating during games. In my opinion, the sport of baseball isn't as fun to watch as it is to play. Sitting in the dugout and watching our teammates play was a huge adjustment for Leroy and me because during football season we were both starters on varsity. As we spectated, it created a lot of idle time for us and we spent most of it joking around and people watching. We began to recognize the faces of the regular spectators in the stands and started to notice that we were getting attention as well. During one of the early games in the season, we were in the dugout as usual just people watching and noticed that people were also watching us! "Hey bro is it me or are those White girls checking us out?" I asked Leroy curiously. "Yea they're definitely checking us out, bro!" Leroy confidently responded. "Do you know them? I don't think I've ever met any of them…" I asked suspiciously. "Nah, I don't think I know them either, but we can get to know them!" Leroy said jokingly.

As we continued making eye contact with the girls sitting on the stands, we began to grow more and more curious. We decided to ask one of our teammates if they knew the girls who were being flirtatious from a distance. We found out that one of the girls' names was Karen, and she happened to be the younger sister of Joseph who also played on our team. The flirtatious looks eventually turned into conversations after the games were over and Karen and I developed a cool friendship. Coincidentally, the following school year, Karen and I ended up in the same Geometry class. Our friendship began to develop even more, and we built upon the foundation that was laid during the previous baseball season. We started off with casual conversations and before I knew it, we were passing notes to each other during class. The attraction for each other grew as the days passed, and eventually, we decided to try and spend time together outside of school and extracurricular events. Around this time, Karen's parents bought her a car, and this made it easy for her to come and visit me at my parents' house whenever she was able.

I remember the awkward silence that took over the room the first time I invited her to my house and had her meet my parents. After she left, my mom pulled me to the side and asked me if her parents knew about us. I told my mom that her parents were okay with us seeing each other because I had no reason not to believe so. Karen told me that her parents knew about me and that they were okay with us dating, but little did I know that I would eventually find out she told them that we were just friends when they confronted her with the rumors about us. Thinking that her parents were okay with her dating a Black guy, my parents allowed her to come visit me regularly, but they never questioned why I was never allowed to hang out at her house. As time went on, we started hanging out frequently on weekends and sometimes after school. Eventually, it got to the point where we would skip a few hours of the school day together. It didn't dawn on me until later that the first time it was ever okay for me to visit her house was when we skipped school and her parents were at work. I remember walking past her parents' bedroom, seeing her fathers' shotgun collection, and realizing what a dangerous situation I was getting myself into.

It wasn't very common for interracial couples to openly date in small-town Georgia, so word started spreading fast. I was fortunate enough to have a cousin named Henrietta aka "Peaches" who worked in the guidance counselors' office at Statesboro High School. I would drop by her office on a regular basis to check in with her and say hello before and in between classes sometimes. During one of my routine visits to her office one morning she scolded me and very concerningly said, "You better be careful dating those White girls. Not all people are open minded to interracial dating and can harbor racist feelings about it." Caught off guard, I assured her that I would grant her request but internally I had no intentions of stopping because Karen made me feel like there was nothing I had to worry about.

Whenever she would visit me at my parents' house, we were on our best behavior in front of my parents and siblings. Eventually, our relationship became sexual in nature. Karen would stay over and presume to be innocent long enough for my parents to let their guard down; oftentimes they would go to sleep and that's when we would sneak off together in a secluded area. We were very creative when it came to finding places to be alone together, whether it be her car, a dark area of the house, trampoline, bedroom, etc. Initially, we started using contraceptives but got more relaxed as time went on. One night, Karen and I were hanging out and she told me that she was on birth control. This was music to my ears because all men know that unprotected sex is the most enjoyable; coupled with the idea that she couldn't get pregnant was intriguing and led to us not continuing the use of any contraceptive measures. I had heard success stories from some of my friends who had unprotected sex with women on birth control and their experiences boosted my confidence and made me comfortable with the idea of not using condoms.

The popularity I derived from sports put a spotlight on our relationship. The fact that what we were doing wasn't common, coupled with me being a jock, made us the talk of the town. All of our close friends knew how much time we spent together and how intimate we were with each other. The idea of a White girl being openly into a Black guy brought about unwanted attention towards Karen that started to create drama in the relationship. Numerous times, I had to address how I felt uncomfortable with Karen providing rides home from school to several friends of mine while I was at football practice. There were also incidents where Karen and I would be hanging out together after school and she would receive flirtatious text messages from dudes that I thought were close friends of mine. One incident that really made me question her loyalty was when I found out that Karen had visited one of my older friend's apartment and stayed overnight when I wasn't there. This friend was an ex-teammate of mine who had graduated high school and moved on to college. He lived in the Georgia Southern University campus with a few other male roommates and he would let me and Karen come hang out at his apartment. This was a party environment every time I was over there, and I felt like it was no place for Karen to be hanging out without me being present—especially overnight. After getting word about the incident, I confronted Karen and she admitted that she had stayed the night at the apartment and ended up falling asleep in a bedroom with a guy I knew but she claimed, "nothing sexual happened".

Another incident that made me question Karen's loyalty to our relationship was revealed to me by my sister JaRissa. JaRissa and her husband also stayed in an apartment complex on campus. Karen and I would also hang out at JaRissa's house from time to time and as a result, my sister became very familiar with the description of the vehicle Karen drove. One day, JaRissa pulled me to the side out of concern. "I saw your girl Karen's car parked a few doors down from my apartment the other day and when I woke up the next morning, it was still there, I don't know the people who live there but I do know it's a guy," JaRissa informed me compassionately. I was devastated to hear this type of news about a girl that I was pretty serious about, and I decided to retaliate by entertaining the attention I was getting from other women. I began to believe that Karen was seeing other people because she began to not answer my phone calls as often and distance herself from me. Karen and I continued to date but I was no longer taking the relationship as seriously as I did in the beginning due to the allegations I had heard.

After roughly six months of dating, pregnancy rumors started to float around. Not sure how these rumors started but whenever I was confronted with them, I would engage with Karen about them out of concern. Confident that her birth control was working like a charm, I didn't allow the rumors to shake up my confidence although I wanted to trust but verify. Karen consistently laughed at the outlandish rumors when I confronted her and denied any possibilities of being pregnant when they first started spreading. Unfortunately, the rumors became more frequent and consistent, so I found myself confronting her about them regularly. Over time my frequent attempts to bust the myth about Karen being pregnant began to agitate her. She went from being humored by the silly rumors to becoming annoyed by them and would get upset with me when I approached her about them.

One day, I came home from school and my mother told me we needed to talk. "Someone told me that Karen is pregnant?!" my mother questioned, bluntly and concerned. "Ma, that's not true at all! It's merely a rumor; I just spoke with Karen about it today and she wouldn't lie to me about something like that," I reassured my mom. Once the rumors got back to my mom, I started to grow more concerned. The next day, I saw Karen at school, told her about the conversation with my mom, and confronted her again to ensure that I didn't feed my mother a lie. This time she immediately became infuriated! "I told you 'no' already a million times. Stop asking me about it!" Karen scolded. Startled by her reaction, I decided to start ignoring the rumors and no longer address them with Karen out of fear of her retaliation. I valued the peace between us and also trusted that she would be truthful with me about such a serious allegation. As the relationship continued, I noticed how she began wearing large sweatshirts to school even during warm weather days. I didn't put two and two together and figured that she was trying to keep herself from getting cold in the classroom. Again, I didn't want to be bothersome about my concerns with whether or not the rumors could be true, so I didn't question her wardrobe choices.

There was one strange reaction I got from her one day that made me feel like she wasn't being truthful. During one of our routine meetups in the hallway at my locker, I gave her a hug as we were briefly visiting with each other before going to our next class. As I was releasing the embrace of the hug, my hand gently grazed across her stomach unintentionally. She immediately jerked her body away from my hand and demandingly snarked, "Don't touch my stomach!" Alarmed by the awkward body language and tone of the statement, I respected her wishes but internally questioned what would make her react that way. She never had a problem with me touching her anywhere before and it was very peculiar to me why all of a sudden, her stomach was off limits. I figured it was possible that she may have been suffering from stomach cramps brought on by her monthly cycle. She would inform me whenever she was in her monthly cycle window by telling me she was "spotting" to ease my concerns about her missing her period. I also considered the fact that she was hiding something from me regarding the rumors that were spreading but trusted that she would inform me if they were true. I decided to remain optimistic and not readdress the possibilities of her being pregnant but was internally worried to death.

CHAPTER 3

THE CALL

"When my father didn't have my hand, he had my back."
—*Linda Poindexter*

*T*hen it happened. A phone call that would change my life forever. On the evening of December 18, 2004 at approximately 10:30 P.M., I was relaxing at my parents' house preparing for bed. As I enter the bathroom to take a shower, the phone rings. My parents were asleep at the time and I didn't want the phone to wake them, so I quickly answered it. "Hello," I said welcomingly. "Hey, it's me!" Karen responded in distress. "What's the matter?" I asked concernedly as I sensed the tension in her voice. "I'm in the hospital and I just had a baby!" Karen managed to say as she started to get emotional. "Karen, stop playing. It's too late to be joking like that," I jokingly said as I was trying to process the seriousness of her message. "I'm not playing, I'm dead serious!" Karen reassured me.

I got completely silent and didn't respond. The voices in my head were in utter disbelief and so many different thoughts and questions started racing through my mind. *The rumors were true! How did I not see the signs? How come she didn't tell me before now?! How am I going to break the news to my parents?! I'm not ready to be a dad! Is the baby even mine? She was sneakily spending time overnight with other guys since we've been involved so is it a possibility the baby isn't mine?! What do her parents think? Will this mess up my football scholarship if I have to take care of a child? I don't even have a job! She doesn't even have a job, how are we going to take care of a baby? What do we name it?*

As I ventured off further into my concerns, I could hear her continuing to speak but couldn't make out what she was saying over my thoughts. I finally came back to reality and finished the conversation with her but don't remember much else from it. After hanging up the phone, the most extreme case of anxiety I've ever experienced came over me. I went to my room, locked the door, and just sat on the floor with my face in the palm of both of my hands. I sat there thinking, *How am I going to tell my parents that they have a grandson waiting for them in the hospital literally right now?!* I was on the verge of a mental breakdown. I knew that word was going to spread fast and I didn't want my parents to hear the news from anyone other than myself.

My parents were asleep when the news broke and I was internally struggling with the when and how I was going to tell them. I suspected that by the morning, the phone would be ringing off of the hook with the news of me being a father. I needed to beat the rumor mill. I began trying to harness the courage to reveal such groundbreaking news to them. I stood in the mirror and tried to rehearse the words that I thought they would be the most receptive to. This conversation with myself in the mirror is one of the few times I remember telling myself, "You can do this!"

After providing myself with false hope, I mustered up the courage to wake my parents up. I kept forgetting the lines that I rehearsed. I must have paced back and forth in my room for an hour before I decided that the only way to get it over with was to just spit it out. I slowly opened my room door as if I didn't want to wake anyone who was sleeping. The irony of quietly opening my bedroom door on my way to the next room just to wake someone still baffles me. As I proceeded to tiptoe down the hall towards my parents' room, the anxiety resurfaced. It felt to me as if I was walking to death row. That's the perfect way for me to describe it. I was certain that they were going to kill me; not for having a child at the age of 17, but for waking them up in the middle of the night when they had to work early in the morning. A walk to my parents' room that was only about 15 feet from my room seemed like it took forever.

Once I arrived at their bedroom door, I froze with my arm and fist in mid-knocking motion. A million thoughts were going through my head. *Will I get hit with another bb gun? Will they kick me out of the house? Should I wait to tell them in the morning? Will they be ashamed of me?* Again, I had to muster up the strength to knock on their door. I was so full of anxiety that I just wanted it to be over with. As a knee jerk reaction, I knocked loudly on their door. The anxiety immediately multiplied by three. I waited a few seconds, and no one responded. At that point, I was already committed so I knocked again even louder. I wouldn't be denied the opportunity to get this burden off of my shoulders. I convinced myself that I was just telling them the news but deep down I was ultimately asking for their help. After the third knocking attempt, I could hear my mother respond half asleep, "Who is it?" she asked aggravatedly. "It's Nick," I whimpered. "Can I come in?" I pleaded. "Yes, what is it?" she questioned as she realized how unusual it was for me to be waking her. Luckily, Jeremy remained asleep as I was talking to my mother.

I entered their room, and I could feel my heart beating out of my chest similar to a male cartoon character that just saw an attractive female character. "I have to tell you something Ma," I managed to blurt out while buying myself some time to try and remember my lines again. I couldn't manage to find the words to say. My mother could tell something was bothering me and she just sat there trying to wake up and give me her undivided attention during the awkward silence I was providing her. "Karen is in the hospital and she just had a baby," I said in a tone between a whisper and my inside voice—that voice you use to yourself when you need to think things through. "What?" she questioned in a way where I could tell she couldn't understand my mumbling. I repeated it a little louder the second time but not loud enough to wake Jeremy up. She immediately opened her mouth and slowly covered it with her hand as if she was trying to stop herself from screaming, but not a sound came out. She was in disbelief. More awkward silence. She sat there staring at me like she knew I was lying about the rumors the whole time. I felt the most ashamed I had ever felt in my life. That was the first time I felt like I had let my mother down. I couldn't bear the way she was looking at me and I just went back to my room. I was expecting her and Jeremy to come into my room at any second and all hell would break loose. It didn't, surprisingly. I didn't get a wink of sleep that night.

The next morning, after my parents woke up, there was an eerie feeling in the air. To my surprise, they weren't as furious as I expected them to be. My mother seemed very disappointed in me, but she was still being very supportive on the matter. After a brief recap of the news I told her while she was sleep, she decided to take me to the hospital to see the baby. Nervous is an understatement! I was aware that her parents didn't know how serious we were prior to her birthing a child but since their teenage daughter just had a baby, I felt they were determined to find out everything about me. That was the worst introduction a young man can have when meeting his girlfriends' parents. Regardless of my hesitation, I had to face my fears. There was an awkward silence as my mom drove me to East Georgia Regional Medical Center. No music was playing, and you could literally hear a pin drop. All I could think was "How the f*ck did this happen?" As we got closer to the hospital, my anxiety grew more and more. I was sweating bullets. I thought back to the time I saw those shotguns in the room of Karen's parents and was afraid I would end up like Emmet Till, after meeting them.

We arrived at the hospital and began walking to Karen's room. When we arrived, her parents were standing in the hallway. My mother introduced herself to Karen's mother Christine first and then to her father Billy. This exchange was pretty awkward from my observation because usually, my mother was very welcoming and energetic when meeting new people. This time my mother had a demeanor and body language like she regretted ever having to meet them especially due to the circumstances. While my mother spoke to her parents, I was timidly hiding in her shadows trying not to make eye contact. I couldn't hold out for very long because there was a pause in the conversation between the parents, moments after the introductions were over. Before I made eye contact, I could feel her parents' eyes burning holes in me.

As I looked up from the spot I was staring at on the floor, I saw Billy surveying me up and down. His look said exactly what I assumed he was thinking, *"So this is the father of my grandson?"* To break the awkward silence and glaring, I decided to take a deep breath and introduce myself. Men normally shake hands when they meet out of respect, so I reached out my hand towards Billy's direction. "Hello, nice to meet you. My name is Nick," I managed to utter as my voice cracked from the nerves. The first thing Billy said to me in response was, "Is there any chance my daughter has AIDS?" with a look on his face that was serious as a heart attack. "No," I confidently responded.

I stood there silently trying to process why he would ask me something like that. My inner voice started going crazy again. *Is that what he thinks of Black people? Does he think his daughter would be involved with someone she thought had AIDS? Do I look sick? Would he have asked me this question if I were White?* I have yet to get an answer for why he asked that question to a 17-year-old kid. In hindsight, maybe it was because I was wearing a hoodie similar to the one Trayvon Martin had on the night George Zimmeran took his life. I wondered if I was being profiled because of the color of my skin. I bottled in the way his question made me feel and pretended that everything was okay. After all, we were all there to see the baby and now that intros were out of the way, I was ready to transition to seeing Karen and the baby. Billy and Christine informed us that the baby was taken to a Neonatal Intensive Care Unit (NICU) in Savannah, Georgia at Memorial Health. The reason he was taken there was because the baby was born two and a half months premature. After learning the severity of the situation, I immediately began to panic. Not only did I just find out that I was literally an overnight father, but the child's life was also in danger.

I keep referring to the child as "the baby" or "the child" because at this point in the story, we still hadn't decided on a name for him yet since everything happened so fast. I began to rewind the hands of time in my head and reminisce on the moments Karen and I spent together during the pregnancy that I was unaware of. Then it dawned on me, usually, women take prenatal medicine and have frequent doctor visits when they are pregnant. Karen hadn't exercised any doctor visits during her pregnancy that I was aware of. In fact, Karen and I were drinking and smoking together on numerous occasions during the time she was pregnant, and I began to feel guilty. Knowing the type of activities that Karen and I were involved in during her pregnancy, I thought to myself *D*mn, that's a miracle baby to survive all that.* Had she told us that she was pregnant, we could have easily gotten her the medical care that she needed. We briefly finished chatting with Karen and her parents after getting updated on the status of the baby. Karen and I didn't do much talking at all—it was primarily the parents having a discussion. After realizing that we had to travel an hour to Savannah to meet the baby, we decided to wait until the next day to make the trip.

The next day came and we made the drive to Memorial Health. When we arrived, there was an extensive hygiene process to get access to the area of the NICU the baby was in. I remember having to wash my hands and forearms very well and only a certain number of people were allowed to have access at a time. Karen and her family had already been at the hospital for a while so when my mother and I arrived, they let us visit him immediately. We were guided back to his cubical by a nurse and I remember approaching what seemed to be like a museum exhibit. This was the first time I had seen an incubator. He was laying in the incubator with tubes that seemed to be coming out of every orifice in his face. He also had a mask covering his face because his eyes were still underdeveloped and were very sensitive to light. The incubator was heated by lightbulbs designed to keep him warm and expedite the development of his underdeveloped skin. Although I was excited to see if he favored me, it was to no avail.

I looked over at my mother and she was grinning ear to ear. The silence and eerie feeling of disappointment suddenly vanished, and it was the first time I had seen her smile in 48 hours. The reality that she was a grandmother had sunken in and from that point on, I knew she had forgiven me. My mother asked the nurse if we could hold the child and they gladly obliged. The nurse carefully removed him from the incubator and slowly placed him in my arms. I had very little experience in knowing how to correctly hold little babies—especially premature ones. I did the best I could to coddle him into my arms without injuring his very small and frail frame. I also had to avoid holding him in a way that would tug on the feeding tube and IV that was inserted into his arm and mouth. It was a very surreal feeling and as I gazed at him in my arms, I was excited and scared at the same time. After about thirty seconds of me holding him, he began to try readjusting his body and squirm around in my hands. He tried to regain his comfort level and after a few unsuccessful attempts, he began to cry.

My immediate response was to try and get help from my mother, so I tried to hand the baby to her. Without hesitation, she took a step back and didn't extend out her hands to receive the child from me. I gave her a puzzled look. She then sternly replied, "No, that's *your* baby." In that moment, I realized what a huge responsibility I had just undertaken. My mother was right. It *was* my baby. By not receiving the child from me when he started crying, she was simply implying that it was my responsibility to care for and nurture the child that I created. Initially, I felt abandoned by my mother as I tried to get her help, but I knew that her intentions were good, and she just wanted me to change my mindset and step up to the responsibility of being a parent. I had to figure out a way to stop the baby from crying without my mother's help. I mimicked techniques that my mother used to soothe my younger sister when she was a baby. I began rocking the baby in my arms and calmly speaking funny phrases and noises. It worked! The baby fell back asleep as a result of me having to improvise on the spot and transform into desperate parent mode. This moment was a huge reality check for a 17-year-old, and I knew I had my work cut out for me.

Since no one was aware of or prepared for the babies' arrival, we didn't have a name reserved. For several days, we addressed the child as "the baby". It took some time for everyone to overcome the shock of the babies' abrupt arrival but after several days, things began to normalize. Karen and I began to discuss possible baby names that we were considering. We finally decided that we liked the name Amarius after going back and forth with several name concepts. Pronounced "uh-MARH-ee-us". Karen and I were excited that we decided on a name that we both agreed on and we were eager to share it with our parents. My parents were very receptive and supportive of the name we decided on and I didn't get any push back from them, after all it was our baby, right? Karen's parents' reaction was a different story.

I received a phone call from Karen shortly after she had a discussion with her parents about the name we decided on. I could hear the disappointment in her voice as soon as she started talking on the phone and I knew some bad news was headed my way. "They like the name Payton better," Karen attempted to inform me convincingly. "Payton? That sounds like a little girls' name to me, I'm not feeling it," I responded defensively. "Why are they suggesting other names?" I asked out of curiosity. "You and I have already decided on the name we want to call our son," I respectfully added. Karen's response was defensive and supportive of her parents' views like they had convinced her to let them give their input about the name we chose. In a roundabout way, Karen tried her best to explain why her parents didn't like the name Amarius.

What I interpreted based on her response, was that the name Amarius was too "ethnic sounding". I was confused as to why they didn't support the name Karen and I agreed on. After a few moments, I began to question... *Would a Caucasian family really have such different views about suitable children names compared to an African American family's views?* I also realized that technically, Karen and I were still children ourselves since neither of us were 18 years old yet. This was a point of contention for me. I really liked the name Amarius. It was different and original, and that's what I liked about it. Karen mentioned that her family was willing to compromise and name him after me. I didn't want my son to be named Nicholas. There are so many people with the name Nicholas and I didn't want him to have such a common name since he was born under very uncommon circumstances.

I knew I was fighting a losing battle. I decided to compromise as well and offered to agree to Payton being his middle name. They accepted my offer and both families agreed that his full name would be Amarius Payton Wedlow. Although I wasn't comfortable with the name

Payton, I suggested that we include it as his middle name to speed up an agreement between both families and avoid any more tension than there already was based on the circumstances. At that point, I knew that it was going to be an uphill battle for me to raise my son in the image of a Black man when his maternal grandparents were already being so insistent in calling the child by a name that is very uncommon for males in the Black community. Internally, I had no intentions of ever calling him Payton, but little did I know, her family members had no intentions of ever addressing him as Amarius. The avoidance by family members to address him as certain names proved to be a major factor in Amarius finding his true identity later on in his life.

CHAPTER 4

ADJUSTING TO FATHERHOOD AS A TEEN

*"A father could be defined as the 3 P's – The
protector, the provider, and the problem solver."*
—*Theodore W. Higginsworth*

s a result of how early Amarius was born, he had to remain in
the NICU for roughly a month and a half. Karen, our family
members, and I would make the hour-long commute to Savannah,
Georgia as often as we could to visit Amarius. After about a week or two
of adjusting to parenthood and visiting the NICU, I was notified that
Karen's parents set up a meeting with an adoption agency. Although it
came as a shock to me, I was semi relieved to hear about it. Prior to the
meeting, Karen and I had a long heart to heart about the possibilities
of adoption. The conversation took a very emotional turn almost
immediately. Life-altering discussions about adoption as teenagers were
almost too much to bear for us. We tried our best to weigh the pros and
cons of being teen parents and discussed possible outcomes as we fought
back emotion. We were still yet to develop a solid plan for how we would
raise Amarius because at that point, we were still trying to figure out life
for ourselves. In addition to the sudden introduction into parenthood,
we were also still adjusting to the integration of a Caucasian and African

American family who would need to be on the same sheet of music in order to provide a stable environment for Amarius.

During our earth-shattering conversation, Karen and I concluded that it was best for Amarius to get adopted by parents who were more stable than we were. It was one of the most difficult decisions I've ever had to consider. As I reflect back on this moment, I now realize that it was very selfish of me to even consider adoption. My mindset at the time was not wanting the unexpected birth of a child to ruin my opportunity to receive a scholarship to play college football. I also knew I had a lot more youth that I wanted to explore before I had to care for a child, and the idea of adoption was intriguing to me because I saw it as an opportunity to disregard my responsibility as a father and continue pursuing my dreams. The adoption meeting was scheduled a few days after Karen and I made our decision. The meeting was conveniently held in a conference room in the same hospital as the NICU Amarius was staying in. We arrived at the meeting and all were present. My parents and I were sitting on one side of the room, Karen and her parents were on the other. I was pretty nervous, but after coming to the agreement with Karen prior to the meeting, I assumed that the meeting would be pretty straightforward.

There was an awkward silence in the room prior to the adoption agency representative breaking the ice. You could almost hear what the combination was to her briefcase as it was being opened. The representative introduced herself and immediately began discussing the legalities of adoption and all possible options. Initially, all family members were on board with the decision. As the meeting developed, Karen's demeanor began to change. I could sense that there was something wrong with her based on her mannerisms as the agent spoke, but I couldn't check on her due to how far away I was sitting. Shortly after the meeting started and before we reached an official decision, Karen stormed out of the room; she looked as if she were overwhelmed and wasn't interested in being present for such a life-changing discussion. You could hear the disappointment in her weeping voice over the thundering footsteps as she swiftly exited the room in tears. The room grew silent again. The removal of herself from the meeting sent a very clear message. Without having to chase after her and inquire about what was wrong, everyone knew that leaving the room in tears was her way of protesting the adoption. I can only imagine how uncomfortable it must have been for a first-time mother to be expected to be okay with giving her baby away to another family. Before Karen returned to the meeting, everyone had a similar look on their face; complete disgust in ourselves for trying to take the easy way out and even considering adoption.

After Karen stormed out of the room, my entire mood changed. Karen was right! We weren't making the right decision. The baby was a blessing and putting him up for adoption just because he wasn't born in the most ideal circumstances wasn't the answer. I internally rallied behind her and commended her strength after she stood up to everyone by storming out in protest of the adoption. I also felt guilty because I was in support of adoption initially only because I knew I was still very immature and not ready to be a father. When are you ever really ready though? Sometimes, you have to just figure things out as you go, and this was a pivotal turning point that was about to help me transition from a boy to a man. Needless to say, after Karen returned to the meeting, it was a unanimous decision amongst everyone not to proceed with the adoption. It was the best decision we could have made!

The birth of Amarius took place over the Christmas school break right at the midway point of the school year. Imagine leaving school for Christmas break as a typical teenager and returning to school after the break as a father! One of my closest friends Zach Sanders called me after hearing the rumors that Karen and I had a child. As soon as I answered the phone Zach questioned me immediately in disbelief, "Wed, you're a dad, bro?!" Zach and I have been close friends since kindergarten, and the impact of what I had gotten myself into really began to sink in after him asking me in the fashion that he did. I responded, "Yeah, bro. I am." My emotions were all over the place. I experienced excitement, shame, fear, proudness, nervousness, happiness, and many other feelings simultaneously when being confronted about being a teenage father.

When I returned to school after Christmas break, people treated me like an urban legend. I remember having a cellphone I brought to class that my cousin Tosha gave me, and it had pictures of Amarius on it. I was in Anatomy class and I reached over to show a friend sitting in the desk next to mine a picture of my son. The teacher overheard what I thought was a quiet conversation between my friend and me as I attempted to show him. I looked up and saw the teacher looking in my direction. I immediately thought I was in trouble. "Is that a picture of the baby?" my teacher asked. "Yeah it is, do you want to see?" I responded. A few moments later, almost the entire classroom was crowded around my desk looking at pictures of the baby. This was an awesome moment for me because this was confirmation that everyone including the teacher had heard the rumors. Instead of approaching me about the rumors, everyone respected my privacy. The moment I volunteered a show and tell opportunity, everyone crowded around in support and curiosity. The teacher could have easily told me to put away my phone and pay attention. Instead, she took a moment to stop instruction and shift the focus to the acknowledgment of my truth as a new teenage father.

Adjusting to parenthood as a teenager was very challenging. My focus and responsibilities shifted away from myself to another human being literally overnight! Everything changed. I was no longer able to go and hang out with my friends on a regular basis. My play days were over in the blink of an eye. I had to grow up and mature a lot faster than I originally planned to. We returned from school after the Christmas break and football season was over. I no longer had to attend football practice after school, so I had to figure out something else to do in my free time. I had a child to provide for and decided to get a job. Luckily, my high school had a Work-Study Program that allowed students to attend school for half of the day and leave early for employment opportunities. Jeremy helped me get a job working at Cleve White Nissan, detailing cars. I would leave school around noon each day to work at the car dealership. This was my first taste of being in the workforce and I hated it. My dream was to play football in the National

Football League (NFL) and there I was washing cars for a living. It was a reality gut check for me. Have you ever washed a car when it was cold outside? Trust me, you don't want to.

I also missed out on tons of other leisure opportunities that my peers were attending regularly. One of the most memorable instances where I realized that my childhood was over was the night of my senior class trip. Traditionally, the senior class of my high school would go on a trip annually. The event was called Grad Night and students would travel out of town to an agreed upon location to celebrate the upcoming high school graduation. The Grad Night event for my senior class took place at Disney World. Prior to learning I had a son; I had planned to attend. After my son was born, I realized that I wouldn't be able to attend the event due to me having to prioritize my responsibilities. My son's wellbeing was much more important than a vacation. However, it was one of the most envious feelings I have ever experienced when I knew that all of my friends were having the time of their lives while I was literally sitting at home changing diapers.

As my senior year came to an end, my goal was still to secure a full scholarship playing football. Karen and I decided that it would be best for me to pursue a scholarship opportunity and try to make it to the NFL in order to provide better for my family. During my sophomore year in high school, I was receiving recruitment letters from the University of Florida and the University of South Carolina. I thought for sure I would attend a college in the South Eastern Conference (SEC), but my dreams were quickly derailed by a knee injury that cost me almost the entirety of my junior season. I recovered from the injury and had a productive season as a senior, but the interest from SEC schools never returned. At the end of my senior year, I was recruited by Ball State University and given a scholarship. Ball State University is a Division 1 school in the Mid-Atlantic Conference. Although it wasn't the ideal school I had dreamed of attending, I was still thankful for a full scholarship opportunity to play football on the collegiate level. Ball State is located in Muncie, Indiana. Muncie is located roughly an hour northeast of

Indianapolis, Indiana. For me, this was very far away from home in Georgia and I experienced culture shock upon my arrival.

The Midwest seemed like another country to me. There was no red clay, no abundance of pine trees, and the humidity wasn't a fraction of what I was used to experiencing in the southern climate I grew accustomed to. There were no parents around to keep me focused and provide structure while on campus. I had to adjust to living in a college dorm, sharing a room with a complete stranger, and showering in community style bathrooms. I had to do my own laundry, prepare my own food, and keep my own pantry stocked. I wasn't fortunate enough to have a car and had to walk to class, practice, and anywhere else I needed or wanted to go. I was presented with major challenges because I didn't have a consistent source of income and I no longer had a cell phone. The only source of income I had was a meal card that only scholarship athletes were privileged to. The meal card would allow you to purchase three meals a day at participating restaurants across campus. I was fortunate enough to have made friends with teammates that had cars who would sometimes assist me with transportation to and from practice but that wasn't always the case. I also had trouble adjusting to the college workload.

The amount of hard work it took to balance a full academic schedule with a full athletic schedule was overwhelming. High school didn't prepare me for that. In high school, I loved lifting weights and sprinting. In fact, I was a state semi-finalist in a high school weightlifting competition. In college, the workouts were so intense that the strength and conditioning coaches would push you beyond your physical limits. In most cases, I would be so physically and mentally challenged that I would vomit after and sometimes during workouts. I'll never forget coach Aaron Wellman. Google him. He was the lead strength and conditioning coach during my tenure at Ball State. He went on to coach at the University of Michigan, San Diego State University, New York Giants, and he's now working at Indiana University. The dude is no joke! Coach Wellman brought intensity to workouts like no other and demanded 1000% from every rep! I never quite adjusted to the high intensity workouts that I endured in college. I simply just tried to survive them. The competition was also stiff on the collegiate level. In high school, I was the stand-out athlete every game. In college, everyone was the best at their respective high schools.

When everyone is a good athlete, there is little room to make mistakes. When Ball State recruited me, they sold me a dream. I was told that they loved my style of play and that I was the perfect fit for their offense. I was told that they needed someone to come into their system and start playing right away and I was their guy. They told me that there were only three running backs that I would have to compete with; but when I got to Indiana, I found out that including myself, there were nine running-backs all competing for the same position! Stiff competition, intense workouts, and structured athletic and academic schedules proved to be an overwhelming adjustment to college athletics. As a freshman that wasn't familiar with the offense, I began low in the depth chart by default. I was very afraid to make a mistake and fall lower in the depth chart which caused me to not be as confident as I was in high school where I had no competition. It took a while to regain my confidence because I was learning a new offense, coaches had little patience, and the game was a lot faster compared to high school.

All the new challenges I was faced with demanded attention to detail, maximum effort, and laser focus. The tempo of the workouts and the 24/7 dedication it took to be successful took the fun out of football for me. It began to feel more like a job, and I started to dread going to practice and workouts. I ended up falling out of love with the game. In the midst of adjusting to an intense athletic schedule, I was also trying to adjust to a very challenging academic schedule. College classes were also fast paced. The first time I attended a college class, I walked into what seemed to be an auditorium and there were 250 other students in the lecture with me. I remember thinking to myself, *If I were to skip this class the professor wouldn't even notice because there are so many people in here!* Sitting in an auditorium with over 200 students listening to a professor with a monotonous voice similar to the way Ben Stein sounded when he filmed the commercials for the Clear Eyes products;

just wasn't my style of learning. As the season continued, the weather began to cool off and then frost over. I was used to the hot and humid weather in the south.

One morning, I rolled over in bed before class, looked out of my dorm room window, and saw that it was snowing outside. I immediately rolled over and went back to sleep. I didn't even own the proper wardrobe to protect me from extremely cold weather and was not trying to walk to class in the snow. I found out the hard way that it wasn't a good idea to skip class because our football coaches did random checks on the athletes to make sure they were attending class. The consequences for getting caught skipping class was a punishment workout the following morning at 6 A.M. nicknamed by the athletes as the "hot six". Imagine being forced to get on the stair master for 45 minutes at six in the morning, then attend all of your classes for the day, then go to practice, and attend mandatory study hall for two hours after practice. Exhausted is an understatement! This was a typical day for me; not to mention having to balance the parties, women, and other distractions that I encountered in college.

The co-parental relationship between me and Karen was very rocky after I left for college. Shortly before my high school graduation, our relationship hit a rough patch and we grew apart; we went our separate ways romantically as I was leaving for college. Scholarship athletes can't legally have a job, but I was fortunate enough to have my mother and other family members help financially support Amarius in my absence for the short period that I was on scholarship. My mother was so helpful in fact, that she would often babysit Amarius when Karen had things to do. It got to a point where my mother felt taken advantage of. One night, Karen asked my mother to babysit Amarius while she went to work; my mom later found out that Karen went to a nightclub instead of work after seeing pictures of Karen partying on Facebook the next day. Karen and I were able to remain cordial initially after the failure of our relationship, but she couldn't understand why I couldn't support her financially during college.

I tried my best to explain that I wasn't allowed to have a job as a scholarship athlete, but she could never comprehend and accept my circumstances. She grew extremely frustrated with me and started researching the process of how to put me on child support. The overwhelming pressure of adjusting to college athletics, academics, and trying to co-parent from a long distance broke me down over time. I fell into a depressive state. I lost focus; I lost my love for football, and allowed my GPA to drop below the minimum requirement to maintain a scholarship. The culmination of those trials and tribulations during my three semesters in college ultimately caused me to lose the scholarship. In what seemed to be the blink of an eye, I was back living in my mother's house; no job, no way to support my child, and no plan B. I needed a change.

As things began to spiral out of control in college, I remember casually saying to one of my close friends, "If this college thing doesn't work out, I'm going to be saluting in someone's military." This statement revisited my thoughts frequently as I sat on the couch at my parents' house trying to get my life together. Regardless of the turmoil my life was in during this time, I still had a son to raise. I spent time with Amarius at my parents' house while Karen would go to work. As Amarius and I spent time together, all I had to offer him was the groceries in my parents' refrigerator. It made me feel like a failure when I didn't have a car or any money to use for taking Amarius on meaningful excursions like getting ice cream or going to see a movie. The threats of child support from Karen continued. I knew I had to establish a plan B immediately in order to provide for myself and my child.

CHAPTER 5

ESTABLISHING MYSELF AS A MAN

"A good father is one of the most unsung, unpraised, unnoticed,
and yet one of the most valuable assets in our society."
—Billy Graham

I was self-aware that I needed structure, discipline, and a steady
source of income. I decided to go speak to a recruiter and try
my luck at joining the military. Initially, I considered all branches of
the military but when I actually weighed the pros and cons of each, I
was only interested in joining the Air Force. I didn't want to be on a
ship over water for six months at a time, so the Navy was out of the
picture. I didn't want to be sleeping out in the field and possibly on the
front lines getting shot at, so the Army and Marines were no-gos as
well. Based on the quality of life rumors I had heard when comparing
the Air Force to other branches, I knew this was the branch for me. In
addition to that, I also like the Air Force's uniforms better than other
branches. The Air Force requires the highest minimum testing scores
on the Armed Services Vocational Aptitude Battery (ASVAB) test to
qualify for entrance, which is one reason why it may be considered as
"the smart branch". This sounded like a challenge to me and I was up
for it. I took the test and scored pretty high on it, which qualified me
to join. That was the start of my military career! I successfully enlisted
into the Air Force and my first day of basic training started on May
29, 2007. I was ecstatic to have a second chance at leaving my parents'

house and establishing my independence. I was determined to make the best of it this time around. After all, Amarius was depending on me.

After getting established into the Air Force, the drama with Karen's family continued. Initially, Karen and I were able to co-parent peacefully, but there was still tension between me and her parents. I remember one day; Billy was on the other end of the phone and he was being very argumentative. I recall him yelling, "You haven't even legitimated him!" At the time, I wasn't aware what that meant. I decided to do some research because I didn't like the way he made it seem like I wasn't qualified to be a father for Amarius. I was young and naïve. I was under the impression that as long as you sign the child's birth certificate, then you had rights to the child. Boy was I wrong. After conducting some research, I learned that Billy was right. In the state of Georgia, when a child is born out of wedlock, a father must legitimate a child before they are able to establish rights, custody, and visitation.

Billy knew I wasn't aware of this legality, which is why he barked it at me over the phone that day. It seemed as if his intentions were to place hurdles in my way to prohibit me from having a say in legal decisions regarding Amarius. Little did he know, he was giving me the blueprint on what I needed to accomplish in order to legally establish myself as a parent and obtain rights to my child. Thanks, Billy! After learning what I needed to do in order to be equally respected as a parent for Amarius, I decided to pursue the legal route. There were a lot of prerequisites I needed to accomplish before going to court. First, I needed a bigger place to live. As a young single Airman, I was required to live in the dormitory on base. My first duty station was Nellis Air Force Base in Las Vegas, NV. In order to obtain the proper living space when Amarius came to visit, I had to show proof of a custody/visitation agreement to the Air Force before they would allow me to move out of the dorms and find my own place. In order to establish custody and visitation, I had to legitimate myself as the father.

One of the easiest ways to legitimate yourself as a father in the state of Georgia is to accomplish a DNA test. I contacted the DNA Diagnostic Center testing facility and scheduled a test date for September 6, 2007. I was nervous about this process because I was afraid that there was a possibility that I wasn't the father due to my insecurities and perception of Karen's infidelity early on in our relationship. Luckily, the test concluded that I was the father and all my concerns disappeared. After getting the test accomplished, I knew it would assist me in legitimating myself as Amarius's father, but I wasn't sure how to get the process started or if I could even afford it.

At the time, Karen and Amarius were still living with her parents. Karen's parents Billy and Christine were very involved with the decisions being made for Amarius. It was weird to me. It was sort of like they considered Amarius as their own child and not their grandchild. I never met a set of grandparents who felt so entitled to a grandchild. I would attempt to make phone calls and coordinate spending time with Amarius when I visited home but was met with resistance in most cases. Now that I had a job, they were applying even more pressure regarding child support. I knew I had to act fast before things spiraled out of control.

Then out of the blue, another "you gotta be kidding me" moment occurred. One day I caught wind of Karen just randomly going on a "church retreat" to California. This was pretty odd to me at the time because of how random it was, and I didn't recall her being involved heavily in church activities historically. I wish I was making this up but... it turns out that Karen had another baby! Crazy, right?! It hasn't been confirmed, but the rumor about the "church retreat" was that Karen flew out to California to give the baby up for adoption to a couple that lived out there but couldn't go through with it because the child had some complications at birth. She birthed a beautiful little girl that she decided to name Ericka. After returning to Georgia with Ericka, the talk around the town was that the child was mine. I was floored by this! Not only did Karen hide ANOTHER pregnancy from everyone, but somehow everyone was convinced that Ericka was mine. I was in a relationship with another woman at this time and obviously this rumor didn't go over very well. I was scared to death! Karen and I had still been sexually involved off and on despite no longer being in a relationship. I knew that deep down there was a possibility that Ericka could be mine, but since I was dating someone else, I wasn't forthcoming with that information. I was defensive and tried to avoid admitting the possibility when I was approached about the rumors.

During another heated telephone conversation I had with Billy, "We're going to put you on child support for TWO kids!" he said in a booming voice. Those words frightened me considering all the horror stories I had heard about men being on child support and how difficult it is to maintain. As a low-ranking Airman, I didn't make much money as it already was and to be on child support for two children would have been a devastating blow. The only way to clear my name was to take another DNA test. I tried my best to avoid getting the test. I thought that my word alone would clear my name. My poker face didn't last very long. So much pressure was applied by Karen and her family, the girl I was dating, and my family members… I couldn't dodge it any longer. Although I was afraid of the outcome, I knew there was no other way to avoid the elephant in the room. Conveniently, the DNA Diagnostic Center keeps your DNA on file for up to a year.

Since they already had a collection of my DNA from Amarius's test, I didn't have to get re-swabbed again; Karen just had to take Ericka to get swabbed to see if I was a match. All I had to do was sign a piece of paper giving consent for my DNA to be used for the test. My mother cornered me with the piece of paper one day at my aunt's house after weeks of me trying to avoid the test. "Baby, if you know for sure the baby isn't yours, why don't you just sign this paper and get it over with?" my mother asked. My heart was pounding, and I was overcome with anxiety again. I valued the relationship I was in at the time and didn't want to face the fact that I had cheated on her. I knew internally that there was a slight possibility, but I felt like the chance of me being the father was pretty slim based on how careful I was the last time Karen and I hooked up. I listened to my mother and signed the paperwork. I put it in God's hands.

This time was one of the most stressful times of my life. I was compelled to write a letter expressing my discomforts of the allegations surrounding me possibly being the father of Ericka and sent it to Karen and her parents. In the letter, I discussed how I had agreed to accomplish a DNA test to bring the allegations to a conclusion and clear my name. Karen and her parents had prevented me from being included in decisions being made for Amarius since I hadn't properly legitimated myself as his father. This led me to expressing in the letter how having a DNA test on file proving that I was the father of Amarius should have been enough to prove legitimation. Furthermore, I addressed my attempts to call Billy on the phone to voice my discomforts man to man, but he wasn't receptive and hung up the phone. Their actions made me feel as if I was being shielded from parenting for Amarius and I was determined to take the necessary steps to overcome these hurdles.

When the results from Ericka's DNA test were returned, I was able to rejoice! The results concluded that there was a 0% chance that I was the father of Ericka. I immediately began to react with an "I told you so" response to all of the people who doubted me. Little did they know, I was internally breathing a sigh of relief and extremely thankful that I wasn't the father of Ericka. Nothing against Ericka, but the idea of being on child support for two children and more drama with Karen's parents wasn't appealing to me.

After clearing my name of the Ericka rumors, I focused on what I needed to do for legitimation. I was still unsure of the process, but I knew having the DNA test proving I am the father of Amarius was a good start. I decided to speak with my Flight Chief, Master Sergeant Michael Spruill, to ask for some guidance. Sergeant Spruill is a brother from New York and as cool as a fan. He had a funny analogy for everything, and I could relate to him easily. Prior to me approaching him, I had overheard him speaking about some custody issues he had previously experienced and I knew he would be a good resource for me. During the meeting with Sergeant Spruill, I expressed the hurdles that I needed him to help me overcome and he supplied me with the perfect resource to remedy my issues. He understood that I was a low-ranking Airman and didn't have much money for lawyer fees. He knew a paralegal by the name of Emily Stevens that had an office in downtown Las Vegas. Emily was familiar with the family law process in all 50 states. She had very affordable rates and was very understanding.

She would listen to your concerns and your intentions, then type up a petition for you to file in court.

Since she wasn't a lawyer, I had to go to court and represent myself, but that's better than not taking any action and getting screwed over by the opposing party. I met with Emily and she typed up a petition that helped me legitimate Amarius, establish joint-custody, child support, and a visitation agreement. She was very organized and had sticky notes with addresses that told me which documents to mail, where to mail them to, and which ones to keep for my records. She charged me approximately $250 to type up the petition and get it filed. I spoke with Karen about my intentions to legitimate Amarius and establish child support. Since we were still able to co-parent peacefully, she was on board. I provided incentive for her to be in agreement by offering to pay her backed child support. I had just received a lump sum of money and I offered to give her the full amount to repay her for the short period of time in Amarius's life when I didn't have a job. Karen's instant receptiveness to my offer led me to believe that she knew it was a great deal for her. Karen agreed to all terms and we were able to attend the court hearing without any lawyers involved.

As the judge reviewed my petition, I remember him asking Karen, "Are you sure you want to agree to this?" He asked her like three times back-to-back. It was as if he felt like I was trying to short-change her or something. I recall thinking to myself, *Bro, why are you slowing down the process? This is a sweet deal for her!* Karen was able to fight through the judge's attempts to make her second guess herself and the judge ended up signing off on the final order establishing legitimation, custody, child support, and visitation all in one hearing! This was a monumental move for me as a father because I was able to finally legitimate myself and legally establish my position in Amarius's life; and I did it in a manner that didn't obliterate my bank account. I felt so accomplished. It also established an opportunity for me to have some leverage as a parent in Amarius's life regarding decision making for him without so much resistance from her parents. I wondered how Karen's parents would react when they found out she sided with me on this one instance in our adversarial conflict? See attachment X to reference a few of the pages from the final order.

STATE OF GEORGIA

NICHOLAS J. WEDLOW,
Petitioner,

vs.   Civil Action No. 1B08DR381W

Respondent

ORDER GRANTING LEGITIMATION OF THE CHILD AND ESTABLISHING CUSTODY AND CHILD SUPPORT

After hearing evidence and agreement of the parties, the Court hereby enters its findings

of Fact, Conclusions of Law and Judgment at follows:

FINDINGS OF FACT

1. AMARIUS PAYTON WEDLOW, male child, born December 18, 2004, is the subject

of this proceeding.

2. The mother of said child is   who has been served with

notice of the within proceeding, and has agreed thereto.

3. The natural father of said child is Petitioner herein, NICHOLAS J. WEDLOW, who

has acknowledged paternity and supported the child.

4. The Petitioner desires to establish custody, visitation and support of the minor child.

CONCLUSIONS OF LAW

NICHOLAS J. WEDLOW, Petitioner, is adjudged to be the legitimate father of said

minor child and he is entitled to an order establishing custody, visitation and support of the child.

JUDGMENT

IT IS HEREBY ORDERED:

NICHOLAS J. WEDLOW is the legitimate father of the minor child, AMARIUS

attachment X

48

IT IS FURTHER ORDERED, ADJUDGED AND DECREED that the parties shall be awarded joint legal custody of the minor child, and shared (equal) physical custody of the child, pending full time enrollment of the child in school, at which time custody shall be reviewed. The parties shall exchange the child monthly, with Petitioner having the child in November, January, March, May, July and September. Upon the child entering school, until further order of the court, custody shall be as follows: Petitioner shall have the child the second weekend of each month, with Respondent delivering the child to Petitioner's mother's home address Friday at 6 p.m. and returning the child on Sunday at 8 p.m.; for a minimum of eight (8) weeks summer vacation annually; Christmas vacation in odd years (which shall include the child's birthday on December 18); Thanksgiving vacation in even years; and other visitation by mutual agreement of the parties.

Petitioner shall be notified at all times of the child's home address and phone number, and any child care providers or school the child attends. Petitioner shall also have telephonic visitation two times per week, and webcam visitation in the future.

Petitioner shall claim the child annually for tax purposes in odd years; and Respondent shall claim the child annually in even years for tax purposes.

Petitioner shall provide Respondent child support in the statutory sum, with an offset for the cost of medical insurance and transportation costs. Current child support shall be set at $275 per month from Petitioner to Respondent.

I _____ has agreed to the following proposal from Nicholas Jerrod Wedlow, concerning the child support of our son, Amarius Payton Wedlow. On April 16, 2008, Nicholas will have given me, the sum of $1259, for the back payment owed in child support. Nicholas has agreed to make child support payments in the amount of $275 on the 15th of each month. Support amount will increase, upon the advancement of Nicholas's pay grade in the United States Air Force. Payments will be made until Amarius Payton Wedlow reaches the age of 18 years old. I am in compliance with this arrangement, and have agreed to drop the child support case filed at the Bulloch County Child Support Recovery, located at 1 Courtland Street, Statesboro, GA 30458 (912-489-8747). For any reason Nicholas does not meet the above agreement to make the monthly payments, I will re-open the child support case.

Sincerely,

_____   4/15/2008
                            Date

Janet C. Peed   4/15/2008
Witness   Date

Things started to smooth out after I legitimated myself as the father, established joint custody, visitation, and child support. This enabled me to have more say regarding the decisions being made for Amarius. Karen began allowing Amarius to fly out to Las Vegas, NV and visit me during my court-ordered visitations. We began to co-parent without issue and work together. We were able to have mature parental conversations; Karen was pretty understanding and flexible in the early years of Amarius's childhood post legitimation. The first summer that Amarius came to visit me in Las Vegas was pretty challenging for me financially. At the time, I was still a low-ranking Airman and struggled to manage some of my financial responsibilities. Any given month, I had to pay child support, a car note, car insurance, rent, power, water, credit card bills, etc. In addition to all of my bills, I still had to purchase airfare and provide entertainment for Amarius during my visitations with him. This particular year, Karen reached out to me around April requesting help. She explained that she had been struggling financially and wanted me to begin my summer visitation early. I was unprepared to begin my visitation with him from April through the end of the summer but remained flexible because I was excited to spend time with Amarius. I explained my financial hurdles and we agreed that I wouldn't pay child support during the visitation; because she knew I would still need to provide entertainment and childcare for him. I didn't realize that this agreement was going to come back to haunt me later on.

Karen didn't provide a lot of details as to why she was struggling financially or what she was going through to make her need me to randomly visit with him early. I also didn't ask questions, but as that particular summer went on, I overheard rumors about what she could have been going through. Karen had also told me that she was moving out of her parents' house. I wondered why she would suddenly be moving out of her parents' home again when historically she hadn't had much stability otherwise. I was also curious as to whether or not she and her parents were having differences that led to her swift exodus from their home. This made me very uncomfortable with returning Amarius to live with Karen in an unstable environment. I decided to reach out to Emily Stevens again for help. Emily helped me file a petition for modification of custody, unbeknownst to Karen. At this time, I was still pretty unfamiliar with the custody modification processes; especially being pro se, which is essentially representing yourself in court without a lawyer.

Emily's job as a paralegal was to help properly file the necessary paperwork, and after that, you were on your own. It worked for me the first time Karen and I went to court for the legitimization because we were in agreeance of all the terms, but this time I knew it would be different. Although Karen was struggling to become a stable parent, she wasn't going to just let me waltz in the courtroom and take full custody. Knowing that I was going to be in for a wild ride, I decided to step out on a limb and use the money that I was going to spend for Amarius's return flight to Georgia after the summer ended to fund the filing of the custody modification petition.

Emily educated me as much as she could on the process and hurdles I could potentially encounter in a custody modification battle. She expressed to me that these cases oftentimes take anywhere from a few months to years; in addition to multiple court hearings prior to getting a decision. This is when it dawned on me that I probably wasn't going to be able to afford going through with a custody modification. I expressed my concerns to Emily and her powerful response resonated with me. "The good ones never give up," Emily said as she attempted to provide me with the willpower to embark on that juggernaut of a task. Emily was implying that good fathers find a way to make it happen! Her words changed my approach to fatherhood overall. I wanted to be considered as a good father and she motivated me to not give up. However, at the time, I simply couldn't afford all the back and forth from Las Vegas to Georgia to attend multiple court hearings while simultaneously maintaining all of my other bills and expenses.

As the summer began to come to an end, Karen inquired about when I was returning Amarius to her. At that time, I decided to inform Karen that I was trying to fight for full custody, and she got pissed. She immediately went into defensive mode. I didn't want to reveal my hand too soon, but I also wanted to manage her expectations on when Amarius would return. Miraculously, everything started to improve for her after I revealed my plans. Her parents let her move back into their home and suddenly she was conveniently "stable" again. I had a big decision to make. Was it really worth going into a tremendous amount of debt and risk losing a contested custody battle that I knew I couldn't afford?

Additionally, I had no experience in law proceedings, and representing myself in court was pretty intimidating, especially since I didn't have a background in family law education. Furthermore, it was going to be hard to make a case that she was an "unfit" mother without gathering some hard evidence to support my position. I decided to forfeit the modification of custody request and return Amarius to Karen. There was only one problem. I couldn't afford to buy him a return flight to Georgia. After a huge argument with Karen and her parents, her father Billy decided to purchase his airfare. Amarius returned to Georgia and Karen was able to reestablish her stability as a parent.

CHAPTER 6

PRINCESS KEIMORA

"A girl's father is the first man in her life,
and probably the most influential."
—*David Jeremiah*

After a few years of the dating scene in Las Vegas, I began to yearn for companionship. Single life was fun for a while, but it began to get old quick. Social media really began taking off around that time and it made it easy to meet new people. I was scrolling on Facebook one day and saw the profile picture of a beautiful woman named Kayla aka "Kay" in the "people you may know" section. It just so happened that she was mutual friends with my younger sister Claire. Her profile picture caught my eye and I decided to investigate further. I reviewed several of her profile pictures and was blown away by her beautiful eyes. I decided to slide into her DMs and the rest was history!

Unfortunately, Kayla lived in Georgia and I was still in Las Vegas, so we were faced with settling for a long-distance situationship. Things heated up between me and Kayla pretty fast. Our phone conversations and video chats would last for hours at a time. It turned out that we had a lot in common. Kayla's biological father wasn't very active in her life as a child either and we were able to relate to each other in that regard. Kayla was the same age as my younger sister Claire, and they were pretty good friends in grade school. Apparently, Kayla had a crush on me back in my high school football days and her previous curiosity about me fueled her interest in pursuing a relationship as our new-found friendship developed. After conversing with each other over a span of roughly six months, we decided to make it official. We established a relationship, despite the challenges of being geographically separated from each other.

In January of 2011, I was tasked with a deployment to Kuwait. I had never been out of the country before, so this was a new challenge for me. Although Kayla and I were already in a long-distance relationship, being in a time zone that was 12 hours ahead of her tested our communication even more. After adjusting to being in a new country and the communication challenges, our relationship continued to prosper. She would set her alarm for 2 A.M. so that we could video chat with each other daily. We talked about future plans, goals, traveling, making money, etc. The anticipation to see each other in person became almost unbearable. My deployment was scheduled for 4 months and afterwards I had planned to fly her to Las Vegas to visit me upon my return to the States.

The opportunity for us to see each other presented itself sooner than we expected but wasn't the most ideal circumstance for a visit. What seemed to be a typical day at work turned out to be a very scary and stressful situation. I remember being told that I needed to go to my commanders' office because he needed to speak with me. It wasn't a routine occurrence to go speak with the commander unless you were in trouble; so, I immediately expected the worse when I got notified that he wanted to see me. I was eager to see what it was about because I didn't recall doing anything that could have gotten me in trouble. I reported to his office as directed while simultaneously trying to mask my nervousness and insecurities.

As I entered his office, I could sense that something was terribly wrong. The look on his face revealed that I wasn't in trouble; however, it was a look of sadness like he had a burden that he was hesitant but obligated to share with me. "Have a seat, Airman Wedlow," my commander stated welcomingly. I sat down slowly and hesitantly on the couch in his office and waited patiently for him to let me know why I was there. After taking a deep breath, he broke the news. "Your father is in the hospital and he's in critical condition right now, we have arranged for you to fly back to Atlanta tonight so that you can go be with your family," my commander informed me. I was floored by this news! This was not what I was expecting to hear, and it suddenly made sense why my commander seemed so uncomfortable before informing me. I was blown away and thankful at how quickly the American Red Cross was able to schedule and purchase travel arrangements for me after a family member had contacted them and informed them of the situation.

I left his office in a complete state of shock and feelings of guilt. The Air Force didn't know that Big Henry wasn't my biological father. I listed Big Henry as my biological father when I completed the paperwork to enter the Air Force because his name was on my birth certificate and it was easier to explain. Plus, Big Henry was more of a father figure to me than Lindsey was, and I didn't want to give credit to someone that wasn't involved. The news about Big Henry's health saddened me because it's tough to receive news about someone you love not doing well. In addition to the sadness, I felt extremely guilty. I felt a sense of guilt because as an adult, I didn't keep in touch with him the way I probably should have. A large part of the lack of communication was due to the fact that he wasn't my biological father. The other part was the "out of sight, out of mind" mentality that people fall into when they live far away. Neither of these reasons justified our relationship declining as I got older, but this is my truth.

While packing my bags and preparing to return to America, I began to reminisce about all of the good times I had when visiting Big Henry as a child. Those memories saddened me even more. I also began to process how I would interact around the Wedlow family during my visit. I was aware that they still didn't know about my true biological father and I didn't plan on breaking the news to them at a time like this. I was also nervous about traveling from a foreign country back to America by myself. I arrived in Kuwait with a large group of Air Force members, so I felt pretty comfortable. This time, I was returning to America by myself and I was pretty uncomfortable checking in at the airport in Kuwait City when everyone barely spoke any English. Luckily, I was able to locate someone that spoke enough English to help me navigate my way through the airport. After literally half a day of flying over the Atlantic Ocean, I made it to Georgia safely.

Despite the unfortunate circumstances, my family members were very excited to see me and welcomed me with open arms. Aunt Carolyn, Big Henry's sister, showed me a ton of hospitality and allowed me to stay at her house during my two-week stint in Georgia. Our joys of reconnecting were derailed by the reason I was visiting; Big Henry was fighting for his life! Aunt Carolyn took me to the hospital to visit him shortly after I arrived. She informed me of his symptoms and they were very concerning. He had several health concerns going on at once, but the primary issue was the fact that he had pneumonia. This was very concerning to me because he had overcome a stroke before that he never fully recovered from, and now, he was faced with more medical adversity. When I entered his hospital room, I remember seeing him lying there with tubes coming out of his mouth, hooked up to numerous machines, motionless, and quiet. The guilt I was already experiencing intensified and I became very emotional. At the time, I wasn't sure if he would pull through this and I was ashamed that I hadn't stayed in contact with him after I became an adult. I feared that I wouldn't be able to rekindle our relationship if he didn't make it through his current medical state. The good news is Big Henry was able to overcome the pneumonia and pull through. Unfortunately, it wasn't until I returned to Kuwait that he was coherent enough to acknowledge his hospital visitors.

In between visiting Big Henry at the hospital and staying at aunt Carolyn's house, I took advantage of being in Georgia and was able to visit Kayla. Aunt Carolyn was pretty understanding about me wanting to visit with other friends and family; she knew it had been a while since the last time I was in Georgia. I was fortunate enough to have a rental car during my stay, and it really assisted me with getting around and connecting with everyone. Although it was a sad visit due to the state of Big Henry's health, I was very excited to see Kayla. Kayla lived roughly two hours southeast of the hospital Big Henry was admitted to. After visiting the hospital, I would make the drive to see Kayla during the nighttime. The chemistry we developed over the phone and through video chat really sparked when we saw each other in person. Those beautiful eyes looked even better face to face than they did in her pictures.

Kayla was still living with her mother Jennifer at the time; I call her "Ma Jen". Ma Jen was nice enough to let me spend the night at her house a few times during my visit. This allowed me and Kayla to spend more time together and get to know each other. They embraced me as family and really made me feel welcomed in their home. Did I mention Ma Jen can cook her @ss off?! Well, she can! I really enjoyed the home-cooked meals that she would provide when I visited, and it really made the two-hour drive even more worth the trip. Kayla and I began to get intimate with each other during visits as well due to the strong chemistry we were now able to act on. Without going into too much detail, we created fireworks in the bedroom, and Fourth of July celebrations didn't even come close. Have you ever had built up anticipation for visiting that special someone after being physically separated from them for a while and then finally being able to see, feel, and experience them? Let's just say that when I was able to finally get my hands on Kayla, our engagements exceeded my expectations and she was definitely well worth the wait.

Unfortunately, my short visit to Georgia came to an end. Big Henry was on the road to recovery prior to me returning to Kuwait to finish my deployment, and that was comforting to me. Aunt Carolyn showed me amazing hospitality and I really enjoyed spending time with Kayla and my other family members. Visiting Georgia was a breath of fresh air and a nice break from my deployment, but duty called, and I had to get back to the grind. After returning to Kuwait, I had approximately two months remaining on my deployment before I could return to the States. It seemed as if time stood still when I resumed my overseas duties. Getting a glimpse of life in the States was a huge tease and made me miss home immensely. Deployment life can get lonely when you are far away from home fighting for the freedom of Americans.

As the deployment began to come to an end, I was informed about some life-changing news! Kayla revealed that she was pregnant! I was excited, scared, and nervous all at the same time. My relationship with Kayla was still pretty new and we were still getting to know each other. Having another child out of wedlock wasn't ideal but God doesn't make mistakes. I knew I was in for a challenge and a tough road ahead. Kayla and I decided to work together and make the best of our new life together.

On November 27th, 2011, Kayla gave birth to a beautiful and healthy baby girl who we named Keimora, aka "Kei"; daddy's little princess. Parents are pretty biased about how their children look but she was honestly the prettiest baby I had ever seen. She had blue eyes and the same complexion as her mother. She was angelic. The first time I laid eyes on her, I completely fell in love. I was blessed to have two beautiful children and it sparked a new level of productivity in me because I knew that I wanted them to be able to depend on me to provide. Kayla and I got settled in Las Vegas, NV together and focused on prospering with our newly formed family.

After a few months of living together, Kayla and I decided to take our relationship a step further. We were enjoying our life together and our beautiful daughter was icing on the cake. We felt as if we were stronger together and we spawned into a cohesive unit with the shared mental model of providing the best for our daughter. On April 07, 2012 we eloped and got married in downtown Las Vegas. Unfortunately, we couldn't afford a huge elaborate wedding with all of our family members involved, but it was still a beautiful ceremony. Being a family man enabled me to eliminate distractions and focus on enhancing my capabilities to provide better for my family. It kick-started a newly-found ambition in me that brought about the necessary growth and maturity that were essential for me to reach new heights.

That was one of the most stressful times in my life. My financial responsibilities increased significantly. I had to pay child support before I even thought about paying all of the other bills I was responsible for. For a while, Kayla was a stay-at-home mom so we had to make do with only one income for the four of us. Money started to become scarce, but we were able to live within our means to survive. These financial hurdles motivated me to increase my work performance to position myself for promotion. Not only did I aspire to achieve more financial compensation for my work ethic, but my family needed it! It took a while to position Kayla where she could seek employment. Due to a single-income household and having to pay child support, we simply couldn't afford childcare for Keimora long enough for Kayla to start receiving paychecks.

CHAPTER 7

AND THE
DRAMA BEGINS

"My father used to play with my brother and me in the yard.
Mother would come out and say, 'You're tearing up the grass.'
'We're not raising grass,' Dad would reply. 'We're raising boys.'"
—Harmon Killebrew

*C*oincidentally, after I got married, my relationship with Amarius began to suffer. My court-ordered telephonic visitations were reduced significantly. Karen never admitted to purposefully not allowing me to speak with Amarius, but her actions said it all. I would routinely speak with Amarius over the phone prior to my marriage, but post marriage, communication with him was like pulling teeth. Karen would allow me to speak with him at times but consistent conversations with Amarius became few and far in between. There always seemed to be an excuse about why he wasn't available to talk. *If Amarius was just outside playing with his friends, then why does it take a week for him to return my phone call? Did she not see my missed calls and texts? Was she dodging me?* These are the types of questions that I couldn't get the answers to and it became frustrating.

Initially, I didn't understand where the drama was stemming from but over time, I began to identify the root of the problem. Karen expressed on several occasions how she wasn't comfortable with Kayla being around Amarius. It was more than just a coincidence to me that all of a sudden, Karen wasn't being a mature co-parent and letting me maintain the relationship I had built with Amarius despite my new marriage. Why this was an issue baffled me because Kayla treated Amarius with the same love and support that any mother would for their child. Kayla had no intentions of replacing Karen as the primary motherly figure in Amarius's life; she was simply being a supportive wife and helping me provide for him.

Whenever I got the opportunity to speak with Amarius, I would inquire with him about why our communication had been reduced. He would respond and say things like, "I don't know, I've just been busy." These types of responses were pretty odd to me because what child is too busy to speak to their father for a few minutes several times a week? Over time, I noticed that he began to have an attitude with me based on how he responded to some of my questions. It seemed as if I was inconveniencing him by wanting to talk to him consistently. I knew that the reduction in respect was due to being geographically separated but it bothered me how comfortable he became with not speaking with me regularly and treating me like I was aggravating him. Out of sight, out of mind is a real thing and it began to affect the relationship between me and Amarius. In addition to the geographical separation, it also bothered me that Karen all of a sudden wasn't necessarily encouraging Amarius to maintain consistent telephonic communication with me. After all, I was only asking for Karen to stick to our court-ordered agreement and have Amarius available for our minimum of two phone calls per week.

As time went on, my attempts to communicate with Amarius became worse and worse. The co-parental relationship between Karen and I became increasingly rocky. We went from being able to have cordial conversations about Amarius to confrontational arguments over the phone regarding co-parenting. When we were in disagreement about different issues, she would get upset and punish me by not letting me speak with Amarius. There were times when Karen would grab the phone from Amarius and just hang up. This brought my blood to a boil because she knew that she had the upper hand and was taking advantage of it. There was nothing I could do about conversations with

Amarius being cut short because I lived so far away. I would attempt to call back and try and finish the call but would get ignored. At times, I felt completely helpless and it was so frustrating to be hung up on and ignored like I didn't even matter as a father. I started to feel like I was just a paycheck to her.

My attempts to negotiate future visitations with Amarius also began to get deflected by Karen regularly. In addition to not being able to talk to Amarius on the phone, there were several other court-ordered provisions Karen wasn't complying with. We were supposed to be alternating years for claiming Amarius on taxes and she was supposed to notify me of any caretakers' name and contact information that cared for Amarius in her absence. Out of sheer desperation, I would attempt to reach out to Karen's parents and try to get them to talk some sense into her when she would ignore my phone calls and attempts to see Amarius. This tactic was also unsuccessful because the type of response I would get from Karen's parents was, "Leave the grandparents out of it, take her to court." I was infuriated by Karen's failure to comply with the court order as well as her family's lack of receptiveness to encourage her to comply with the order; which made it difficult for me to be a father to my son. It hurt to hear them encourage me to take Karen to court, but they were right. If I had an issue with Karen not complying with our court order, I needed to take it to trial to resolve it. Sounds easy right? The only problem was I simply couldn't afford it; so, I tried to take the civil route and negotiate my way into some cooperation.

My attempts at peaceful negotiation with Karen and her parents fell on deaf ears. I continued to receive resistance during my attempts at the court-ordered telephonic and physical visitations. During the spring of 2012, the summer was fast approaching, and I wanted to prepare for a summer visitation with Amarius. Tax season positioned me financially and enabled me to afford the airfare from Georgia to Nevada and I was excited to take advantage of it. I scheduled his airfare for travel in early June of that year because I wanted him to arrive in Las Vegas in time for Father's Day; that would have been the first Father's Day I would have had with both of my children. Despite the communication hurdles with my son, I didn't think Karen had the balls to deny me a physical visitation if I presented her with proof of purchased airfare. After purchasing a plane ticket in the spring of 2012, I provided Karen with a copy of the itinerary in hopes that it would give her incentive to take my visitation seriously. This was another miscalculated assumption of mine.

My proposal for a summer visitation was met with immediate rejection by Karen. "You still owe me child support for the previous two summers where he came to visit you and you didn't pay me!" Karen responded defensively to my request. "Are you serious?! You had no problem with me not paying you while he was with me but now all of a sudden, I owe you?!" I barked frustratingly. I was in disbelief how she suddenly and conveniently brought back up child support that she had agreed to not requiring me to pay because she understood my financial situation at the time. It was obvious that Karen was trying to place financial hurdles in my way to reduce my chances of being able to afford a summer visitation with Amarius. From Karen's actions, it appeared that she was bound and determined not to send him for the summer. The words from her parents began to reincarnate themselves in my thoughts after the buildup of frustration and lack of cooperation; "Leave the grandparents out of it, take her to court." A court hearing started to sound more and more appealing; I just needed to figure out how I could afford it.

As the scheduled summer visitation neared, Karen stuck to her guns and didn't budge. I practically begged her to allow Amarius to visit me despite the previous child support arrears she was demanding that I recoup. I wasn't in a position financially to repay her a lump sum of $1,375 ($275 x 5 months) so all I could do was hope that she voided her demands out of sympathy for a struggling father. She remained unsympathetic to my pleas to see my son. She elected not to take him to the airport and avoided any negotiations with me about it all the way up to the day he was supposed to fly out to visit me. I couldn't believe how bold and arrogant she was being about my visitation. I thought it was extremely petty for her to conveniently request child support money that we had previously agreed on me not paying. I was in complete shock that she wasn't going to take him to the airport. I even tried to get one of my family members to take him to the airport for her since she didn't want to, but Karen didn't answer the phone for either of us around the time he was supposed to fly out. I was outraged by her lack of cooperation! I was frustrated, disappointed, let down, and quite frankly, pissed off! What was I supposed to do about the airfare I had just purchased? Hundreds of dollars down the drain just because she didn't want him to come?! Wow! I couldn't believe it. My dreams of having the perfect Fathers' Day were completely squandered and at the time I felt like there was nothing I could do about it because I couldn't afford to go to court.

After a few days of sulking in my misery, I tried to force myself into accepting the fact that I wasn't going to be able to see my son for the summer and never recouping the money for the lost airfare. Not only did I have to deal with losing money and not seeing my son, but the ignoring of my phone calls to speak with him continued. For a father who just wanted to spend time with his kid, that was the worse feeling in the world. Kayla spent a lot of time trying to keep me focused on the positive. I did have a lot of positives to focus on and I was thankful that I could at least have a beautiful Fathers' Day with my gorgeous wife and daughter. I decided to accept the fact that I wasn't going to see Amarius and focus on making the best of the summer with Kay and Kei. Roughly a week from Father's Day, Kayla started planning a wonderful Father's Day for me to cheer me up. She planned to cook my favorite meal, an itinerary of places for us to sightsee, and some family activities. My spirits were lifted, and I was eager to make the best of it. Father's Day weekend arrived, and we were blindsided by some devastating news!

It was a quiet Friday night in the Wedlow household. Kayla and I were relaxing in our living room with Keimora watching television. Keimora was in charge of the TV so we were watching her favorite cartoon show. I pretended to be interested but in reality, I was on my phone scrolling my Facebook newsfeed whenever I noticed Keimora wasn't paying attention to me. Then out of nowhere, I randomly receive a phone call from Karen. This was odd to me because I had been trying to contact her about Amarius's visitation but she didn't answer or return any of my calls or texts. I answered right away because it had to be important if she was finally returning my phone calls. "Hello?" I answered curiously. "Hey, it's me, Amarius just got attacked by my boyfriend's dog! He is okay but I just wanted to let you know. He is about to have surgery on his shoulder, I will call you and give you all the details later once the procedure is complete."

This news elevated the built-up resentment that I was already experiencing from the way Karen had been dodging me about telephonic and physical visitations. My anger went to a whole new level; I had reached my tipping point! You mean to tell me that my son was viciously attacked by Karen's boyfriend's pit bull on Father's Day weekend when he was supposed to be visiting me?! I was so *insert curse word* mad that Kayla had to physically restrain me and calm me down. How could this be possible?! This situation had karma's name written all over it! I later found out the details of the situation. Amarius was swimming in a pool at Karen's boyfriend's house and he dropped his goggles on the ground. Her boyfriend's dog then picked the goggles up, Amarius tried to retrieve the goggles from the dog's mouth and the dog attacked. He locked on to Amarius's shoulder and began shaking him violently. Amarius was only about 7 years old at the time and he was still a tiny little guy. What if the bulldog locked onto his neck?! He could have been killed on Fathers' Day had the dog aimed for his throat! Literally a matter of inches is what saved his life! To this day, Amarius still bears a gruesome scar on his shoulder from that vicious life-threatening attack.

Bulloch County Animal Shelter/Animal Control

81 MILL CREEK RD
17245 HWY. 301 N
STATESBORO, GA 30458
Phone: (912) 764-4529
Animal Control (912) 489-6911

Incident REPORT

Complaint ID:	4108			
Status:	Complete		Printed:	06-26-2012 10:49:20 AM

Origination

Date:	06-15-2012 06:40:00 PM	Logged by:	Joseph Sanders- 1120
Reason:	Vicious,Bite Case,Anonymous: No,Other		
Area:	COUNTY		
Location:			

Notes:
1-BLUE PITBULL MALE: Animal attacked and injured child, child transported to ER.

Citizen Making Report   **Owner of animal at origination**

Dispatch and Outcome

Assigned to:	Joseph Sanders- 1120	On	06-15-2012 07:27:00 PM	Priority	1
Final Outcome:	Animal Picked Up	On	06-15-2012 08:41:00 PM		

Officer/Outcome Notes for Complaint ID: 4108

Upon arrival to ER meeting with victim and mother, they advised they were at mothers boyfriend resident and child was playing in back yard when child was attacked on back deck causing serious injuries. upon arrival to owner resident animal was up-to-date on rabie vac; and was contained in pen, because animal was so aggressive towards myself Officer Sanders and the vicious attack with dog trying to basically trying to kill child for no reason animal is considered a Dangerous dog, animal was transported to shelter and will be held for a 10 day rabies observation period and the destroyed.

Animal Information - Animal Number: 1

Species		DOG ID#: 6431	Pet Name	MAXIMUS	Current Owner
Breed		AMERICAN PIT BULL TERRIER	License		
Crossbreed			Vacc ID		
Gender		MALE/NOT STERILIZED	Microchip		
Color		BLUE/WHITE	Registration		
Age		DOB: 04-15-2011 (1 yrs, 2 mos)	Collar Type	NO COLLAR	
Size		LARGE	Collar Color		

Photos for Complaint ID: 4108

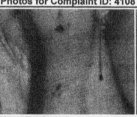 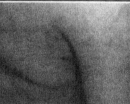 

Bulloch County Animal Shelter/Animal Control
81 MILL CREEK RD
17245 HWY. 301 N
STATESBORO, GA 30458
Phone: (912) 764-4529
Animal Control (912) 489-6911

Incident REPORT

Complaint ID:	4108	
Status:	Complete	Printed: 06-26-2012 10:49:20 AM

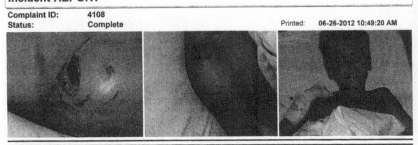

Customize this form text
End of Complaint Report 4108

CHAPTER 8

CONTEMPT OF COURT!

"Every father should remember, one day his son
will follow his example, not his advice."
—Charles Kettering

The audacity of Karen to prevent me from my court-ordered visitation caused my son to encounter a near-death experience. This infuriated me and motivated me to take action. The numerous violations of the court order had to be addressed! I was aware that I needed to start the paper trail instead of allowing Karen to continue violating the court order. I started conducting research on how I would collect enough money to hold her in contempt of court. I didn't have very much money in my savings account so that wasn't an option. At the time, I was banking with Navy Federal Credit Union and I had heard of coworkers that had gotten personal loans from them before, so I decided to give it a shot. Kayla and I went to Navy Federal and began the loan request process. Their customer service was topnotch and they listened with engaging sympathy as I explained why I needed to borrow the money. Luckily, I had maintained a decent credit score over the years which enabled them to swiftly approve my request. I was in and out of the bank in under thirty minutes with $3,000 at my disposal. This was a victory within itself but there was still a lot of homework to be done.

My cousin Adrienne has always been one of my closest supporters and I would vent to her about my frustrations with Karen and the custody issues. Adrienne showed a ton of empathy for my situation and she took it upon herself to assist me in finding an affordable attorney who could represent me in a contempt case. She found an attorney on Google from southeastern Georgia named Casey Reichanadter and forwarded her information to me. Casey was still pretty new in family law, but I decided to take a chance because she was more affordable than other attorneys that Adrienne provided for me. I reached out to Casey and conducted a consultation with her about my case. After reviewing the facts, Casey reassured me that I had a strong case and offered to represent me. We discussed the process and I paid her a retainer fee of $1,500. Casey promptly filed the petition for contempt with the Bulloch County Courthouse and we were provided with a court date approximately thirty days later. I used the rest of my personal loan to purchase airfare for myself, Kayla, and Keimora to fly to Georgia to attend the hearing.

After Casey filed the petition for contempt, Karen had thirty days to respond to the petition. I was primarily only concerned with recouping the money I lost for the plane ticket, but since Karen had violated other provisions of the court order, it was convenient for us to address the other issues simultaneously. Karen retained a lawyer and filed a counterclaim to the petition. Karen's attorney filed a response requesting that I be held in contempt for failing to pay child support for the previous two summers that Amarius visited me. She also requested that I repay Billy for the return flight he purchased for Amarius after I attempted to get full custody. How convenient of her, right? I was appalled by her last request in the counterclaim which was for me to repay her lawyer fees! The audacity! I didn't even know that was a thing but apparently, you can do that. That seemed like a petty tactic Karen was trying to use and the perception that I got from that request was that she was trying to punish me financially for inconveniencing her by taking her to court.

I was nervous about her counterclaim because I knew it would appear to a judge that I've been neglecting to pay Karen consistently, regardless of whether or not we had an agreement about summer child support. A wise man once told me, "An agreement is only as good as the piece of paper it's not written on." From that point forward I knew I needed to document any future agreements between me and Karen in writing. I was also afraid that I would end up having to pay her lawyer fees if her request was granted. Karen's counterclaim only had enough ammunition to rebut the airfare I was trying to collect but the other issues, she had no response for other than denial. Let's see how that held up in court...

As we arrived in Georgia and prepared for the contempt hearing, Kayla and I were experiencing feelings of anxiety and uncertainty. This was only the second time I had been to court for any reason up until this point in my life and didn't know what to expect. My lawyer and I prepared well but not knowing what the opponent had in store was nerve-wracking. Aside from the court hearing, we were excited to be back around our family in Georgia and their support put our nerves at ease. As we arrived at the hearing, I met with Casey and we conducted a final review of our game plan. Unbeknownst to me at the time, it is encouraged for the petitioner and the defendant to negotiate terms prior to presenting the case to the judge. This provides an opportunity to reduce the amount of litigation in the courtroom and shortens the hearing. Casey and I met with Karen and her attorney prior to entering the courtroom and discussed the issues.

After some brief back and forth discussion of the terms, we came to an agreement on all but one issue. It was agreed that Karen would drop her request for owed child support and the return flight if I didn't hold her accountable for the money received from annually claiming Amarius on taxes. Her lawyer also offered to provide make up visitation dates for the time I missed during the summer Amarius was supposed to visit me. Another one of her chief complaints was her suddenly feeling like eight weeks during the summer was too long and wanted to reduce my summer visitation time with Amarius to five weeks. The only issue we couldn't come to an agreement on was Karen's request for me to provide proof of a round trip plane ticket prior to allowing Amarius to visit with me. I didn't want to agree to this because it was more affordable for me to purchase a one-way ticket on separate occasions. I was aware that the reason for this request was to prevent me from keeping Amarius with me longer than agreed; she was afraid I would attempt to keep him longer than my court-ordered visitation time like I did when I was planning to pursue a change of custody a few years prior.

We entered the courtroom and prepared for the hearing to begin. I was nervous and curious about how it would go. I feared that the judge would agree with Karen about how she felt I needed to provide her with proof of a round trip plane ticket prior to any visitations. If the judge required this proof, it would have decreased my ability to afford future visitations significantly. Although I was worried, I kept the faith and was ready to plead my case. The judge called me to the stand for cross-examination. I got sworn in, took the stand, and both lawyers proceeded to question me. While I was being questioned by Karen's lawyers, he tried his best to criminalize me by discussing the time that I took it upon myself to keep Amarius longer than the court order specified for my summer visitation.

Of course, he failed to mention how Karen requested me to begin my visitation early and how she was struggling for stability as a parent. I tried my best to justify my reasoning, but the judge wasn't convinced. The judge interrupted the cross-examination and asked, "Mr. Wedlow, do you realize you can go to jail for that?" Startled by his question I responded, "Actually, no, sir, I didn't know that." I was blown away by how the focus of the hearing transitioned from holding Karen in contempt for not letting me see Amarius recently to me being threatened with jail time for something that happened two years prior. I thought to myself, *Wait, aren't we literally here in court today because Karen wouldn't let me see Amarius this summer?* The hypocritical judge never addressed Karen and her failure to cooperate with my summer visitation, but he was ready to throw me in jail? Wow! Right then and there I lost faith in the court system.

The hearing eventually reached the matter of contention. Was it a reasonable request to demand that I show proof of a round trip plane ticket prior to future visitations with Amarius, or not? As the judge reviewed the evidence that surfaced during the cross-examination, he asked Karen a question that played to my favor. "What if Mr. Wedlow decided he wanted to drive his son out to visit?" the judge asked curiously. This question stumped the defense. Although I never planned on making the 30-hour drive to Georgia, I was grateful that the judge assisted me and solidified that flexibility into the final order. The judges' final decision was that I wasn't required to provide proof of a round trip ticket and this verdict was a huge weight off of my shoulders. I was extremely grateful that I got my make-up visitation dates scheduled and didn't have to pay her lawyer fees. I was also pretty bummed out that my summer visitations got reduced from eight weeks to five. Although it felt like a win, I was stretched thin financially after the hearing. I had to pay my lawyer, child support, and purchase airfare to travel to Georgia to attend court all in the same month with a one-income household. I was broke to say the least. I've included a snapshot of the final order from this contempt hearing.

IN THE SUPERIOR COURT OF BULLOCH COUNTY
STATE OF GEORGIA

NICHOLAS J. WEDLOW,	)
	)
Plaintiff/Movant,	)
	)
vs.	) Civil Action Number: 1B08DR-381-W
	)
,	)
	)
Defendant/Respondent.	)

FINAL ORDER

The parties having come before this Court for a hearing on August 9, 2012, both parties having been present and represented by counsel, and evidence having been presented and heard; it is HEREBY ORDERED as follows:

1. Findings of Fact

On December 22, 2008 the Superior Court of Bulloch County, State of Georgia, Civil Action No. 1B08DR-381-W, issued an Order Granting Legitimation of the Child and Establishing Custody and Child Support for the parties' minor child, to wit Amarius Payton Wedlow, born on December 18, 2004.

On April 4, 2012 the Plaintiff-Father filed a Petition for Contempt against

Page 1 of 6
Nicholas J. Wedlow v.
Civil Action No: 1B08DR-381-W
Superior Court of Bulloch County

the Defendant-Mother. The Plaintiff then filed a Second Amended Petition for Contempt on August 2, 2012 alleging that the Mother violated said Order by denying him summer and telephone visitation, failing to notify him of the minor child's caretaker's name and contact information, and claiming the minor child on her taxes every year.

The parties resolved all but one issue, regarding whether the Father would be required to purchase a round-trip ticket for the minor child's visits. A hearing was held for the Court to resolve the outstanding issue.

2. Visitation

a. The Father will have the following visitation schedule to make-up for the lost summer visitation:

1) Fall Holiday, beginning on October 13, 2012 and concluding on October 20, 2012.

2) Thanksgiving, beginning on November 17, 2012 and concluding on November 24, 2012.

3) Christmas Holiday, beginning on December 26, 2012 and concluding on January 5, 2013.

4) Winter Holiday, beginning on February 9, 2012 and concluding on February 16, 2013.

The Father shall pay all travel costs for these make-up visits. The Mother shall release her claim to any and all reimbursements for travel expenses incurred prior to the date of this Order.

b.   Beginning March 2013 and going forward until the minor child reaches eighteen (18) years old, the visitation schedule will be as follows, pursuant to the child's school calendar:

Odd Years

MOTHER	FATHER
Fall Holiday	Thanksgiving
The first Saturday before the week-long holiday until the following Saturday.	The first Saturday before Thanksgiving until the following Saturday.
First Half of Christmas Vacation	Second Half of Christmas Vacation
The day after the end of the first semester until December 26.	December 26 until the Saturday before the second semester resumes.

Winter Holiday	Spring Break
The first Saturday before the week-long holiday until the following Saturday.	The first Saturday before the week-long holiday until the following Saturday.

Even Years

The above schedule shall be reversed as to Father and Mother.

The Father shall have five (5) consecutive weeks of summer visitation every year. The Father shall pay all travel costs for visitation.

c.   The Father shall be entitled to a minimum of two (2) phone calls a week with the minor child. When the minor child is in the Father's custody, the Mother shall be entitled to a minimum of two (2) phone calls a week with the minor child.

d.   The Father is not required to purchase a round-trip ticket for the minor child during any visits, and the Father may use any reasonable mode of transportation for said visits.

3.   **Child Support**

a.   The Mother shall release her claim for any child support arrears incurred prior to the date of this Order.

b. Each party shall be responsible for one-half (1/2) of the minor child's extracurricular costs.

c. Each party shall be responsible for one-half (1/2) of the minor child's unreimbursed medical costs.

4. **Taxes**

The Mother shall claim the minor child on her taxes every year.

5. **Attorney's Fees**

Both parties shall release any claim for attorney's fees in the above-captioned matter.

6. **All Other Provisions**

All other provisions of the parties' Order Granting Legitimation of the Child and Establishing Custody and Child Support not specifically modified by this Order remain in full force and effect and unmodified by this Order.

[Signatures on page 6]

Page 5 of 6
Nicholas J. Wedlow v.
Civil Action No: 1B08DR-381-W
Superior Court of Bulloch County

While I was in town for the contempt hearing, I decided it would be a good idea to tap in with his teachers before I returned to Nevada. I precoordinated a parent-teacher conference before I arrived so that I could get a glimpse of how Amarius was performing academically. I didn't trust Karen to provide me with accurate information and I wanted to see for myself. After all, I am his father and I wanted to exercise my rights by forcing the school to grant me access to his grades like I'm rightfully allowed. During the conference, I was shocked by what was revealed. Amarius had been performing poorly in school. His grades were subpar, and this was alarming to me because he had so much academic potential. The teacher explained that he had behavioral issues such as excessive talking and overall silliness. She also informed me that she had been trying to schedule a parent-teacher conference for Amarius for quite some time but for one reason or another Karen had not been able to deliver. I apologized to his teacher for not being involved as much as I would have liked to, but she also understood that I didn't live in Georgia. I assured her that his behavioral issues and lack of effort academically seemed like a lack of discipline issue that I needed to address with Karen. Those issues would not have existed had he lived with me but since he lived with his mom, it made sense.

After hearing through the grapevine that I attended a parent-teacher conference, Karen reached out to me as soon as she could and angrily sent me a text message that read, "How are you going to attend a parent-teacher conference without me?!" I calmly explained to her that I wasn't required to coordinate with her to meet with Amarius's teachers. Karen had barely returned my phone calls and text messages. What made her think that I felt confident enough in her communication to coordinate her attending a parent-teacher conference that I scheduled? Furthermore, if the teacher had been trying to schedule a parent-teacher conference for quite a while then it obviously wasn't high enough on Karen's priority list to accomplish one. It didn't make sense to me that I could fly from out of town and attend a parent-teacher conference, but Karen lived in the same city as his school and hadn't already scheduled one herself. I didn't want to go back and forth with Karen about the parent-teacher conference. I took the initiative to schedule a conference for my son and Kayla was in attendance. I could see how this did not put Karen in the best light considering that she had failed to take that initiative herself. Either way, I disregarded her attempts to argue and killed her with kindness.

CHAPTER 9

FINANCIAL VENGEANCE?

"I've said it before, but it's absolutely true: My mother gave me my drive, but my father gave me my dreams. Thanks to him, I could see a future."
—Liza Minnelli

*K*ayla and I returned to Las Vegas a few days after the hearing and began to continue building our life together. The contempt hearing temporarily set us back financially and we committed to recovering from it. Kayla was still unemployed, and I was barely able to cover all of our expenses. We were living in a decent-sized two-bedroom apartment right outside of Nellis Air Force Base at the time because I didn't want a long transit to work to minimize money spent on gas. Although we weren't in poverty, I wasn't content with my finances and I began to focus on seeking opportunities for promotion. My opportunity to test for Staff Sergeant was fast approaching and I wanted to take advantage of it. Kayla did a phenomenal job of helping me buckle down and assisting me with studying for the promotion test. We spent hours reviewing flashcards, taking practice quizzes, and Q & A sessions regarding Air Force history and job specialty knowledge.

Our preparation paid dividends when the list of selected promotees was announced and my name was on it! We were overjoyed with my selection for promotion and celebrated our victory together. I was informed that I had to wait several months before I could sew on my new rank and actually start getting paid more but it was a huge sigh of relief to know that financial help was on the way! We were still repaying the loan that I borrowed from Navy Federal Credit Union to attend the contempt hearing but being selected for promotion was the blessing that we needed to stop the financial bleeding.

When good things are happening in your life, word travels fast! I'm sure Karen must have gotten word that I was being promoted because shortly after the announcement, I got served with a petition for a child support modification. I couldn't believe my eyes! I had just literally attended the contempt hearing in Georgia a few months prior and was still financially recovering, and she was already trying to go back to court?! I was blown away by this news. Karen knew I had a wife and child to care for in addition to Amarius, and I felt like the child support I was currently sending her was fair and affordable for me. It was such a coincidence to me that Karen all of a sudden wanted more child support after news of my promotion rang out. The fact that I recently held Karen in contempt of court did nothing to endear me to her.

After being served with a legal document demanding that you attend a court hearing, you have thirty days to respond. The pressure was on. I had to begin researching the legal process all over again, and admittedly I wasn't financially prepared to do so. I was aware that the original child support agreement that Karen and I negotiated suggested that as my pay increased, so would my child support. I also only had one child when we negotiated that initial agreement; I wanted to ensure that my wife and daughter were factored into a fair child support agreement in the future. Since I was still making payments on the loan recently taken out for the contempt hearing, I didn't want to request another one. I also didn't have enough money in my savings account to retain a lawyer for a child support modification hearing. It was decided that I would attend the hearing pro se. I realized that representing myself in a child support modification hearing wasn't the smartest decision, but my choices were limited due to finances. Traveling via airplane back and forth from Las Vegas to Georgia for civil litigation with lawyers all within a few months was a very expensive process for a low-ranking Airman.

I informed my supervisor about getting served with the petition and let them know that I would need to fly back to Georgia to attend the hearing. Although they were supportive of my custody matters, the military has a "mission first" mentality. During this period of time, our squadron was at minimum manning and we couldn't afford for anyone to take vacation time. Basically, I was told by my supervisor that I wouldn't be able to attend the hearing and they wanted me to request that the hearing be held at a later date. Since I was representing myself, I wrote a letter to the judge explaining in detail why I wasn't allowed to attend. Surprisingly, the judge responded and granted me an extension! I was very thankful because the extension worked out in my favor. The hearing was rescheduled for April 03, 2013, which gave me several months to prepare. I was temporarily relieved, but I was also aware that I still had a huge legal battle ahead of me.

April came around faster than I expected it to; what initially felt like months available to prepare, turned into what seemed to be a matter of weeks! As time passed, I was able to conduct some research and discovered a company named AboutTheChildren.org (I suggest you Google it). About the Children is a team of lawyers who are available to help fathers (and mothers) that are pro se. They specialize in providing legal guidance, preparing and filing paperwork in preparation for your hearing, and they have very affordable pricing. Their service is also phenomenal! I reached out to them, provided them with a copy of the petition I was served with, my current pay stub, and financial budget. I completed my budget as honestly as I possibly could. After reviewing my budget, they were able to help me calculate an amount of child support that was more than I was currently providing for Amarius; but not such an increase that would affect the current quality of life for my wife and daughter. The state of Georgia calculates the amount of child support each parent has to pay based off of both parents' incomes.

I was prepared to offer Karen $400 in child support, which is an increase of $125 per month. This amount would allow me to grant her request for more child support while simultaneously enabling me to continue affording all the other bills and family expenses I had to cover. Karen also had to submit a budget prior to the hearing, and we had the opportunity to review it. She obviously wasn't being honest and the audacity of what she included was pretty disrespectful. There were several items on her budget that stood out as completely bogus to me. Let me put it in perspective for you; if Karen is living with her parents without a job, how can she afford to pay for lawncare? When Karen and I were dating in high school, her family would maintain their yard themselves but now that she wanted to increase child support; all of a sudden Karen was paying for monthly lawn service?

Karen also listed that she was paying $120 a month for gifts to other children. Really?! How is that even possible if you don't have an income and why would you even consider doing that if you're supposedly saving money to move out of your parents' house? One of the most frustrating factors regarding Karen's request to increase child support was the fact that on numerous occasions, JaRissa informed me about seeing Karen in a work uniform that resembled medical scrubs around this time. Smells fishy how she was suspiciously reporting that she was unemployed on her budget. If her being seen in scrubs correlated to being employed, then it would appear that she was purposely not reporting her income; which affected the amount of child support I had to pay. After all, if a parent doesn't have a job, how can they provide for their children? If you can't provide as a parent, do you really deserve to have custody?

Having the hearing rescheduled for April conveniently positioned the court date to right after Kayla and I received our tax return for the year 2013. This helped us repay the loan I had taken out for the contempt hearing and enabled us to reduce some debt that we had been battling with. Unfortunately, we didn't have enough money left over for Kayla and Keimora to travel with me to Georgia for the hearing, so I went alone and unafraid. I was confident in the preparation that I had conducted with AboutheChildren.org and I decided to stick with them as my legal aids. Additionally, I didn't want to take out another loan from the bank and decided to take my chances pro se. I flew out to Georgia to attend the hearing assuming that fair justice would prevail, and I would return with a reasonable amount of child support increase agreement. Unfortunately, I was wrong… again!

Prior to the hearing, Karen's lawyer approached me to negotiate before our hearing began. He and I were the only two people in what seemed like an interrogation room. He said to me in an honest business style tone, "If I were representing you, I would argue that your child support obligation shouldn't increase since you have another child but since I'm representing Karen, I'm going to ask for the max increase in the amount of child support you pay based on both of your incomes." Of course, Karen conveniently wasn't employed at the time of the hearing so minimum wage would be imputed into the child support worksheets for her income; which caused me to pay more money to support the child. Her lawyer proposed that I pay $675 per month! This was almost $300 more than what I was planning to offer! I explained to him that the amount Karen was requesting was way too high for my budget and I declined. I offered $400 and he said that she wouldn't accept anything lower than $600. At that moment I knew I was at a disadvantage by representing myself. Since we couldn't agree on an amount, we had to take our hearing in front of the judge for a decision.

Once I sat on the witness stand for cross-examination, her lawyer tried to make me look like the ultimate deadbeat father! He presented the budget I submitted as evidence and brought up the fact that I was paying for cable. "Did you know that Karen doesn't have cable? Why do you have cable, Mr. Wedlow?" Her lawyer asked curiously. "Because I live in Las Vegas, NV, which has a higher crime rate than Statesboro, Georgia, and I want my family to have entertainment while they're in the house when I'm at work instead of being outside in potential danger," I responded in a cocky manner. "Did you know that Amarius doesn't have any socks?" He asked me as if I was clueless. "Actually, no I wasn't aware of that, but I send her child support monthly so if he needs clothes, she could easily buy him some socks," I responded instinctively.

I could tell that her lawyer was getting frustrated with me at this point based on my witty responses. I decided to defend myself by saying "Sir, prior to the hearing didn't you mention that if you were representing me you would fight for me to get a credit for having another child which would help me get a reasonable amount of child support compared to what Karen is requesting?" He looked at me as if I had just been released from a psych ward. "No, Mr. Wedlow, actually I don't recall discussing any of that with you." He responded. I was floored by the way he denied our conversation prior to going in front of the judge. That's when I realized that attorneys have a duty to zealously represent their clients without regard to how they may feel personally. His words from our prior conversation indicated that he was putting me in a position that would cause my family to endure a financial hardship, but it was business to him; since he was representing Karen he was fighting for his client.

Unfortunately, I was the one on the defense; and I was currently losing. I pled my case as best I could about me having to provide better for my wife and our daughter. Her lawyer stated, "Mr. Wedlow, no one told you to go and have another child, you knew about your obligation to provide for your son." This guy was cutthroat. Although he was right, it's not like I planned to have another child. Her lawyer painted a picture to the judge that gave a perception of me that seemed like I was just completely neglecting my son; which wasn't the case. I gave it all I had but I was flailing. I thought the judge would factor in the higher cost of living in Las Vegas compared to Statesboro, the fact that I had a wife and child to take care of, and travel expenses for visitation with my son. I was sadly mistaken.

I remember sitting on the witness stand during cross-examination in my full-service Air Force uniform and the judge asked me, "Have you ever thought about getting a second job?" "No, your honor." I responded in disbelief! Thinking to myself, *Does he not see me sitting here in a military uniform? Does he think being in the military is like working at McDonald's?! I work twelve-hour shifts most of the time, is it really necessary for me to work two different jobs when Karen doesn't even have one job? Wow!*

At that point, I was in complete disbelief and appalled that a judge would ask me about getting a second job when it was obvious that I was serving my country! I was enraged with the justice system and lost all faith in family court in that moment. I remember looking around and realizing that I was the only African American in that courtroom in small-town Georgia. That's when it dawned on me that despite my service to this country, I stilled looked like a second-class citizen in the court of law. This increase in child support would make it more difficult for me to afford visitations with Amarius, and it seemed that I was the only one in the courtroom who cared about that. Oftentimes, I would even pay more than the $275 when I could, but the court didn't care about that. During that hearing, her lawyer tried to make it seem like I had neglected my son and favored my wife and daughter over him. Her lawyer also portrayed me as if I was living a fabulous lifestyle in Las Vegas with my other family while my son and his mother were in Georgia suffering financially.

Prior to conclusion of the hearing, I had already made up in my mind that I had lost. The hearing didn't go anywhere near the way I had envisioned it going. I didn't realize that family law could be so cutthroat, especially when it came to child support. I was a law-abiding citizen who had good intentions and just wanted to care for my family. I just couldn't believe that Karen testified that she didn't have a job and it didn't seem like a red flag to the judge. After the hearing was over, the judge informed us that he would get us a decision shortly. I was disappointed that I left Georgia not knowing how much my child support would increase and had to wait patiently to receive the final order in the mail. It was painstakingly uncomfortable to be held in suspense for roughly a week not knowing the fate of my finances. I did my best to keep the faith and hope that the judge would consider what it would do to my budget if he raised my child support to an amount I couldn't afford. It was out of my hands at that point and all I could do was pray. So, I did. Then I checked the mail one fine evening and saw this!

IN THE SUPERIOR COURT OF BULLOCH COUNTY 2013 APR 11 AM 8: 18
STATE OF GEORGIA

CLERK OF COURT

——————,   §
                 §
　　Plaintiff,   §
                 §
vs.   §   CIVIL ACTION NO. 1B12DR329w
                 §
NICHOLAS J. WEDLOW,   §
                 §
　　Defendant.   §

FINAL ORDER:
MODIFICATION OF CHILD SUPPORT

Plaintiff _ _ filed a Complaint for Modification of Visitation and Child Support. Defendant Nicolas J. Wedlow filed a timely response. The Court held a hearing on this motion on April 3, 2013, and now, having given full consideration to the argument of counsel, the record in this case, and the law, the Court finds and concludes as follows:

The Court finds that there has been a substantial change in the income of the Defendant which has increased his ability to pay child support as previously ordered by this Court on February 4, 2009. In determining child support, the Court gave the Defendant an adjustment or deviation for medical and dental expenses, as referenced in Schedule D, and special expenses for child rearing as it pertains to travel, as referenced in Schedule E, but declined to give an adjustment under Schedule B for a qualified child. As referenced in the attached Child Support Worksheets and Child Support Addendum, the Defendant shall pay to the Plaintiff the sum of $688.00 per month in child support beginning on May 1, 2013 and continuing on the 1st of the month thereafter.

SO ORDERED, this _____ day of April, 2013.

_____
WILLIAM E. WOODRUM, JR.
Chief Judge, Superior Court of Bulloch County
Ogeechee Judicial Circuit

I almost fainted when I read the final amount: $688?! We were devastated to say the least! How could the court have the audacity to deny me an adjustment in the amount I had to pay when I had another child who qualified for a credit?! I was appalled again. Kayla and I began to panic! How would we manage to pay all of our bills? How would we afford groceries? Gas? Rent? How would I budget in future visitations with Amarius? It blew my mind how the court had no sympathy for my finances but didn't even bat an eye when Karen was testifying that she didn't even have a job! It didn't make sense to me at all! No matter how you break it down, it just didn't seem fair. I actually started contemplating obtaining a second job. Kayla and I had some serious brainstorming to do, despite how upset we were, we still had to figure out how we were going to make ends meet.

At that particular time, I was applying for a job within the Air Force that required a higher security clearance than the one I already had. The background investigation for this new job opportunity required a detailed credit check. That being said, I couldn't afford to start missing payments to creditors and having arrears in child support if I wanted to give myself a shot at being accepted into this new job. I had to eat more than just one slice of humble pie. Kayla and I decided that the best way to afford the increased amount of child support in addition to all our other expenses was to downgrade our living arrangements. We were currently paying $650 per month in rent for our two-bedroom apartment.

We knew of some studio apartments on Oasis lane that weren't too far from where we currently lived, and we decided to go see what they had to offer. This particular neighborhood wasn't the most ideal place to raise a family. Honestly, it was smack dab in the middle of the ghetto. It was literally a rock throw's distance outside of Nellis AFB, which is an entirely different conversation within itself. I wasn't afraid to live in a low-income community because I haven't forgotten where I came from, but this neighborhood was the last place I wanted my wife and daughter to be in all day while I was at work. I knew that we would have to heighten our security measures if we were to ever feel comfortable in the hood.

We spoke with the housing office about our intentions and they gave us a tour. The studio apartment was only about 400 square feet. This was a major deal breaker for me, but we were also desperate to find some affordable living arrangements. The model unit they toured us around was very tiny but had all the amenities that met our needs. The living room and the bedroom was the same area, there was a small kitchenette, and a small bathroom—that's it! They were only charging $425 for these units and this was a surefire way to budget in some of the additional child support I was now responsible for paying. I also planned to end our contract with the cable company which freed up an additional $200 per month, enabling me to cover the entirety of the child support amount of $688. Although we hated every minute of this downgrade in living arrangements, I convinced Kayla that this was a "minor setback, for a major comeback." The front office ran my credit, and I was instantly approved for the studio apartment. One of my coworkers was gracious enough to allow me to use his pickup truck and we began the moving process the very next day.

After viewing the studio apartment, we quickly realized that we had too much furniture in our two-bedroom apartment and we wouldn't be able to take it all with us to the studio. I didn't have the finances to afford a storage unit monthly, so I had to make a crucial decision. Unfortunately, we had to either sell or throw away couches and other furniture that was too large for the studio. Our bed frame was too big to fit into the living room/bedroom area, so we had to get rid of it. Imagine going from having a living room with a comfortable couch and a love seat to a small area with your bare mattress on the floor and a futon beside it as your living room and bedroom all in one. This was a very painful and humbling process; I'll never forget how it felt as we were moving from a decent neighborhood into an area that could qualify as Section 8. The feeling, I can only imagine, must have been similar to what the Native Americans experienced when they traveled the trail of tears.

As soon as we finished moving in, the apartment revealed its true colors. The moment we lied down on the mattress to relax and take the load off, something grabbed my attention out of the corner of my eye. I glanced over in the direction of the movement and saw a cockroach crawling on the counter! Great, not only do we have to reduce our living space, live in the ghetto, and pay more money in child support... now we were faced with overcoming a cockroach infestation! As a child, I grew accustomed to ignoring cockroaches but as an adult, I never imagined I would have to experience those conditions again; but here we were. Not to mention the apartment complex had community washers and dryers that looked like they hadn't been cleaned in months and were barely serviceable. Just when I thought things couldn't get any worse, Kayla discovered that she was pregnant, again! It was one of the most humbling experiences of my life helping my pregnant wife ease her way down onto a mattress that was laying on the floor hoping that a cockroach doesn't crawl its way up into the covers and snuggle up beside her.

CHAPTER 10

THE DRAMA CONTINUES

*"An almost perfect relationship with his father
was the earthly root of all his wisdom."*
—C.S. Lewis

Karen's confrontational approach with matters concerning Amarius started to worsen around that time. Her increasingly difficult co-parenting approach was keeping me in a financial struggle and was ultimately limiting my ability to visit with him. Despite the obstacles in my way, I wanted to stay relevant in his life. My attempts to speak with Amarius on the phone were rarely entertained on a consistent basis. My persistence with initiating communication seemed to frustrate Karen even more. On the rare occasion when I was able to get Amarius on the phone, it became a routine thing for her to end the call prematurely before I could even discuss the reason I was calling. Not only was she confrontational with me—she would also engage disrespectfully with Kayla. One evening I was speaking with Amarius on speakerphone; Kayla tried to be sweet and say hello to Amarius. Karen immediately grabbed the phone from him and yelled, "Nick you need to tell your other head to be quiet!" Of course, this didn't go over well with Kayla. In fact, situations like that created animosity between Kayla and Karen that resulted in more obstacles in my journey to parent Amarius.

I fell into a depressive state and became demotivated to continue putting forth so much effort when my willingness to be a father to

Amarius didn't seem appreciated. The drama between me and Karen had an adverse effect on my marriage and my relationship with Kayla began to suffer. I became consumed with fighting for my parental rights and couldn't focus on being the husband and father Kayla and Keimora needed me to be. Kayla expressed on numerous occasions how she felt like I loved Amarius more than her and Keimora. At one point, Kayla began entertaining a divorce if things didn't improve between us; my passion for being a father to Amarius started driving a wedge between me and my wife. Not only did it affect my household family members, but other immediate family began to empathize with me and grew concerned about my mental health. They were tired of reaching out to me and hearing about all of the latest drama between me and Karen due to my frustrations with not being able to spend time with my child. The situation wasn't improving, and it had reached a tipping point.

Close family members would contact me and provide guidance. One day my mother called and tried to assist by saying, "Just leave her alone; just pay your child support and don't try to call or get visitations because it always ends up in drama, you've done all you can do." Kayla overheard my mother telling me this and agreed. I couldn't believe what I was hearing. The most important women in my life were encouraging me to give up on my son and instructing me to do the bare minimum—pay child support. Despite how much it pained me to listen to them, they were my closest supporters and at the time it felt like good advice. Maybe if I listened to them, my overall mood would improve. After all, nothing else was working so maybe giving up was the right answer.

I attempted to take their advice and actually stopped calling and texting. There is a saying that goes "You find out how strong your relationship is with someone when you stop being the first one to initiate communication." During this period of time, I learned just how true that saying is. I had to force myself to not pick up the phone and reach out to Amarius. All the while, I was internally hoping that one day I would receive a phone call from him; it never happened, and that made it hurt even more. It seemed as if I didn't matter or exist to my own son. Granted, he was still young and the phrase "out of sight out of mind" is a real thing. It wasn't his fault; I couldn't blame him. I ultimately blamed Karen. I was puzzled by the fact that she had no problem receiving child support and the medical benefits I provided for him but wouldn't encourage him to have a relationship with me. Seriously, how hard is it to dial my number and hand him the phone?

My hiatus from trying to communicate with Amarius consistently lasted about two months. It ate at me that I was allowing myself to just give up on my son. I became ashamed of my actions and disgusted with myself for allowing someone else to encourage me to go against my gut instinct, regardless of how close of a supporter they were to me. I reached a point where I couldn't take it anymore and started trying to call again and get more involved. Not to my surprise, I began experiencing the same lack of acceptance that influenced me to take a step back in the first place. Only this time, I didn't allow it to deter me from continuing to try.

When my court-ordered visitations rolled around, the circumstances only fueled my depression and anger. It was heartbreaking to come to the realization that even if Karen were being cooperative with coordinating a visitation, I couldn't afford to pay for Amarius's travel arrangements after paying child support. Faced with this reality, I had to forfeit several visitations due to the inability to afford them and the lack of cooperation from Karen. Additionally, a studio apartment wasn't enough living space to accommodate myself, a pregnant wife, Keimora, and Amarius even if he was able to visit. I started to question whether or not things would ever improve. There seemed to be no relief in the foreseeable future. I internally began to accept the circumstances and convinced myself that I deserved what was happening to me even though I knew deep down I was being wronged as a father.

Out of sheer desperation, I began to vent and post my frustrations on Facebook and other social media platforms. I had numerous contacts on social media that were neutral parties to my custody situation. Karen and I weren't friends on Facebook, but we had mutual friends who could see both of our pages and the things we posted. The community heard my cries of frustration and came to my aid by being supportive and helping me in any way they could. Unbeknownst to me at the time, I was friends with a teacher who worked in Amarius's school and she was familiar with who he was. Her name is Mrs. Katrina Brunson Archie, and being connected with her was a blessing in disguise. After spewing out my frustrations on a post one day, Mrs. Archie sent me a direct message on Facebook. She mentioned that she sees Amarius on a daily basis at school and could easily pass a message to him for me if I needed her to. This provided so much hope for me and I want to publicly thank Mrs. Archie for her helpful and gracious ways! This was one of the first times I felt Amarius was accessible to me without Karen interfering and making it difficult for me.

Mrs. Archie was able to engage with Amarius at school, pass a message to him on my behalf, and help me bridge the communication gap. This was a huge breakthrough! Mrs. Archie took a picture of Amarius and encouraged him to write a letter so that she could take a picture of it and send it to me, and he did; included below:

Conversation started September 17, 2014

Nick Wedlow   9/17, 6:14pm
did you see him today?

Katina Brunson Archie   9/17, 6:14pm
I did and I told him that you tried to call him.

Nick Wedlow   9/17, 6:14pm
awesome thank you! what was his response

Katina Brunson Archie   9/17, 6:15pm
He smiled when I told him that I knew his dad. And that I had a message from you. He seemed excited!! Wish I could do more but don't want to overstep my boundaries!!

Nick Wedlow   9/17, 6:18pm
you are not overstepping your boundaries at all! What does it hurt to relay a message? I really appreciate the help though, i just feel like i have to exhaust all my resources in order to stay in contact with him

Katina Brunson Archie   9/17, 6:20pm
I completely understand!! Feel free to send a message here for him and I'll sneak and let him read at school!!!!

Nick Wedlow   9/17, 6:21pm
ok lol i will type one up when i get done with my homework

Katina Brunson Archie   9/17, 6:21pm
Ok. No problem!!!

Nick Wedlow   9/17, 7:31pm
ok just finished my homework , when you get a chance i would like you to let him read this message....

Nick Wedlow 9/17, 7:35pm
Whats up MARI??!! How are you son? Just wanted to let you know that I have been trying to video chat with you but for some reason your mother isn't cooperating. I don't want to cloud your day with negativity though. I just want to let you know that I Love you and I miss you! I also want to tell you that I am proud of you and I would like you to keep up the good work!! call or Skype me when you get a chance! Also its this cool new video chat system named Google Hangouts that works better than Skype encourage your mom to contact my email on there at

———————————— September 18, 2014 ————————————

 Katina Brunson Archie 9/18, 2:11am
Got I. Will let him read it this morning. 😊

———————————— September 18, 2014 ————————————

 Nick Wedlow 9/18, 5:49am
thanks 😊

 Katina Brunson Archie 9/18, 6:10am
I told him to write you a note and I will take a pic of it and send it to you on messenger. When I get it from him. I'll send it!! 😊

 Nick Wedlow 9/18, 6:11am
you are awesome!

 Katina Brunson Archie 9/18, 6:12am
No problem!!

 Katina Brunson Archie 9/18, 6:10am
I told him to write you a note and I will take a pic of it and send it to you on messenger. When I get it from him. I'll send it!! 😊

 Nick Wedlow 9/18, 6:11am
you are awesome!

 Katina Brunson Archie 9/18, 6:12am
No problem!!

 Katina Brunson Archie 9/18, 7:14am

 Katina Brunson Archie 9/18, 7:14am

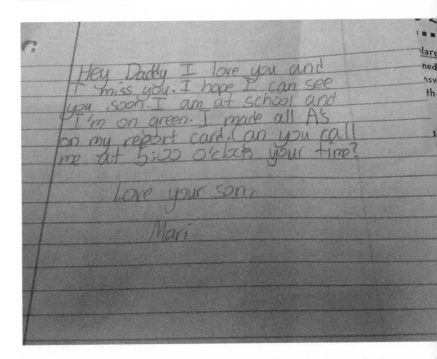

Hey Daddy I love you and I miss you. I hope I can see you soon. I am at school and I'm on green. I made all A's on my report card. Can you call me at 5:00 o'clock your time?

Love your son,

Mari

Receiving this letter from Amarius reaffirmed that we had a special bond, and I knew that he really did love me despite my inability to speak with him consistently. I was temporarily relieved because it seemed as if I found a way to reach Amarius without having to go through Karen. Mrs. Archie allowed me and Amarius to pass a few messages to each other through her Facebook profile and it was a blessing to reconnect with him. Unfortunately, the euphoria I experienced after receiving a letter from Amarius and holding a conversation was short lived. I'm assuming that Amarius had a conversation with Karen after he arrived home from school that day and informed her that I had reached out to him; because the next day, drama erupted.

Karen reached out to me all pissed off and threatening to get Mrs. Archie in trouble with the Principal, Mr. Hill, for helping me speak with Amarius! I was puzzled by Karen's pettiness! Why was it such a big deal to her that someone was helping me stay in communication with my son? For some reason, it irritated Karen when people would help me interact with him. At that point, I knew that she was trying to control every bit of communication between me and Amarius. The audacity of Karen to prevent me from speaking with him regularly and then get upset when someone assisted me with communicating with him was mindboggling to me. After receiving Karen's response, I reached out to Mrs. Archie to warn her about the potential drama that could be headed her way.

There was another employee at Amarius's school that I knew very well. Her name is Mrs. Debra Minick, who also happened to be my science teacher in 7th grade. Word must travel fast because soon after Karen caught wind of the situation, Mrs. Minick reached out to me on Facebook as well. I gladly explained the situation to her, and she was in complete support of Mrs. Archie helping me. It turns out that Karen never reached out to the principal and was just bluffing after threatening to do so. I'm assuming she came to her senses and realized that had she let me communicate with him regularly, people wouldn't reach out to me and help me maintain my relationship with him.

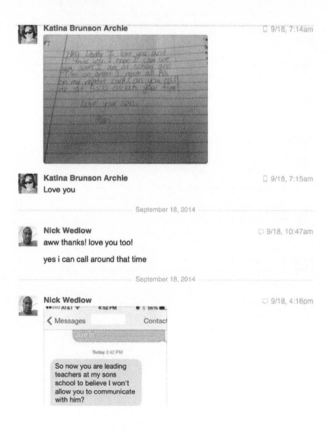

> If you have something to say to him, you can call him @ 9125319640. Do not interrupt his school day to try and make me look bad. I'll be sure the staff

> gets the message too. And my lawyer will be mailing you some important papers so be sure to check your mail.

Text Message   Send

 Nick Wedlow   9/18, 4:19pm
take a look at the attachment when u get a chance please... I guess he got home and told his mom about google hangouts and she started asking him questions... i hope this doesn't cause too much trouble for you I'm really sorry i forgot how   she was.... now u see what I'm dealing with? on a good note I'm on the phone with him now and he said he didn't have a problem with you helping me stay in contact with him so she just on some power trip shit right now

 Katina Brunson Archie   9/18, 4:30pm
Oh my God.   . I will go to Mr. Hill in the morning and explain so it won't be a surprise for him. Thanks for the heads up!!!

 Nick Wedlow   9/18, 4:32pm
no problem man I'm soooo sorry tho i hope mr hill can understand...

 Katina Brunson Archie   9/18, 4:33pm
It's fine!!!

 Nick Wedlow   9/18, 4:36pm
cool please let me know how it goes

 Katina Brunson Archie   9/18, 4:38pm
No problem.

 Nick Wedlow   9/18, 7:02pm
make sure u talk to ms minick too she knows me and our situation

 Katina Brunson Archie   9/18, 8:01pm
Ok I will talk to her as well.

Glad you got a chance to talk to him !!!

 Nick Wedlow   9/18, 8:02pm
me too thanks to you!

———————————— September 19, 2014 ————————————

 Katina Brunson Archie   9/19, 1:11pm
Everything is fine. Talked to both administrators and neither heard from her today. Unless this is the quiet before the storm!!! He wouldn't look me in the eye today so I guess she told him not to talk or speak to me anymore. Either way I'm glad you had a chance yo talk to him!! 😊

Nick Wedlow   9/19, 2:35pm

yea ms minick contacted me and asked what was going on and didn't mention there being a problem, yea she probably scared him into not communicating with you about me anymore

either way I'm thankful for your help but sad i have to go to these extremes to keep in contact with him

--- October 2, 2014 ---

Nick Wedlow   10/2, 7:29pm

havent talked to him again since you helped me out that once smh

Katina Brunson Archie   10/2, 7:31pm

Awe. I'm sorry. He still won't speak to me. But I did see her last week at the book fair. She didn't say a word to me!! Maybe she'll come around!!

Debra Finch Minick   9/19, 8:30am

Nick. What is going with

Nick Wedlow   9/19, 9:03am

she's been non cooperative for the most part when it comes to me keeping in touch with amarius via video chat and phone so i posted on facebook that if anybody saw him let him know i was trying to get in touch with him and Mrs Archie commented on the status because she sees him all the time so i told her to tell him to contact me which he did, he wrote me a letter and she took a pic of it and sent it to me, i guess he went home to tell his mom i asked him to video chat me and she got mad

since i have more options than her to contact him she got upset. i honestly dont know why she is like that but all im trying to do is keep in contact with him

Nick Wedlow   9/19, 10:40am

is there a problem?

Debra Finch Minick   9/19, 11:16am

No Katina just told me that you told her to talk to me and I would handle but I have heard nothing today

Debra Finch Minick   9/20, 5:19am

Nick the only bad thing about this situation is that I would have done the same thing Katina did. I told our principal this

Nick Wedlow   9/20, 7:57am

yea I'm so glad my son has teachers and administrators like you and katina!! I really appreciate the support i get from you guys! you know i don't have any bad intentions, at this age a boy needs his father to develop into a man and i want to keep in contact with him for his mentorship..... it just sucks for me that i have to go through these extremes just to keep in contact with him.

CHAPTER 11

ALLOW ME TO INTRODUCE PRESTIGIOUS!

"A father is a man who expects his son to be
as good a man as he meant to be."
—Frank A. Clark

s we approached the end of year 2013, Kayla was getting closer to giving birth to a baby boy. We were still living in a studio apartment at the time and struggling to maintain our finances. The job I had been applying for got approved and I was scheduled to attend training in San Antonio, TX on January 7, 2014. Timing couldn't have been any worse because Kayla's due date was January 18, 2014. The training I was scheduled to attend for the new job was approximately 45 days; with a graduation date of February 14. Once I completed the training, I would be eligible for a bonus of $30K. Completing this training would provide an opportunity to stop the financial hemorrhaging for me and Kayla. This scenario presented a ton of incentive to attend the training despite the fact that I would miss the birth of my son. Although Kayla was pretty upset that I was going to miss our son's birth, she understood the bigger picture and supported my decision because she knew securing that bonus check would provide a better quality of life for us. We only had one problem; who would help care for Kayla and the new baby in my absence?

After brainstorming on how we would execute our plan for me to attend training, I developed the perfect solution. I was aware that my mother wasn't working at the time and decided to reach out to her. Before I could even explain all of the details, my mother agreed to provide her assistance. I was transparent with her about our small living space that happened to be in a less than ideal neighborhood, but she didn't care; the only thing that mattered to her was that there was a new grandbaby involved! We worked out the logistics of my mom's travel and flew her out to Las Vegas on January 5, 2014, which was the day before I had to depart for training. Her flight arrived late in the afternoon and we got her settled into our small apartment so that she could get some rest. I had an early morning flight the next day, so I finished packing and planned to go to bed early. Kayla, Keimora, and I, nestled in together on the mattress while my mom prepared to sleep on the futon. The plan was for Kayla to drop me off at the airport and afterwards show my mother around the area and the hospital that she would be delivering the baby in. Unfortunately, things didn't go as planned.

At approximately 2:30 A.M. on the morning of January 6, Kayla woke me up frantically in agonizing pain. She was having contractions! Initially, she assumed she was experiencing Braxton Hicks, so I stayed up to comfort her. Her contractions started getting closer and closer together as we noted the time during each occurrence. A few hours went past, and we became increasingly more concerned that she could possibly be in the early stages of labor. My flight was scheduled for 6 A.M. It was fast approaching the time for me to make my way to the airport. My completion of the training was a priority for our family since it would yield huge financial dividends. Kayla's due date was still roughly a week away, so we didn't expect that she was going into labor early. We decided to have Kayla and my mom drop me off at the airport and then go to the hospital afterwards for her to get checked out. They drove me to the airport, we said our goodbyes, and they immediately went to the emergency room. They admitted Kayla into the hospital to ensure she and the baby were ok. They informed her that although she was dilating, she wasn't in active labor and sent her back home.

I boarded the plane and began my journey to San Antonio, TX. I had a layover at another airport prior to arriving to San Antonio and I called Kayla as soon as I could after my first flight ended several hours later. She mentioned that she was still in pain and having contractions that were increasingly getting worse. I instructed her to go back to the emergency room if her condition worsened. I consoled her on the phone as long as I could prior to boarding my next flight. As I boarded the flight, Kayla had decided that she was going to go back to the emergency room due to the amount of pain and the frequency of her contractions. I felt so vulnerable and helpless because my flight was about to take off while my wife was suffering in pain and possibly going into labor. I obviously couldn't communicate with her while in flight and I was worried to death. What was only a two-hour flight seemed like an eternity. Our flight finally landed and as soon as the wheels hit the runway, I called Kayla to check on the status. Kayla answered the phone immediately and I could barely make out what she was saying over her heavy breathing. I was only able to make out bits and pieces at first but after a few minutes of me encouraging her to remain calm, I was able to interpret that she was at the hospital and in labor!

I was overwhelmingly excited and disappointed at the same time! We didn't expect her to deliver until a week later but the fact that the baby decided to come on the day I left was an unbelievable coincidence! I tried to convince myself that the decision to attend training for my new job over attending the birth of my new child was the right move; it just didn't feel that way at the time. I felt terrible for not being there to support her, but I also knew that she was in good hands with my mother and it eased my anxiety a little. Kayla's contractions were rapidly coming more frequently, and it was only a matter of time before the baby arrived. Luckily, we had video chat capability on our phones and my mother planned to hold the phone for Kayla so that I could watch the birth. As I deboarded the aircraft and rushed to baggage claim, I could only hope that she held the birth off long enough for me to get to my hotel room so that I could watch the birth in my own privacy. By the time I got my luggage off of the baggage claim, Kayla's contractions were minutes apart. I quickly flagged down a taxi and gave them the directions to the hotel I was going to be staying in for my training.

I instructed my cab driver to get me to the hotel as quickly and safely as possible. My heart was racing! Kayla was struggling through the contractions so frequently she could no longer hold the phone. My mom decided to start the video call because we knew it was about to go down. I watched Kayla squirm around in the hospital bed in agonizing pain. It reminded me of that scene from The Exorcist when the girl was chained to the bed screaming out inaudible words and jerking around dramatically. I watched in suspense as I witnessed the beautiful gift of life begin to unfold. I arrived at the hotel, checked into my room, and rushed to the elevator. I ran down the hallway dragging my luggage behind me. I got to my room, opened the door, and threw my luggage on the second queen bed. As soon as I got into my room, Kayla was giving birth! I made it just in time! After a few intense pushes, I heard the faint cries of a newborn infant and saw the nurse holding up a handsome baby boy like Rafiki did Simba in The Lion King. I was speechless. It was a beautiful thing to watch; I just hated that I wasn't physically there to witness it in person. My mom allowed Keimora to cut the umbilical cord, and I felt a tear roll down my cheek as I saw how exhausted Kayla was from creating a new life. After the chaos settled and the medical staff got the baby all cleaned up, we decided to name him Prestigious. We chose this name because we wanted something original with a powerful meaning and Prestigious was the perfect fit.

Over the next 7 weeks, I was able to complete the rigorous training I had to undergo for my new job. I learned a lot about my new career field as an aircrew member, met some great people, and established some lifelong relationships. I graduated from training on Valentines' day and flew back to Las Vegas to meet Prestigious for the first time. It was a huge relief to be back home with Kayla, my mom, and our two beautiful children. Not only was I happy to be back home—I was excited about completing training and being eligible for a bonus paycheck! The day after returning home from training, I took my completion certificate to the personnel office on base and started my reenlistment paperwork.

With proof that I completed training, I was now able to extend my contract in the Air Force into my new career field as an MQ-1 Sensor Operator. The Sensor Operator career field had a hefty bonus attached for the members who were eligible to reenlist into it. After the paperwork was processed, I was able to secure a $30K bonus! They provided me half upfront and scheduled the rest to be annually deposited into five equal increments over the next five years.

This financial breakthrough was a blessing from above and we took full advantage of it! Kayla and I sat down together and strategized how we would utilize the bonus check to improve our quality of life. We decided to use the majority of it to pay off the remaining balance for the Chevrolet Monte Carlo I owned. Paying off the existing car loan provided us with the financial flexibility to purchase another vehicle. Having two cars would increase our maneuverability and reduce the travel limitations Kayla and I experienced early on by having just one vehicle between the two of us. I was able to convince Kayla that I would take her car shopping for her Valentines' day gift a few days after I returned home from training and received the bonus check. Kayla started conducting research online to find cars within our budget that she was interested in. She was drawn to the 2014 Jeep Patriot model and we headed to the dealership to go check them out. Up until that point, I had never seen a bigger smile on her face.

Kayla had never owned a car before so taking her car shopping for the first time ever was a huge milestone for both of us. We pulled up to the Jeep dealership on Sahara Ave in Las Vegas giddy with excitement. We parked and started walking around the lot to view the inventory. Kayla immediately spotted the Jeep of her dreams! As she stood there marveling at the make and model she had been researching online, a sales rep approached us, and the rest was history. We had already gotten preapproval for an auto loan through Navy Federal Credit Union, so we were able to seal the deal effortlessly! We completed the paperwork and Kayla was able to drive away in her brand-new Jeep.

The financial relief didn't stop here though. It was also tax season around this time, and we received our tax return shortly after purchasing he new Jeep. We strategically used our tax return to pay off more credit ard and loan debt to free up more money in our budget monthly to ssist us in affording a bigger place to live. Finally, after about 8 months f living in a slummy studio apartment, we were able to pay off enough lebt to afford a one-bedroom apartment in northwest Las Vegas that vas within our budget. It still wasn't the most ideal size living space or our newly expanded family, but it was a step up compared to the tudio apartment. It was challenging to find a larger place to live while aying $688 in child support with a one-income household, so we took vhat we could get.

Although we were blessed with some temporary financial relief, Kayla was still unemployed, and we had two young children to raise ogether. After sacrificing a few visitations to save money and rebuild inancially we were at a point where we would have enough space to ccommodate Mari if he were to visit. Comfortably housing five people n a one-bedroom apartment was a challenge, but we were determined o sacrifice a little comfort to spend time with him. Shockingly, we vere able to negotiate with Karen and successfully exercise one of our nake-up visitations with Amarius in November of 2014. This visitation vent pretty smoothly, and it provided hope that Karen would continue ccommodating future visitations. I later found out that this was a nisperception of mine.

CHAPTER 12

THE FLIGHT THAT CHANGED IT ALL

"A father is someone you look up to no matter how tall you grow."
—Unknown

Summer of 2015 was fast approaching, and I didn't want to miss another Father's Day with Amarius. My plan was to use the money from my tax return to purchase plane tickets for Amarius's summer visitation. However, a very unfortunate event occurred and took priority. Grandma Della passed away! I decided to use the money I set aside for Amarius's visitation to fly my entire family to Georgia to attend her funeral. This was a very sad time for my family, and I didn't want to miss the opportunity to pay my respects to my grandmother. After returning to Las Vegas from her funeral in Georgia, I no longer had the money to purchase airfare for Amarius's summer visit.

I was still determined to exercise my upcoming visitation with Amarius because I had missed the last three summers consecutively, and I didn't want to miss another! Kayla and I brainstormed different ways that we could accumulate the money to purchase airfare but none of them seemed feasible. After almost giving up on the visitation, I was scrolling on Facebook one day and I saw people advertising a website called Go Fund Me; which is a tool to help people raise money. This seemed like the perfect option, but I wasn't comfortable asking people for financial help publicly. I was embarrassed at first but decided to swallow my pride because I truly needed the help. I established a profile on Go Fund Me and created a fundraiser for my cause. My plan was to share the link to the fundraiser on Facebook in hopes that family and friends would see it and decide to donate. I attached a picture of the letter Mrs. Archie had Amarius write for me as the profile picture for the fundraiser. I also had to include a description of the fundraiser and I wrote the following paragraph as my pitch for why I could use the extra money:

"Hello, world! Thanks for taking the time to read this post! My name is Nicholas Wedlow. I am a member of the United States Air Force stationed in Las Vegas, NV. I am married with three children who go by the names of Amarius aka "Mari" (10), Keimora (3), and Prestigious (1). Unfortunately, not all my children live with me. Amarius is my oldest child and he resides in Georgia with his mother, a woman who I had a past relationship with. Amarius is a very smart outgoing child who loves to play baseball. I have joint custody of Amarius, as well as: a visitation agreement, provision of child support, health insurance, and I also finance half the costs of his extracurricular activities. I understand as a father that I have created a lot of responsibility for myself and I am proudly doing the best I can so that my children can have more than what I grew up with. If you are reading this and you have other children who belong to you but do not reside in the same household as your family, you can relate to how difficult it is to finance and maintain relationships with your child while in long-distance setups. In no way, shape, or form is this intended to slander, discredit, or tarnish the character of my child's mother. Although… I didn't have any trouble communicating with or having my son visit until I got married to my now wife. I would love to provide more background on how I feel like I am being kept out of my oldest son's life, but I do not want to cross any legal boundaries. Long story short, the amount of child support I send wasn't an issue until I got married. Once child support was increased, it was so dramatic that it brought the visitations to a halt because of my inability to afford them in addition to my family's expenses.

The result of that has caused me to miss the past three Fathers' Days with Amarius. I do not want to miss another one. Along those same lines, since I have to pay child support; I cannot afford childcare for my other two children so that my wife can begin working to help out with finances. In order for her to go out and find a job, I would have to take off a month from work to stay home with the kids so that she can begin bringing checks home so that we can afford to put them in childcare before I go back to work. Since I'm in the military, our current manning will not allow me to take a month off of work. I am creating this donation page today in an effort to attempt to raise money so that I can afford to exercise my summer visitation with my son Amarius and have the first Father's Day where all my children are present. Earlier this year I attempted to save money from my tax return to finance his summer travel cost. Unfortunately, before I was able to do so, I got notified that my grandmother passed away in early March, may she rest in peace. After receiving this news, I chose to use the money I set aside for my son to fly my family to Georgia so that I can pay my respects to my grandmother. With all of this going on, it has been hard to save up money for airfare. I sat and contemplated on what I should do knowing Father's Day and summer visitation is around the corner. Out of sheer desperation, I posted on Facebook stating that I had been thinking about starting a 'Go Fund Me' donation page for my situation and encouraged people to like the status if they wouldn't mind donating. I ended up getting more support than I thought so I decided to go for it! Besides, what do I have to lose? Thanks for your time, and any donation you decide to provide will be greatly appreciated!"

Within minutes of sharing the link to the fundraiser, support started pouring in! I was overwhelmed by the amount of support we got from friends and family! My pitch for help worked like a charm and within a few days, enough money was raised to purchase a ticket. The community heard my cry and sprang into action immediately to provide whatever help they could. I was humbled by their generosity and my desire to be a good father was vindicated by the community support. They knew my character and my true intentions.

I'd like to take this moment to give a special shout out to everyone that donated to the Go Fund Me in support of my cause! From the bottom of my heart, I appreciate your support and generosity!

Kalonji Holmes

Lakendra Braziel

Michael Correa

Jessie Givens

Faith Thomas

BJ Hill

Adrienne King

Prentis Martin

James Holloway

Christian Walton

Eli and Renee Thompson

Jessica Classens

Debra Palmer

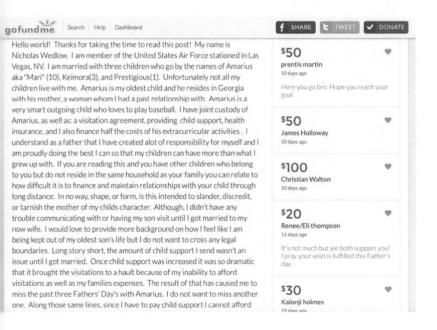

gofundme   Search   Help   Dashboard   **f** SHARE   **t** TWEET   ✔ DONATE

Hello world! Thanks for taking the time to read this post! My name is Nicholas Wedlow. I am member of the United States Air Force stationed in Las Vegas, NV. I am married with three children who go by the names of Amarius aka "Mari" (10), Keimora(3), and Prestigious(1). Unfortunately not all my children live with me. Amarius is my oldest child and he resides in Georgia with his mother, a woman whom I had a past relationship with. Amarius is a very smart outgoing child who loves to play baseball. I have joint custody of Amarius, as well as: a visitation agreement, providing child support, health insurance, and I also finance half the costs of his extracurricular activities . I understand as a father that I have created alot of responsibility for myself and I am proudly doing the best I can so that my children can have more than what I grew up with. If you are reading this and you have other children who belong to you but do not reside in the same household as your family you can relate to how difficult it is to finance and maintain relationships with your child through long distance. In no way, shape, or form, is this intended to slander, discredit, or tarnish the mother of my childs character. Although, I didn't have any trouble communicating with or having my son visit until I got married to my now wife. I would love to provide more background on how I feel like I am being kept out of my oldest son's life but I do not want to cross any legal boundaries. Long story short, the amount of child support I send wasn't an issue until I got married. Once child support was increased it was so dramatic that it brought the visitations to a hault because of my inability to afford visitations as well as my families expenses. The result of that has caused me to miss the past three Fathers' Day's with Amarius. I do not want to miss another one. Along those same lines, since I have to pay child support I cannot afford

$50 ♥

prentis martin
10 days ago

Here you go bro. Hope you reach your goal

$50 ♥

James Holloway
10 days ago

$100 ♥

Christian Walton
10 days ago

$20 ♥

Renee/Eli thompson
11 days ago

It's not much but we both support you! I pray your wish is fulfilled this Father's day .

$30 ♥

Kalonji holmes
19 days ago

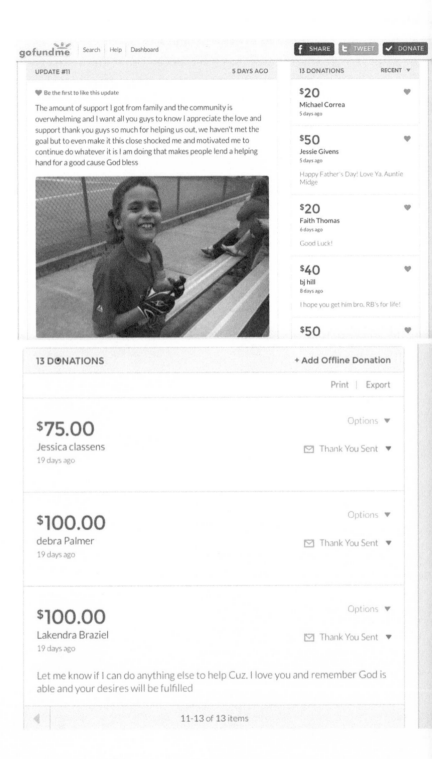

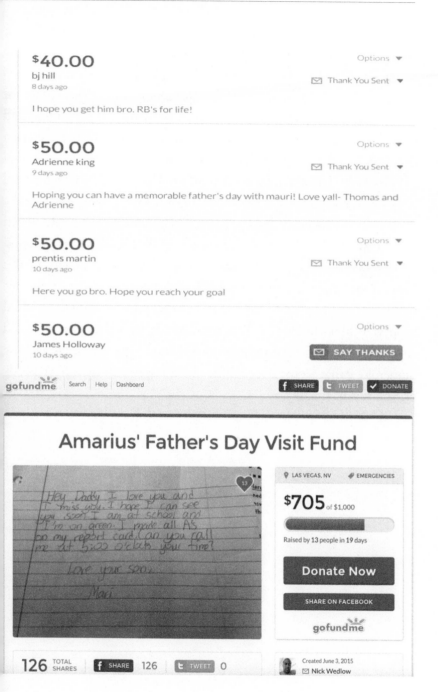

$40.00   Options ▼

bj hill

8 days ago   ✉ Thank You Sent ▼

I hope you get him bro. RB's for life!

$50.00   Options ▼

Adrienne king

9 days ago   ✉ Thank You Sent ▼

Hoping you can have a memorable father's day with mauri! Love yall- Thomas and Adrienne

$50.00   Options ▼

prentis martin

10 days ago   ✉ Thank You Sent ▼

Here you go bro. Hope you reach your goal

$50.00   Options ▼

James Holloway

10 days ago   ✉ SAY THANKS

gofundme   Search   Help   Dashboard   f SHARE   t TWEET   ✓ DONATE

Amarius' Father's Day Visit Fund

Hey Daddy I love you and I miss you. I hope I can see you soon. I am at school and I'm on green. I made all A's on my report card. Can you call me at 5:00 o'clock your time?

Love your son,

Mari

📍 LAS VEGAS, NV   ⚑ EMERGENCIES

$705 of $1,000

Raised by 13 people in 19 days

Donate Now

SHARE ON FACEBOOK

gofundme

126 TOTAL SHARES   f SHARE 126   t TWEET 0

Created June 3, 2015
✉ Nick Wedlow

After the astounding support from the amazing people above, their efforts combined for a total of $705 raised! Without them, purchasing airfare wouldn't have been possible. Their efforts exceeded expectations and armed me with more than enough money to purchase airfare for Amarius's summer visitation with us. I immediately got online and started searching for plane tickets for the timeframe of the visitation dates I was court-ordered to have. Prior to purchasing the airfare, I tried to negotiate a date and time for Amarius to fly to Las Vegas that would work best for both parties. Of course, my attempts to communicate the details weren't acknowledged by Karen so I decided to just go ahead and purchase the ticket before prices got too high. I couldn't wait around on Karen to cooperate, so I decided to press forward with the purchase. I found the perfect flight and booked it without hesitation. Ironically, the ticket price was $688 which was the exact same amount as my child support. Still to this day, I believe the coincidence of the ticket price and child support being the same amount was some type of weird foretelling numerology that set the stage for life-changing events regarding custody of Amarius in the future.

Reservation Confirmation

no-reply@flyfrontier.com <no-reply@flyfrontier.com>   Thu, Jun 4, 2015 at 2:21 PM
Reply-To: no-reply@flyfrontier.com
To: youngthorobread@gmail.com

SAT, JUN 20, 2015 - SAT, JUL 25, 2015   Trip Confirmation Number: MZU53L

ATL ATLANTA, GA ➢ LAS LAS VEGAS, NV

Depart: Sat, Jun 20, 2015

Flight	Departure	Arrival	Duration
F91457	08:40 PM ATL, ATLANTA, GA	10:00 PM LAS, LAS VEGAS, NV	NonStop

Passenger Name	Seats	Bags	Special Services
AMARIUS PAYTON WEDLOW		1 Checked	Unaccompanied Minor Unaccompanied Minor

Depart: Sat, Jul 25, 2015

Flight	Departure	Arrival	Duration
F91456	10:15 PM LAS, LAS VEGAS, NV	05:10 AM ATL, ATLANTA, GA	NonStop

Passenger Name	Seats	Bags	Special Services
AMARIUS PAYTON WEDLOW		1 Checked	Unaccompanied Minor Unaccompanied Minor

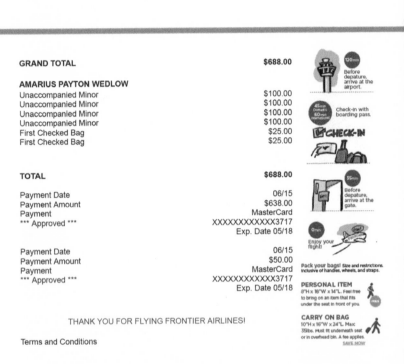

INVOICE

KNOW BEFORE YOU GO!

SUMMARY

Airfare	$185.86
Options	$450.00
Taxes & Fees	$52.14

GRAND TOTAL $688.00

AMARIUS PAYTON WEDLOW

Unaccompanied Minor	$100.00
Unaccompanied Minor	$100.00
Unaccompanied Minor	$100.00
Unaccompanied Minor	$100.00
First Checked Bag	$25.00
First Checked Bag	$25.00

TOTAL $688.00

Payment Date	06/15
Payment Amount	$638.00
Payment	MasterCard
*** Approved ***	XXXXXXXXXXXX3717
	Exp. Date 05/18

Payment Date	06/15
Payment Amount	$50.00
Payment	MasterCard
*** Approved ***	XXXXXXXXXXXX3717
	Exp. Date 05/18

THANK YOU FOR FLYING FRONTIER AIRLINES!

Terms and Conditions

I notified Karen of the details of the airfare immediately and looked forward to coordinating a summer visitation. Once I provided her with the details via text message, she surprisingly acknowledged it. Initially, his mother seemed open to the idea of him visiting for the summer but as time got closer to the flight departure date my attempts to communicate about the travel arrangements began to fall on deaf ears. I saw her lack of acknowledgement as a red flag but didn't think that she would be bold enough not to cooperate, especially after holding her in contempt of court before. Days leading up to the visitation I emailed her a copy of his itinerary and texted her the details again because I wanted to document all communication leading up to the visitation "just in case".

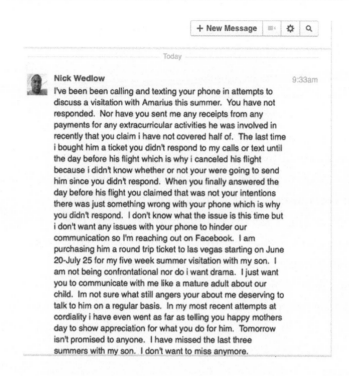

Today

Nick Wedlow   9:33am

I've been been calling and texting your phone in attempts to discuss a visitation with Amarius this summer. You have not responded. Nor have you sent me any receipts from any payments for any extracurricular activities he was involved in recently that you claim i have not covered half of. The last time i bought him a ticket you didn't respond to my calls or text until the day before his flight which is why i canceled his flight because i didn't know whether or not your were going to send him since you didn't respond. When you finally answered the day before his flight you claimed that was not your intentions there was just something wrong with your phone which is why you didn't respond. I don't know what the issue is this time but i don't want any issues with your phone to hinder our communication so I'm reaching out on Facebook. I am purchasing him a round trip ticket to las vegas starting on June 20-July 25 for my five week summer visitation with my son. I am not being confrontational nor do i want drama. I just want you to communicate with me like a mature adult about our child. Im not sure what still angers your about me deserving to talk to him on a regular basis. In my most recent attempts at cordiality i have even went as far as telling you happy mothers day to show appreciation for what you do for him. Tomorrow isn't promised to anyone. I have missed the last three summers with my son. I don't want to miss anymore.

She was still not very responsive to my attempts to communicate about the upcoming visitation. I figured that she was just out of excuses this time and her lack of maturity didn't allow her to communicate cordially. I remained hopeful and stayed optimistic that she was going to take him to the airport on time. The day for him to fly to Las Vegas arrived; my family and I were so excited! We had everything in place; his sleeping arrangements, family activities planned, bought his favorite foods from the grocery store, etc. The only thing left to do was pick him up from the airport and we were jumping off the walls with excitement. A few hours before his flight was scheduled to take off from Georgia, I wanted to make sure they were on the road heading to the airport. I called Karen to check on the status but got no answer. Seconds later, I received a text from her that said, "driving". I interpreted that message as she was driving him to the airport for his flight and couldn't talk on the phone. Little did I know she was implying a completely different message with that text. I would have liked more details from her about their positional status in relation to the airport, but I assumed she was trying to be a safe driver and accepted that text message as confirmation that they were on schedule to make the flight.

I tried reaching out to her again shortly before his flight was scheduled to take off to make sure they made it safely, but again no response. This was a huge red flag! I assumed she was just being stubborn because she didn't like the idea of him staying with me and my wife for an entire summer, which would have been a first for us. I tried not to stress over her lack of communication during such a critical time to communicate but I knew something just didn't seem right. I searched his flight details online and discovered that the flight had taken off. I still needed confirmation that he actually made it on the flight, but Karen was still not being responsive. The flight from Georgia is 4 hours long; which seemed like an eternity when I didn't hear from Karen the entire flight. I tried not to think anything of it and prepared to go pick him up from the airport. I arrived at the airport shortly before his flight was scheduled to land. When an unaccompanied minor is traveling by themselves, the receiving parent or guardian has to go through airport security and wait at the applicable gate to receive the child. Being familiar with this process and excited to see him, I arrived at the airport early to make it through security in time to pick him up from the gate. I was completely unaware that some devastating news was headed my way. I approached the check-in counter of Frontier Airlines to present my I.D. and get my gate pass to get through security. I had a huge smile on my face when I handed the representative my I.D. card and provided them with my sons' information. The rep started to search their computer system and after about thirty seconds of awkward silence I could tell something was wrong. "Is everything ok?" I asked, highly concerned. "Mr. Wedlow, it appears that your son Amarius never boarded the aircraft," the representative informed me regrettably.

Confused at first, I asked her to double-check the system because I genuinely hoped that there was no way he didn't board the aircraft. The representative double-checked and again confirmed that Amarius never got on the plane. I was infuriated! I felt completely taken advantage of, belittled, finessed, bamboozled, etc.! The representative could see me fuming and before I let the airline personnel see me lose my sh*t I walked away angrily. I immediately called her phone and of course she didn't answer so I left a voice mail and all I can remember saying is, "Really, are you f*cking serious?!" and a few other expletives. I couldn't believe that not only did she disregard my summer visitation again, she made me lose the money that people donated to me. This was a new low for her—the ultimate low blow. I think the idea of an entire community supporting me financially in efforts to help me spend time with my son fueled her to be even more vindictive.

I rushed home to break the news to Kayla and she immediately broke down crying in anger and frustration. The audacity of Karen to not send him for another visitation was beyond comprehension to us. Extreme embarrassment, disbelief, disappointment, and anger are just some of the emotions that I was overtaken by. I was at my wit's end with Karen. I wanted vengeance immediately. I literally had to snatch the phone out of Kayla's hand to stop her from sending a few of her friends to Karen's address to inflict harm on her. Although I supported Kayla's retaliation, I was able to control my emotions and think clearly about how we would approach accountability for Karen's actions. I didn't immediately come to a resolution, but I knew I wasn't going to rest until Karen answered for this ugly act of disrespect in court. I had to send out a public apology on social media to all the people who contributed to the Go Fund Me. This was one of the most vulnerable and embarrassing times of my life. I explained to everyone what happened but also had to regrettably inform them that I didn't have the money to pay them back for their contributions.

Days later, Karen still wasn't answering my phone calls or texts. Out of desperation, I began conducting research online and discovered what is called a welfare check. A welfare check can be accomplished by police free of charge to visit an address of your choice to verify the safety and wellbeing of someone. I got on the phone with the Statesboro Police Department, explained the situation, and provided them with Karen's address. For court purposes, I needed documentation that would prove Amarius was supposed to be visiting me for the summer, but he was still in Georgia. Since I hadn't seen or heard from him, I was well within my rights to get someone to check on him. After conducting the welfare check the officer called my phone and explained to me what he discovered. He mentioned that Karen told the police that the reason that she didn't take him to the airport was because she didn't have a ride. Complete BS! The officer went on to say, "I recommend taking her to court because I think you have a case." Little did he know, I was already on top of it!

STATESBORO POLICE DEPARTMENT						Printed Date: 06/29/2015 Page 1 of 2 Printed Time: 11:35 AM	
Dispatch Report							
Dispatch No. 2015 6 3748	Dispatched By sryall	Dispatch Originated TELEPHONE TO PD	Received Time 06/22/2015 13:46	Dispatch Time 06/22/2015 13:49	Closed Time 06/22/2015 14:16		
Dispatch Location Address 201 HART STREET			City STATESBORO	State GA	Zip 30458		
Secondary Location			Business Name HART STREET				
Signal Code 1025	Description WELFARE CHECK						
Complainant WEDLOW NICHOLAS							
Complainant Information (Street Address, Secondary Address, City, State, Zip, Phone Number) 0						(702)569-2083	
Status AR 1 RENDERED ASSISTANCE		Patrol Area	Zone	Sub-Zone	Location 201 HART STREET	Sub-Location	
CRN NUMBER				Lattitude 0	Longitude 0		
Unit 244 APO GAWTHROP JUSTIN							
Dispatch 06/22/2015 13:49		Arrived 06/22/2015 14:00			In Service 06/22/2015 14:16		
Unit 222 CPL SAMPLES PHILIP ANDREW							
Dispatch 06/22/2015 14:01		Arrived 06/22/2015 14:01			In Service 06/22/2015 14:16		

Remarks		
06/22/2015 13:47:28	sryall	ATTEMPT TO MAKE CONTACT WITH THE COMPLAINANT'S
06/22/2015 13:47:42	sryall	10 YEAR OLD SON AMARIUS WEDLOW
06/22/2015 13:47:55	sryall	HAS JOINT CUSTODY WITH
06/22/2015 13:48:15	sryall	SON WAS SUPPOSED TO ARRIVE IN LAS VEGAS FOR VISITATION
06/22/2015 13:48:30	sryall	ON THE JUNE 20 AND NEVER ARRIVED AND HE IS UNABLE TO MAKE
06/22/2015 13:48:48	sryall	CONTACT WITH HIS SON, THE MOTHER OR ANY OF MOM'S FAMILY
06/22/2015 13:49:20	sryall	BELIEVES SHE DRIVES A BLACK GMC ACADIA
06/22/2015 13:51:46	sryall	ADVISED SUBJECT WE CAN CHECK HIS WELFARE BUT WE CAN'T
06/22/2015 13:54:05	srvall	ENFORCE THE CUSTODY AND MAKING HER CALL HIS DAD

STATESBORO POLICE DEPARTMENT			Printed Date: 06/29/2015 Page 2 of 2 Printed Time: 11:35 AM	
Dispatch Report				
06/22/2015 14:04:08	cfoy	244- SPEAKING TO MOTHER AND CHILD THEY WERE UNABLE		
06/22/2015 14:04:20	cfoy	TO GET TRANSPORTATION TO THE AIRPORT		
06/22/2015 14:15:50	cfoy	244- FATHER HAD NOT SPOKEN TO THE SON IN A WHILE		
06/22/2015 14:16:02	cfoy	THEY ARE STILL ATTEMPTING TO MAKE ARRANGEMENTS FOR		
06/22/2015 14:16:16	cfoy	VISITATION		

A few days later, my cousin Tank, who was friends with Karen on Facebook, sent me a picture of a post she shared on the day he was supposed to be traveling to visit me. I still wasn't friends with Karen so I couldn't see her post on my timeline and Tank was aware of this. The reason Tank sent the picture was to inform me of a suspicion he had for

Amarius not getting on the plane. The photo Tank sent was a picture of Amarius wearing a baseball uniform holding a trophy. What I gathered from the time and day she posted this picture was that Karen allowed Amarius to participate in a baseball tournament (that I was never aware of) instead of taking him to the airport like she was supposed to. The audacity of Karen to completely disregard our court order and my attempts to communicate while she was attending a baseball game was a whole new level of disrespect. She had no issues accepting the child support I sent regularly though. Keep in mind that the photo I was sent didn't match up very well with what she told the police during the welfare check. Couldn't the same mode of transportation that she used to take Amarius to the baseball tournament have been used to take him to the airport? My mother was on standby ready to take him to the airport if Karen wasn't able to do so. How hard would it have been to let me know that she didn't have a way to get him to the airport? I could have easily gotten my mother to assist.

CHAPTER 13

A SECOND
CONTEMPT

*"By the time a man realizes that maybe his father was
right, he usually has a son who thinks he's wrong."*
—*Charles Wadsworth*

I felt completely helpless in this situation. I decided to lean on my primary support group and would vent to my cousins Adrienne and her sister Alysia. Alysia was a very close family member in my life while growing up. One special thing about Alysia was her drive to be great. She was the type of cousin who would come and spend the Christmas holidays with our family. While all the other kids were outside playing hide and go seek, she would be inside doing homework. I didn't understand it at the time but after we became adults, she passed the bar and became a lawyer. I saw how her studious ways came to fruition and admired her dearly. Adrienne also contributed to the Go Fund me, so I felt obligated to apologize sincerely about losing the money and not being able to pay her back. Adrienne was fuming but she wasn't necessarily upset about the money; her empathy and frustrations were centered around me losing more time with Amarius. Once again, Adrienne volunteered her services to help me secure legal counsel. Adrienne was aware that I was too depressed to think clearly and wasn't motivated enough to research attorneys for myself; plus, I trusted Adrienne. Adrienne was adamant about being selective and only referring me to a lawyer who is aggressive in nature. Her exact words were, "You need a bulldog for this case!"

After conducting some extensive research, Adrienne sent me the contact information for an attorney named Elizabeth Branch. Without blinking an eye, I reached out to Elizabeth, conducted a consultation about my case, and decided to retain her as my attorney. Elizabeth agreed that I had more than enough evidence for a contempt case and informed me that her retainer fee was $1500 and her rate was $200 per hour. There I was again faced with a tough decision. I didn't have $1500 just laying around. I had to figure out how I would come up with the money to retain Elizabeth. Setting up another Go Fund Me account was out of the picture due to the public embarrassment I had already experienced. I decided to give Navy Federal another try. By now, the Navy Federal Loan officers knew me by first name. I sat down with a loan officer named Nick. I described in detail what I was going through and why I desired a loan. I was in good standing with Navy Federal because I had already repaid the original loan I borrowed previously. Nick also empathized with me about my custody battle and apologized for me having to go through this. He then proceeded to the back office to speak with the head loan officer.

Upon return, Nick notified me that my timely repayment history with Navy Federal allowed him to approve me for a $3K loan on the spot, without hesitation. This loan enabled me to pay the retainer for Elizabeth, purchase airfare for myself to Georgia, and coordinate a ride from the airport to attend the hearing. To you, it may seem unnecessary to spend $3K to pursue $688 for a lost plane ticket, but it's the principle of the matter for me. If I didn't hold Karen accountable for her actions, she would continue the confrontational behavior and not want to co-parent peacefully. Time missed with my son is something I can't get back. I wanted Karen to explain herself to a judge and show her that I wasn't playing games about spending time with my son. I paid Elizabeth the retainer and she immediately filed the motion for contempt petition. Karen had 30 days to respond to the petition before the judge would establish a date for the hearing. I expected Karen to retain a lawyer and try to defend herself, but I was shocked to see her response to the motion pro se.

Response for Motion for Contempt

I, I   , am writing this in response to a Motion for Contempt filed in The Superior Court of Bulloch County by Nicholas Wedlow.

The movant, Nicholas Wedlow, states that he purchased a plane ticket for our son, Amarius "Payton" Wedlow, in the amount of $688, on or about June 4th 2015. The flight was for summer visitation which was to last 5 weeks. The movant also states that he sent gas money to myself on June 16th 2015. The movant alledges that I intentionally refused to send our child. The movant is asking that I be held accountable for his attorney fee's, the cost of the flight, that I be found in willful contemp of the court, that I be ordered to immediately release the child into his custody and that I explain my actions.

There are several reasons why the movant was unable to have his summer visitation. I, in no way, wish to keep our son from his father and I only want the best for our son. Since this court entered a Final Order on August 9, 2012, in which I agreed to giving the movant more visitation time, the movant has not gotten our child for any of his visitations. In April of 2014, the movant sent copies of a plane ticket to me for June of 2014 for our child to visit for summer visitation. I attempted to make contact with him the entire week before our son was supposed to leave. The movant refused to answer my calls or texts. The day before the flight, while packing my son's luggage to leave, the movant text to say he did not want to get our son.

In January of 2014 the movant sent multiple messages stating his desire to cause deadly harm to myself. He has since made the same statements over the phone. Due to this violent behavior, I have become concerned for the safety of my son.

In April of 2015 the movant stated that he would not be getting our son for summer visitation. Due to him stating this, I allowed our son to try out for All Star baseball. Our son made the team and the movant was made aware of it. The movant then decided in June of 2015 that he wanted to get our son for summer visitation. I made him aware that our sons last baseball tournament would be on June 20th 2015 and that ANY date AFTER this would be good for him to leave. Without considering what I had told the movant or without consulting me, the movant bought the plane ticket for June 20th 2015. I told him this date would not be good but he refused to compromise.

The movant sent money to me on June 16th 2015 and has stated in the complaint that it was for gas. The money that was sent was for half of our son's extracurricular activities.

The movant has continuously refused to compromise with me about our son.

I, therefor, ask that the court reinforce the Final Order and see that the movant, in this matter, has been unwilling to compromise on the matter at hand.

Prior to the hearing date, Elizabeth and I prepared our strategy for the contempt case. Elizabeth had a legal assistant named Mark Smith who was very helpful in preparation for my case. Elizabeth wanted to know the entirety of my history with Karen and our parental relationship. I provided Elizabeth with prior court orders, proof of purchased airfare for Amarius, text messages, emails, etc., that were applicable to the case. I also informed her about the incident where the dog attacked Amarius and shared a newspaper article with her that included a police report where Karen had gotten a DUI. Additionally, I relayed info about Karen's inability of keeping a steady job, suspended license issues, and multiple contempts of court; it was checkmate! My goal was to expose Karen's character to the judge so that they would be more inclined to hold her accountable in court for her actions. After showing Elizabeth all the evidence I amassed against Karen, the trajectory for the legal outcome we were seeking began to shift. Elizabeth advised me sternly, "Nick, I think we should petition the court for a change of custody; it's obvious that Karen is never going to follow the court order and I think you have enough evidence to support a change of custody." Hearing this advice from Elizabeth was music to my ears! I rejoiced and felt vindicated by the fact that I had found "a bulldog" that would help me seek the appropriate justice! There was only one problem. How would I afford a change of custody? Elizabeth informed me that her retainer fee for a change of custody was $3K. In my mind, there was no way I could afford this, but I didn't want to miss the opportunity to pay someone who could help me pursue more time with Amarius. I was at yet another financial crossroad.

There was only one option; Navy Federal Credit Union! I decided to visit Navy Federal again to attempt securing the money for a change of custody. Although I wasn't in a rush to accrue more debt, I needed to act on the legal advice provided by Elizabeth. I was greeted by Nick again upon my arrival at Navy Federal. He was surprised to see me back so soon but provided the great customer service that they always had. I explained to Nick how my lawyer advised me to go for it all. Nick could feel the desperation and sincerity in my voice and demeanor as I presented my request for needing more money. I explained how the retainer for a change of custody was $3K and humbly asked him for another loan for that amount. I didn't know how it would affect my finances and my ability to repay the loan, but

I knew that I always find a way and decided to worry about the how at a later time.

Nick listened to me with the intent to help and mentioned that he couldn't guarantee that I would be approved but he would see what he could work out. Nick told me to wait a few moments while he went to the back office to negotiate with the head loan officer. As I waited for him to return, I had already made up in my mind that if I wasn't approved, I wasn't going to pursue a change of custody. A feeling of depression and frustration took over me as I sat there wondering how I reached this point of desperation when I only desired more time with my son. I actually thought about just walking out of the bank before Nick returned because I knew it was going to be a huge challenge to repay the money, especially if I wasn't successful in the change of custody.

Before I could gather the strength to leave the bank, I saw Nick return from the back office with a huge grin on his face. The look of good news on his face immediately made me perk up and attentive to what the head loan officer had decided. "Nick, I have great news for you!" Nick said informatively. "Not only did I get you approved for the loan you are requesting, but even better! You are approved for a revolving line of credit for $10K!" I couldn't believe the words that had just come out of his mouth! "I was approved for what?!" I yelled at Nick as I almost jumped out of my seat. "You have a line of credit for $10K," Nick repeated with affirmation. "That sounds like good news, but what is a line of credit?!" I asked curiously. "The way a revolving line of credit works is, you can spend up to $10K and once you pay it off you can use it again and again. The best part is that your monthly bill for the line of credit will never exceed $200. Your credit is in good shape and you have such a good repayment history with us that we are providing you with the financial flexibility that you are going to need for your custody battle." Nick informed me assuredly. I literally started to tear up as Nick explained what I was approved for and how the line of credit works. This had to be a blessing from God. I was at a loss for words! Nick stopped talking and awaited my response. There was an awkward silence as I sat there trying to process what just happened. I could feel all my financial worries exit my body as I sat there awkwardly staring at Nick fighting back the tears. This was one of the few times that I considered it okay to hug another man that had no relation to me. I entered the bank expecting not to get approved for another loan and I left out of there with more than enough money to pursue a custody battle. To me, this was a sign that I was headed in the right direction and was deserving of more time with Amarius.

Kayla and I celebrated as I broke the news that we were going to be able to pursue the change of custody. We were in disbelief how easily it was to secure the financial ability to pursue justice and were adamant about taking advantage of the opportunity. I immediately reached out to Elizabeth to begin the process. I paid Elizabeth the $3K retainer she requested to file the petition for change of custody. I knew at this point there was no turning back. We were still waiting to attend the hearing for the upcoming contempt case, and we were now preparing to request another court date for the change of custody. At that point, I had already paid Elizabeth $4,500 and I intended on getting my money's worth in justice. Elizabeth and I finished preparing for the contempt hearing and she filed the petition for the change of custody. The next step was to have Karen served with the change of custody petition. I feared that once Karen found out I was pursuing a change of custody it would affect my ability to speak with Amarius. I was eager to get both hearings underway and felt several steps closer to my goal.

The date for the contempt hearing rapidly approached and I grew more nervous as it got closer. Although I had airfare purchased, I didn't have the expenses for a hotel room during my stay in Georgia. Since I had family in the area, I decided to reach out to my ace boon coon, JaRissa! I consider JaRissa as my best friend outside of the brother-sister relationship we have together, and I knew she would be more than willing to let me stay at her house while in Georgia. I flew into Atlanta, Georgia and my cousin Dominique Meridy picked me up from the airport. Dominique was excited to see me and expressed how proud he was of me for my legal pursuit of being a good father. The plan was for Dominique to take me to Macon, Georgia where JaRissa met us and took me the rest of the way to her house in Statesboro. We arrived at JaRissa's house, I unpacked and reviewed the details of my case once more to ensure I was prepped for the hearing the next day. The next morning, JaRissa prepared a phenomenal homecooked breakfast and took me to the courthouse to attend the hearing.

I entered the courtroom ready for war! I was looking forward to watching Karen try to dance her way around the facts as she sat on the witness stand during cross-examination. Unfortunately, I didn't get my opportunity to witness her shenanigans under oath. As always, the expectation is for the petitioner and defendant to have a discussion prior to the hearing to attempt a resolution before presenting the case to the judge. During this particular hearing, Karen didn't have an attorney representing her; she was *pro se*. I'm not sure if she just couldn't afford an attorney for the hearing or if she chose not to retain legal counsel but she was at a clear disadvantage. Elizabeth was familiar with the outcome I was seeking for the hearing and I was confident that we would prevail based on the evidence we had against Karen. Prior to the start of the hearing, Elizabeth politely asked Karen to have a discussion with her in the meeting area right outside of the courtroom. I remained in the courtroom and waited patiently because Elizabeth was my voice, and I was confident in her ability to pursue an outcome that was beneficial to me. As I waited, I couldn't help but visualize Karen being confrontational with my lawyer and trying to weasel her way out of the legal heat that she had gotten herself into. After about 15 minutes, Elizabeth returned to the courtroom to brief me on the results of their negotiation. To my surprise, Karen agreed to most of the terms I was requesting. Karen was eerily cooperative with Elizabeth and I was caught off guard at her receptiveness to the terms of agreement. I was relieved that I would be able to recoup the money from the airfare that I lost and excited to be granted some make up visitation dates with Amarius. Details from the case below:

IN THE SUPERIOR COURT OF BULLOCH COUNTY
STATE OF GEORGIA

NICHOLAS J. WEDLOW,

    Petitioner,

v.

    Respondent.

Civil Action No. SU15DR264W

ORDER ON MOTION FOR CONTEMPT

This matter was came before the Court for a hearing the on August 10, 2015. The Petitioner Father was present and represented by his attorney, Elizabeth A. Branch. Respondent Mother appeared *pro se*. The parties reached an agreement which was announced and recorded before the Court, and the Court on hearing the parties' announcement and considering the facts presented, now finds that the parties announced agreement is an appropriate resolution of the case and hereby orders as follows:

1.

The Court finds that the Respondent Mother is in contempt of this Court as alleged in the Petitioner Father's Motion for Contempt.

2.

The Petitioner Father's right to visitation with the minor child is modified as follows:

(a) Petitioner Father's Summer visitation will begin on the first Sunday after school is released for the Summer vacation period and the child will be returned to the Respondent Mother seven (7) days before school commences again at the end of the Summer vacation period.

1

(b) On the first Sunday after school is released for the Summer vacation period the Respondent Mother will bring the child to the home of the child's paternal grandparents in Statesboro, Georgia at 2:00 p.m. The respondent Mother will then be relieved of any responsibility for putting the child on a plane to fly to the Petitioner Father's residence in Nevada.

(c) Seven days before school commences at the end of the Summer vacation period the Petitioner Father will return the child to the home of the Respondent Mother at 6:00 p.m. The Petitioner Father is responsible for ensuring that the paternal grandparents or other responsible members of his family deliver the child to the Respondent Mother's home on behalf of the Petitioner Father at 6:00 p.m.

(d) The costs of the child's flight to Nevada for the Summer visitation will be split between the parties with the Petitioner Father paying for the plane ticket to Nevada, and the Respondent Mother paying for the plane ticket to return to Atlanta, Georgia.

(e) The Petitioner Father will be responsible for ensuring that the child is met and picked up at the airport by the paternal grandparents or other responsible members of his family when the child arrives in Atlanta, Georgia.

(f) All other provisions of the Court's previous Custody Order, including provisions for Holiday visitation remain unchanged.

3.

The Petitioner Father will never discuss child support or other litigation related matters with the child.

4.

The Respondent Mother will never tell the child to lie to the Petitioner Father.

2

5.

Both parties will complete the Parenting Class required for divorcing parents by the Rules of the Superior Courts of Georgia and both parties will file their Certificate of Completion within 30 days from the date this Order on Motion for Contempt is signed by the Judge.

6.

Pending the outcome of the Petitioner's separate Petition to Modify Custody and Child Support, which was filed in this Court on or about August 28, 2015, the parties will complete a Parenting Plan consistent with the custody provisions of this or any new custody order that the Court may issue.

7.

If another motion for contempt is filed against her, the Respondent Mother will pay the Petitioner Father's reasonable attorney's fees.

8.

Petitioner Mother will pay one half (1/2) of the costs of the child's flight for the Summer of 2015 in the amount of THREE HUNDRED AND FORTY FOUR AND 00/100 DOLLARS ($344.00) which was lost by the Petitioner Father in the total amount of SIX HUNDRED AND EIGHTY EIGHTY AND 00/100 DOLLARS ($688.00) after the Respondent Mother failed to put the child on the plane as ordered by this Court.

9.

The Respondent Mother will notify the Petitioner Father of all of the Child's doctor appointments and visits. The Respondent Mother will notify the Petitioner Father by text or e-mail whenever the child is sick or suffering from any illness, whatsoever.

3

10.

The Respondent Mother will not drive without her driver's license, and she will provide proof of her driver's license to the Petitioner Father on his demand.

SO ORDERED this ___ day of _____, 2015.

_____
William E. Woodrum, Jr., Judge
Superior Court of Bulloch County
Ogeechee Judicial Circuit

Order prepared by:

Elizabeth A. Branch
Attorney for Petitioner
Branch Law Firm
124 Savannah Avenue, Suite 2B
Statesboro, Georgia 30458
(912) 871-5968

Certificate of Completion

This certifies that the person named below has completed a
4 Hour Parent Education And Family Stabilization Course

Nicholas J. Wedlow
8250 N Grand Canyon Drive #2116, Las Vegas, NV 89166
Date of Birth: 02/24/1987
Date of Course Completion: 08/25/2015
Certificate Number: 7506

Course for Parents
Parent Education and Family Stabilization Course

Ms. Shera S. Aldridge,
Course Instructor

After a successful contempt hearing, I was excited to get back to Las Vegas and finish preparing for the upcoming change of custody case. Karen had agreed to repay half the amount of the plane ticket that I lost within 90 days. Unfortunately, my lawyer didn't include the "90 days" stipulation in the final order and Karen took full advantage. Initially, I didn't want to agree to her paying me $344 because it was only half the plane ticket's original cost, but like I said, the paper trail and consistency were what was most important. Karen also had to provide proof of her license upon my request in addition to taking the parenting course. Karen's cooperation in court during the contempt hearing was a breath of fresh air in comparison to her historical difficulty in co-parenting. It was only a matter of time before she started showing her true colors again.

The 90-day time limit for Karen to repay me the money for the plane flight was quickly upon us. As time neared, I began to grow concerned that she wasn't going to meet the deadline. A few weeks before the 90-day period was up, I reached out to Karen via text message to check in on the status. Of course, in true Karen form, she was difficult about it.

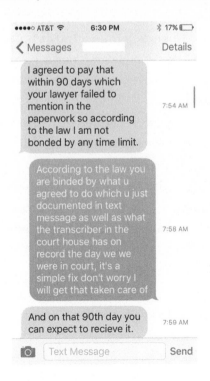

> **I agreed to pay that within 90 days which your lawyer failed to mention in the paperwork so according to the law I am not bonded by any time limit.** — 7:54 AM

> According to the law you are binded by what u agreed to do which u just documented in text message as well as what the transcriber in the court house has on record the day we we were in court, it's a simple fix don't worry I will get that taken care of — 7:58 AM

> **And on that 90th day you can expect to recieve it.** — 7:59 AM

Needless to say, Karen failed to repay me within 90 days. I was immediately angered and frustrated by her audacity to not repay me as agreed. At that moment, the words that Elizabeth uttered about how Karen will never follow the court order were never truer. It was also even more frustrating how Karen would portray the role of a damsel in distress with a nice polite personality in the courtroom but behind closed doors in our interactions, she was the exact opposite. This fueled me to prepare even more for the change of custody hearing because I was fed up with her inability to cooperate.

I grew impatient with the announcement of a hearing date for the modification of custody; it took forever (literally months) to get a court date. I grew frustrated and even took it upon myself to call the judge's secretary directly to see if there had been any development on my case. Several times I called and never got an answer, so I left voice messages. Word got back to my attorney and apparently, she didn't like the way I was approaching the situation. "If you want to piss the judge off, keep calling his office!" Elizabeth scolded. My intentions were good, but this was the first time I had ever had to wait months to get a court date established. I needed to know well in advance because I was trying to plan out my itinerary. As a member of the Air Force, I had to schedule and request leave, buy a plane ticket, and the sooner I purchased airfare the cheaper it would be.

As we awaited a court date, I continued to receive support from friends and family members that were aware of my custody circumstances. One of the most memorable instances of community support came in the form of someone I consider a guardian angel to me. My former high school football teammate Chester J. McBride reached out to me on Facebook one day and randomly sent me a picture of my son. Chester knew both me and Karen, and he was very familiar with the struggles I had experienced with not being able to consistently spend time with Amarius. Chester was one of the most talented people I've ever met. He was book smart, athletic, goal oriented, and a very humble human being. I also had something in common with Chester other than high school and sports; Chester was also a member of the United States Air

Force serving as a Special Agent in the Air Force's Office of Special Investigations. It meant the world to me to have people like Chester going out of their way to help me stay in tune with my son's life despite the hurdles Karen had placed in front of me.

 CJ CJ

9/22/15, 8:03 PM

 Hey I saw this pic of your son bruh and I think you might have not saw it. Buf if not here it goes.. I hope everything is going well for you man and remember to stay positive and work hard.

CJ CJ

Preciate it fam! Where did you get this pic? Yea she don't be sending me pictures so this is definitely a good look thanks man

Her and Travis wife friends on FB and had a pic of Travis little girl and her daughter and I clicked on the pic. I saw the pic with others on her page. So I was damn I remember you posted that you didn't see his pics really so I thought about you man.

Man I appreciate that bro bro! I'm bout to go for full custody... Just waiting in the judge to set a date... This would be a life changing experience for me so fingers crossed

I hope you get it man.. Every child need there dad man. I pray things go well for you and your family. I got to speak to coach p team tomorrow ..

When I run at millcreek I see all the midget league teams out there practicing

CHAPTER 14

THE CUSTODY MODIFICATION

"A father carries pictures where his money used to be."
—Steve Martin

In early December of 2015, I finally got notified of a court date for the modification of custody hearing; set for January 04, 2016. Although I had been eager to get a court date established, I couldn't believe it was happening! Upon notification of the hearing date, I immediately let all of my closest supporters know. It felt like the OJ Simpson trial by the amount of attention and support news of the hearing received. Honestly, I didn't think I had a good chance based on Elizabeth being familiar with the judge who was seeing the case. "This judge usually favors women," Elizabeth informed me during hearing prep. I feared that I was at a disadvantage after hearing this news about the judge, but I convinced myself, "You miss 100% of the shots you don't take," and this powerful phrase helped me remain optimistic about the hearing. I was prepared to give it all I had despite the outcome. I knew deep down in my soul that I would never forgive myself if I didn't at least try. After all, if I didn't win, it wasn't meant to be; but if I did win, it would be all worth it! I remember telling myself: *"Win, lose, or draw, I'll always be content with trying instead of giving up and letting myself continue to be alienated from my child."*

Because I already had a court date, I began planning my itinerary. Fortunately, I was entitled to a New Year's holiday break visitation with

Amarius in December of 2015. Kayla and I agreed that if I coordinated with Karen, I could potentially arrive in Georgia a few weeks early and spend time with Amarius during my New Year's visitation prior to the hearing. This scenario would allow me to kill two birds with one stone, so to speak. I reached out to Karen and informed her of my plans. Karen expressed how odd she thought it was for me to come to Georgia to spend a visitation with him but was surprisingly receptive to this idea and agreed to my request. Karen agreed to my request so quickly that it was obvious that she hadn't been notified about the date of the hearing yet; assuming because she still hadn't retained a lawyer. In reality, my intentions were to position myself in Georgia early, spend some time with Amarius before the court hearing, and explain to him what was about to take place. Karen later found out about the court date and reached out to me highly upset because she realized I was really coming to Georgia because the court date had been set.

Shortly before I was able to travel to Georgia, I was informed of some devastating news. My classmate Chester J. McBride was killed by a suicide bomber in Afghanistan on December 21, 2015. This was a devastating blow for me! Hearing this news felt surreal because literally just a few months prior to his death, he sent me a picture of Amarius. Chester passed away serving his country, but I just couldn't understand how such an upstanding citizen was taken from us so early. It just so happened that his funeral arrangements were scheduled in Statesboro around the time of my custody hearing and I made it a priority to attend his beautiful homegoing services. This time was very emotional for the entire Statesboro community and social media was filled with people posting their condolences and appreciation of Chester and his family. RIP Chester J. McBride! Gone but never forgotten...

Remembering CJ CJ ✕

We hope people who love CJ will find comfort in visiting his profile to remember and celebrate his life. Learn more about the legacy contact setting and memorialized accounts on Facebook.

Remembering
CJ CJ ✓ Friends ▼ 💬 See Messages ⋯

Timeline | About | Friends 374 Mutual | Photos | More ▼

Office of Special Investigations ✓ ⋯
December 20, 2017 · 🌐

~ Remembering Our Fallen ~

On Dec. 21, 2015, AFOSI Special Agents Adrianna Vorderbruggen, Michael Cinco, Peter Taub and Chester McBride and Air Force Security Forces Defenders Tech. Sgt. Joseph Lemm and Staff. Sgt. Louis Bonacasa were killed when their joint patrol, Hustler 6, was attacked by a suicide bomber riding a motorcycle near Bagram Air Field, Afghanistan. Their memories live on...

Nick Wedlow
December 21, 2015 · 👥   •••

RIP to my former teammate/colleague ...still having a hard time accepting this and I don't want to believe a person with his good morals, ethics, potential, and future aspirations could be taken so early... My dude was an OSI special agent and those qualifications are hard to come by, a monster in the weight room, and did I mention he had a masters degree? When I last spoke with him he was preparing for one last deployment then separating from the Air Force because he had already started the application process for the FBI... Forgive me for sharing so many personal details but I have watched him reach these accolades and I am truly proud of his accomplishments and his legacy needs to be heard and respected... My last words to him were "be safe in that sandbox" ...I'm tearing up as I write this... Rest easy bro ... We lost a great role model

Using the line of credit, I was able to book airfare for my trip to Georgia and planned a detailed itinerary that would allow me to spend time with Amarius and attend the hearing. My sister JaRissa came to my rescue again and offered to open up her home to me for my brief

tay for the holiday with Amarius and the court hearing. As time got closer, Elizabeth and I began to prepare for our case via telephone and email. Elizabeth was very thorough with the court preparation. We went through every detail like a fine-toothed comb. We prepped to a T. Initially, Karen wasn't represented by a lawyer, but we were notified during our preparation time that she had retained legal counsel.

I was in no way, shape, or form intimidated by Karen getting a lawyer, as far as I was concerned, she was going to need it. I was informed by Elizabeth that it was wise to get people who knew me well to complete character references about me to provide the judge with information that would help him learn more about the type of father and person I was. Luckily, I was fortunate enough to have a vast amount of people to choose from who were willing to write a character reference for me. Among those people were:

Connie Alston – my beautiful mother. Love you, Ma!

Brad Mauger – a Math tutor who helped me during college coursework.

Adam Runquist – a former supervisor who I had the pleasure of working for.

Debbie Palmer aka Mama Deb – a lifelong supporter who has become family.

Joeseph Blackburn – my wife Kayla's grandfather.

Colonel Vinnie Powers – a former Commander at the 17th Attack Squadron (Bulls!)

*Disclaimer: If you provided me with a character reference letter and I didn't include you on this list, I apologize but memories have begun to fade, and I tried to recollect as best as I can.

5 April 2017

MEMORANDUM FOR CHILD CUSTODY COURT

DEPARTMENT OF THE AIR FORCE
17TH ATTACK SQUADRON (ACC)
CREECH AIR FORCE BASE NEVADA

FROM: 17 ATKS/CC

SUBJECT: Character Reference Letter for SSgt Nicholas Wedlow

1. I am the commander of the 17th Attack Squadron at Creech AFB, Nevada. Nick is an MQ-9 Remotely Piloted Aircraft Sensor Operator in my squadron. For 13 months, I have overseen his career from this position.

2. As an MQ-9 Sensor Operator, Nick is responsible for operating the advanced multi-spectral targeting system. From the ground control station located here at Creech AFB, Nick is responsible for operating this specialized equipment across the globe in support of remotely-piloted aircraft combat operations with the highest consequences at stake. In this assignment, he has exemplified the Air Force Core Values of integrity, excellence, and service which recently resulted in his hand-picked selection to enroll in the Instructor Sensor Operator Upgrade training course. Nick is also the non-commissioned officer in charge of the scheduling section for our squadron where he oversees a team of six personnel coordinating 24/7 combat operations manpower requirements. I have had the pleasure of witnessing Nick emerge as a leader at the top of his peer group.

3. Contact me directly at   or   @us.af.mil with questions.

POWERS, Lt Col, USAF
Commander

I also subpoenaed Amarius's academic records and submitted a public records request for Karen's arrest history and the pit bull attack incident. Our goal was to compile as much factual evidence as we could against Karen to prove alienation, character issues, and to portray her as an unfit parent. We were simultaneously aiming to provide factual evidence that I was in a better position to parent Amarius by presenting information about my Air Force Career, ability to maintain a security clearance, deans' list academic achievements, honors, no arrest history, a stable living environment with a two-parent home for Amarius, etc. In situations like this, you have to pull out the big guns. Keep in mind, Karen brought this on herself. In the famous words of the old timers, "God don't like ugly." At one point, my wife and I were content paying the $688 in monthly child support as long as we were able to exercise our holiday and summer visitations with Amarius. When Karen started taking away our court-ordered telephonic and physical visitations from us, sh*t got real.

During litigation matters, the petitioner and defendant are provided with copies of each piece of evidence that is filed by the opposing party. This means that Karen was supplied with a copy of every document that my lawyer and I filed in support of the hearing and vice versa. I was disturbed after becoming aware that Karen and her legal team filed a witness affidavit that was supposedly written by Amarius. This particular affidavit doesn't read like the words of an 11-year-old and it was obvious to me that Karen's legal team was pulling out all the stops to prevent me from getting custody. At that point, I knew that the gloves were going to come off during this custody battle.

IN THE SUPERIOR COURT OF BULLOCH COUNTY, GEORGIA.

NICHOLAS S. WEDLOW,

    Plaintiff,   :   Civil Action No. SU15DR303W

v.   :

    Defendant.   :

FILED
BULLOCH COUNTY CLERK'S OFFICE
Jan. 4 .2016
Teresa Wales
CLERK BULLOCH COUNTY
SUPERIOR COURT

ELECTION AFFIDAVIT OF CHILD 11 YEARS OF AGE

COMES NOW the undersigned and after having been first duly sworn deposes and says as follows:

I am AMARIUS PAYTON WEDLOW, and I am Eleven (11) years old. My year of birth is 2004.

As I understand the law, I have the right, because of my age, to express to the judge my desires about which with whom I wish to live, and it is my desire and I wish to live with and be in the primary custody and control of my mother,

I also wish to emphasize that my mother has in no way influenced me to keep me from remaining primarily with my father in his home in Las Vegas, Nevada.

I want to say that I love both of my parents and this statement in no way reflects that I do not love and care for my father. I wish to have reasonable visitation with my father as I choose.

I am making this statement freely and voluntarily and understand that this document will be presented to the Court regarding whether my mother will have legal and physical custody of me.

Amarius Payton Wedlow
AMARIUS PAYTON WEDLOW

SWORN TO and subscribed before me
this 4th day of January, 2016.

_____
Notary Public, State of Georgia
My commission expires:

I was completely aware that the odds were stacked against me. I knew the judge favored mothers, I knew that Amarius didn't want to leave his mom, and I also knew that I was a Black male going against a Caucasian woman for child custody in South Georgia. Although it was an uphill battle, I never let negativity occupy my mind—even for one second. I also knew what I brought to the table for Amarius and the amount of preparation we completed would compel any judge to make an intervention after reviewing the facts of my case.

The time came for me to travel to Georgia for the holidays. A few days after Christmas, I flew to Georgia. Dominique picked me up from Hartfield-Jackson Atlanta International Airport again and JaRissa met us in Macon. We arrived at JaRissa's home in Statesboro and the countdown to the hearing began. As planned, I coordinated with Karen so that I could retrieve Amarius from her so that he could spend the New Year's holiday with me at JaRissa's house. It was an awesome feeling to finally spend some father-son time together with Amarius in person. JaRissa has two sons, Zion and Jaceon who are around Amarius's age, with whom he has a great relationship with. JaRissa's younger twin sister Anna and brother Marvin were also present for the holiday break we spent together.

During this holiday break, I had a heart to heart with Amarius. I sat him down and tried my best to explain to him about the upcoming court hearing and what was about to happen. Zion and Jaceon sat and observed while I had this heartfelt conversation with Amarius. I emphasized to Amarius how important it is for his development to have his father in his life and how my goal is to be the best I can be for him. We discussed how we have a great time with each other when we're together and how we want to increase our opportunities to spend time together. Amarius wasn't aware of the arguments that went on behind the scenes between his mother and me. He was naïve to the fact that his mother had shielded me from several visitations and wasn't in compliance with the court order on numerous occasions. I didn't want to involve him in litigation, so I didn't go into too much detail, but I did touch on the importance of a father heavily. I began to get emotional during the conversation.

As I sat there speaking to Amarius, I couldn't help but notice that Zion and Jaceon were being attentive. At that moment it dawned on me that not every child has the luxury of a father. Zion and Jaceon's father had passed away in a horrific four-wheeler accident while they were very young. RIP, Freddale Brown. The opportunity for them to spend time with their father was stripped away from them early on in their lives. I broke down crying and couldn't finish my sentence because the look on the faces of Zion and Jaceon were saying, *"I wish my father was here with me right now."* Amarius wasn't old enough to understand the luxury of having a father, but I was determined to make sure he appreciated my eagerness to be there for him; winning the custody battle was the first step.

Amarius and I ended up having a blast together during our holiday break. We had an amazing time with JaRissa, Zion, Jaceon, Marvin, and Anna. We spent time listening to music, dancing, watching movies, playing video games, eating good food and socializing. Time flies when you're having fun and the holiday break abruptly came to an end. Unfortunately, I had to return Amarius to Karen prior to the hearing. I knew that Karen would possibly try to brainwash Amarius into thinking that he hated to spend time with me to gain an edge for herself in court but there was nothing I could do to stop it from happening. The court date was upon us before we knew it and it was time to handle business. The day before the hearing I went to Elizabeth's office to review and conduct final preparation for the final hearing. We ensured all the evidence and supporting documents were available and in order. We prepared talking points that we wanted to highlight during the hearing, and she coached me through what to expect, dos and don'ts.

As we began wrapping up preparation, Elizabeth began reviewing her notes and practicing what she would say to the judge during her closing remarks. She didn't realize that I was watching and listening to her, but this was one of the most powerful moments that I've witnessed from her. Elizabeth pretended that she was talking to the judge on my behalf and her words were so powerful I could feel a few tears roll down my cheek. I was moved by the way she was prepared to stand up for me and help me spend more time with my son. I wish I could have recorded it. Unfortunately, I don't recall her exact words, but I was so touched by her closing remarks that I genuinely felt like she was taking my case personally and I wasn't just a client to her. Seeing her in action made my confidence go through the roof. I knew that if she nailed her closing remarks in front of the judge the way she did in front of me, any human being overseeing my case would be moved in a manner that insights change.

The morning of the hearing, I woke up with butterflies in my stomach. The big day was here! All the preparation and anticipation was complete, and it was time to execute! JaRissa cooked us an all-star breakfast and afterwards, we drove to the courthouse. We arrived at the courthouse early; my mother and JaRissa were in my entourage. It was game time. I met with Elizabeth and we waited outside the courtroom. Alysia also accompanied me to court that day. Prior to the hearing, I introduced Alysia to Elizabeth. Alysia began discussing strategy with Elizabeth and providing her with insight. Elizabeth recognized how educated Alysia was regarding court proceedings and asked what her background was. Alysia explained that she also practiced law and Elizabeth embraced her input and became receptive to her suggestions. It was the coolest thing ever to me because it was like having two lawyers for one case!

We saw Karen and her attorney enter the building and gather around the entrance to the courtroom where we all waited in awkward silence for the bailiff to open up the doors. I could feel my heart racing with anticipation. I knew that there would be no negotiation prior to the hearing this time. It was an obvious fight. Karen didn't want me to have primary custody, period. No negotiation tactic was going to convince her otherwise. Both sides were prepared to present their case to the judge for a decision.

After about fifteen minutes of waiting, the bailiff opened the doors to the courtroom and instructed everyone to enter and have a seat on the pews. We all rose for the judge's entrance, he took his seat on the bench, and began roll call. There were several cases he had to see that day. There were two cases which were being heard before ours. We got the opportunity to sit and watch several trials before ours and listening to the drama of their case calmed my nerves a little. It was comforting to know that I wasn't the only father experiencing difficulties seeing their children but sickening at the same time. Upon conclusion of the cases prior to ours, the judge announced the start of our hearing. My nerves immediately started going erratic again. The judge began with requesting opening statements from both lawyers. After the opening statements, it was time to call witnesses to the stand.

The first witness Elizabeth called to the stand was Karen. Karen approached the stand, got sworn in, and Elizabeth immediately began her questioning. Elizabeth addressed her questions in chronological order and strategically asked questions that would lead into the evidence we had against her. Elizabeth knew that Karen still hadn't repaid the $344 for the lost plane ticket so she targeted her with questions that would expose Karen's character. Karen testified that she supposedly tried to mail me a money order via priority mail but didn't have any tracking information. Sounds believable, right? She also testified that she had taken the parenting course that she was ordered to complete from the contempt hearing, but the clerk couldn't find any record of it the day of the hearing. Elizabeth was sharp that day. Her style of questioning was forward thinking. Her questions seemed innocent initially until she presented evidence to support that Karen's testimony wasn't truthful. It was very entertaining to watch. It really exposes a person's character after they answer a question and get presented with evidence that proves that they just lied under oath.

For example: Elizabeth asked if Karen could briefly explain her work history. Karen informed the court of all the places that she has worked over the past few years in detail. Then Elizabeth followed up with another question, "Do you remember testifying in court in 2012 that you weren't working? But you were working—you just said that you were working in 2012." Her testimony was contradicting in nature like this on multiple occasions during the hearing on various different subjects. Her honesty about her employment is important because child support is based off of both parents' incomes in Georgia. If Karen says that she isn't working, then I automatically have to pay more child support. Elizabeth targeted her early to expose that she hasn't been truthful about her finances over the years in order to receive more money from me. Karen also claimed that she paid all her bills using student loans. Sounds fishy, right?

1	Q	What's the company?
2	A	Straight Talk.
3	Q	And who pays for that cell phone?
4	A	I do.
5	Q	With what?
6	A	Obviously the money that I get from my student loans.
7		That's how I pay all my bills.
8	Q	Is that what your student loans are for?
9	A	Yes.
10	Q	Get a cell phone for your kid?
11	A	If that's what I choose to use them for, yes.
12	Q	Why didn't you put your student loans down on your
13		financial affidavit?

During cross-examination, Karen was being very snarky and responded with smart-aleck answers to Elizabeth's questioning. It was pretty sad to watch how aggressively Karen was defending her testimony when Elizabeth kept exposing her dishonesty and character issues. I was relieved to finally witness the court's reactions as they were introduced to the type of person she was. I could see her portrayal of a cooperative co-parent crumbling before everyone's eyes. It was very hard for Karen to defend herself when we brought the receipts we had against her to court—ones that displayed all of the issues I've had with her historically. Elizabeth also exposed Karen's traffic citations, her arrest history, DUI/reckless driving incidents, check fraud, multiple contempt hearings, frequent relocations of living arrangements, Amarius's low grades, and numerous other issues.

After completion of questioning for Karen, I was the next witness called to the stand. Elizabeth began to ask me questions that would present my side of the story in response to Karen's dishonest answers. The only difference was, we were able to provide more receipts. We presented text message history between me and Karen that didn't reflect Karen's testimony. We submitted concerningly low grades that I was able to retrieve from the Parent Portal application that I had access to as his parent. I submitted records of purchased airfare, the incident report from the pit bull attack, evidence from the Go Fund Me account, phone records, parent-teacher conference documents, etc. We pulled out all the stops! Elizabeth also asked questions that led to testimony about what I do for a living, my academic success, my nonexistent arrest history, my relationship with Amarius, and all the other positive factors. Elizabeth concluded her questioning and it was time for me to get cross-examined by Karen's attorney.

As soon as Karen's attorney began to question me, I was immediately pissed off. His job was to try to prove that I was a terrible person, and although he wasn't successful, he tried his best, that poor lil thing (in my mom's voice). I'm going to include a few screenshots from the transcript of the temporary hearing to give you an idea of how the hearing went. The court transcript is 307 pages long, so I've included several excerpts of the most interesting moments of the hearing.

2	<u>CROSS EXAMINATION BY MR.</u> :
3	Q Mr. Wedlow, I'm . I represent Ms.
4	obviously. I want to thank you for your service in the military.
5	But I have a question: do you wear that dress uniform all the
6	time?
7	A No.
8	Q You just wore it today?
9	A Yes.
10	Q I mean, have you worn it while you've been on
11	Christmas break here or just to impress the Court? I'm just
12	asking why you wore it today instead of like khakis and a shirt.
13	A Because I feel like this is a formal setting and these
14	are my formal clothes.
15	Q Okay. Those are your formal clothes. Okay. I was
16	just asking. I'm not trying to demean the air force in any way.
17	I'm just asking. Have you ever told Ms. that you've
18	missed father's day -- the last three father's days because of
19	your inability to afford visitation?
20	A No, not the last three. Just one.

Off the bat, Karen's attorney tried to imply that I was wearing my Air Force uniform to impress the court. This immediately made me get upset. Even if I didn't wear my uniform, I would have worn something more formal than khakis and a shirt. Seriously, bro? Give me a break. I immediately knew that I was going to grow increasingly upset as the questioning progressed, but I was also aware of my surroundings and couldn't afford to display any unprofessional body language. I remained as composed as I could, but it was very difficult to not get out of character when a lawyer is trying to make you look like a piece of sh*t to the judge. Karen's lawyer didn't really have a leg to stand on other than a few text messages I sent to her from past years. Admittedly, I've said some mean things to Karen in the past; I've since apologized. Also, in my defense, I only said those things out of frustration due to her attempts to alienate me from my child. To this day, I've never

nflicted any harm on Karen and never will. I was also questioned about
ny living arrangements. At the time, Kayla and I were living in a one-
bedroom apartment. Karen's lawyer tried to corner me about my small
iving arrangements, but I was prepared for this question.

1	A	Yes.
2	Q	How big is it?
3	A	Right now I'm not sure of the square footage.
4	Q	One bedroom?
5	A	Yes.
6	Q	So you're married with a wife, two children and you've
7		got a one bedroom apartment?
8	A	Yes. That's because I have to pay $688 in child
9		support and --
10	Q	So it's because of child support?
11	A	No.
12	Q	Somebody made you have that child?
13	A	No one made me had a child.
14	Q	Uh-huh (nodded).
15	A	Yeah.
16	Q	But you have a one-bedroom apartment? So if this
17		child goes with you, you're going to have a five-member
18		household living in a one-bedroom apartment?
19	A	I've spoken with my landlord and they know about the
20		case, and I will immediately be able to move into a bigger space
21		and I will be able to afford more if I am granted custody.

Karen's lawyer concluded his questioning of me and decided to
call Karen to the stand next. As her lawyer questioned Karen, she
revealed some shocking news that I wasn't aware of. It saddened me that
during her testimony, I learned that my son had been diagnosed with
ADHD. I was floored by this information. The audacity of Karen to
withhold information regarding my son's medical health and wellbeing
for over four years baffled me. On top of that, she lied about having
informed me about this prior to the hearing. I was fuming at this point

as I watched her discuss the details of him being prescribed Adderall and taking it for years without me knowing. As I listened, my mind started racing with questions that I needed answers to. *Why hasn't she ever packed medication in his bag during his visits with me? How could she bring herself to not tell me this information while simultaneously using my military health insurance to cover the price of the doctor visits and medication? Did he really need the medication or was his energetic behavior in class due to a lack of discipline at home?* Karen tried to imply that Amarius's ADHD diagnosis was the reason his grades were subpar to mediocre at best. I completely disagreed. I knew in my heart that Amarius just needed more structure and discipline in his life so that he could excel academically; I was prepared to provide that for him if custody was handed to me.

Of course, her lawyers' job was to save face and try to help Karen's character recover in the eyes of the court. He asked her questions which led to answers that portrayed me as an overaggressive type of guy that bullied her in court. The only real substance they could use as evidence against me was the mean text messages I sent to Karen in the past out of anger. Those were isolated incidents and if I were really the type of person they tried to make me out to be, I wouldn't have been able to attain the clearance needed for my job.

Here's how he questioned Karen:

18	Q	Have you felt bullied by him in the past?
19	A	Yes.
20	Q	Have you felt belittled by him in the past?
21	A	Very much so.
22	Q	Have you felt controlled by him in the past?
23	A	Very much so.
24	Q	Do you feel that he still tries to bully and control you?
25	A	Yes.

135

1   Q   I lost my train of thought. What's Mr. Wedlow's
2 general demeanor been with you? How would you describe his
3 personality?

4   A   Narcissistic.

5   MS. BRANCH: Your Honor, I'm going to object.
6 She's not a professional and has no right to characterize
7 his personality. These are psychiatric. She basically just
8 made a psychiatric diagnosis on him.

9   THE COURT: Any response, sir?

10   MR.   : Your Honor, I think she's just
11 giving a lay opinion of her experience with him. I really
12 wasn't looking for a psychological eval -- I mean, a
13 psychiatric --

14   MS. BRANCH: Your Honor, she has no
15 expertise.

16   THE COURT: The Court will sustain the
17 objection.

9   Q   Did he get any cards for his birthday?

10   A   No.

11   Q   So this was the first year a card was mailed?

12   A   Uh-huh (nodded).

13   Q   Okay. Have you ever intentionally -- you may have
14 already said this and I'm sorry. It's all running together. Have
15 you ever intentionally not checked your mail or not entered a
16 forwarding address with the post office?

17   A   No.

18   Q   Okay. Your son has -- is it ADHD; is that correct?

19   A   Yes.

20   Q   When was he diagnosed with that?

21   A   In 2012.

22   Q   Okay. Is that -- do you think -- well, I can't ask you if
23 you think. And he has a little bit of attention -- problems paying
24 attention in class?

25   A   (Nodded.)

1   Q   Okay. Does he take medicine for ADHD?

2   A   He does.

3   Q   What does he take?

4   A   Adderall.

5   Q   Okay. Does it seem to help?

6   A   It does.

7   Q   I mean, from what you've seen?

8   A   Uh-huh (nodded).

9   Q   Okay. Is Mr. Wedlow aware of that?

10   A   Yes.

11   Q   Of his diagnosis and medication? I didn't think to ask

12 him that.

13   A   (Nodded.).

6   Q   Okay. You say that Amarius has been on Adderall

7 since 2012; correct?

8   A   Correct.

9   Q   But you never told his father that he was on Adderall,

10 did you?

11   A   Yes, I did tell his father.

12   Q   And you never sent a single -- you never sent any

13 Adderall with him when he went to visit his father, did you?

14   A   He doesn't take it during the summer or when he's on

15 breaks.

16   Q   Okay. Who's the doctor that prescribed that

17 Adderall?

18   A   Dr. Gorsi.

19   Q   How do you spell that?

20   A   G-O-R-S-I.

21   Q   Where is he or she?

22   A   He's no longer at Statesboro Pediatrics and Family

23 Healthcare. All of that is in the medical paperwork that I have.

24   Q   So he's no longer there? So who's currently

25 prescribing this Adderall?

The audacity of Karen to get on the witness stand and be dishonest so effortlessly was beyond belief. She lied about repaying me the $344, why she didn't take Amarius to the airport, her employment history, notifying me of her address changes, and numerous other factors of the case. I knew Karen had issues with being truthful prior to the hearing but it was a whole new level of dishonesty to see her lying under oath. During her testimony, her lawyer admitted the affidavit they had Amarius sign. To me this was the ultimate low blow because according to my lawyer, an 11-year-old couldn't submit an affidavit as evidence and there was some confusion about whether or not it should be allowed. It was disturbing how far they were willing to go to ensure that I didn't get custody.

3	Q	Can you identify this document?
4	A	It's an affidavit that my son signed.
5	Q	When did he sign it?
6	A	This morning.
7	Q	And you witnessed it?
8	A	I did.
9	Q	I mean, you witnessed him signing it?
10	A	I witnessed him signing it.
11	Q	And it's an election affidavit to live with you?
12	A	Yes.
13		: Have you seen this?
14		MS. BRANCH: Again, Your Honor, if His Honor
15		is going to talk to the child, I think that basically solves that
16		right there. And I don't see -- an 11 year old doesn't really
17		have the right to elect, so I don't know why he needs --
18		why you would file an affidavit for an 11-year-old.
19		I think, certainly, Your Honor has the right to talk
20		to an 11-year-old, and I think that basically is the way to
21		find out what the 11-year-old wants, not to file an affidavit
22		that his mother and lawyer may have coached him on.
23		: Your Honor, number one, that is a
24		gross misstatement of the law. As far as I know, an 11-
25		year-old to a 13-year-old has a right to sign an affidavit.

1   The Court can take it into consideration. Age 14 and older,

2   then there's a presumption. The Court doesn't have to

3   follow it, but there's a presumption to overcome.

4   And I didn't serve this 24 hours in advance

5   because, as I said before, this is not a witness affidavit.

6   There's nobody to call or cross examine.

7   I've drafted affidavits for children between 11

8   and 13 for as long as I've practiced law, and I have

9   McConaughey right here that says a child can make an

10   election. I've never even known this to be an issue. This

11   is the first objection I've ever come across on this issue.

12   MS. BRANCH: Well, I don't --

13   : The Court's going to go ahead

14   and admit it over the objection. It will be part of the record

15   in the case.

16   **(NOTE: Whereupon, Defendant's Exhibit Number 6**

17 **was admitted into evidence.)**

18   : And for the record, I didn't coach

19   him. I just said, you can sign it if you want to.

20   THE COURT: Further questions, sir?

21   : That's it.

As the hearing went on, the judge also interjected and asked questions of his own directly to me and Karen as we were on the witness stand. When he questioned Karen about her arrest history and suspended license issues, I knew that the wheels were turning in his head and he was concerned about her character. I remember thinking "checkmate" as he asked her some concerning questions.

4   Q   Mill Creek. Where was your last place of
5 employment?
6   A   T.J. Maxx.
7   Q   And when was that?
8   A   In 2012.
9   Q   2012. And you've not worked since 2012?
10   A   No, sir.
11   Q   Why have you not tried to work since 2012?
12   A   I've been in school.
13   Q   So you've been doing your schooling that you testified
14 to earlier?
15   A   Yes, sir.
16   Q   You have a series of citations there. Why do you
17 have so many driving citations? Are you just in the wrong place
18 at the wrong time or what is it?
19   A   I just -- I don't -- I can't -- I don't know how to answer
20 that. Just a mistake, I guess. I mean...
21   Q   Well, a lot of them maybe you don't even have your
22 driver's license on you. That's what I saw. Maybe it was
23 reduced down to not having your driver's license and they had a
24 suspended license. You don't carry your driver's license on you
25 when you're driving?

1   A   I do. In those cases, I may not. I have -- I didn't have
2 it on me.
3   Q   You don't learn from all these citations that you can't
4 realize that apparently you're a candidate for being stopped and
5 being cited?
6   A   Yes, sir.

The judge elected to speak with Amarius in his private chambers
after we returned from a recess for lunch. I was worried to death about
what Amarius would say to the judge because I knew that deep down,
he didn't want to move to Las Vegas with me. I also knew that Karen

155

had potentially coached him and influenced his mindset about the case. This was the most nerve-wracking moment I experienced during the entire hearing because I felt completely vulnerable and helpless. I could only hope that Amarius spoke highly about me to the judge. I strongly felt like the meeting between Amarius and the judge would make or break the case.

The hearing lasted all day! We began at approximately 9:30 A.M. and after our quick recess for lunch, the hearing progressed up until late in the afternoon. There were several people in the courtroom observing that had cases which were supposed to be heard after the conclusion of ours. Unfortunately, those people had to reschedule their hearings for another day because ours lasted so long. After several cross-examinations, the meeting between Amarius and the judge, and the judge asking all of his questions, we were finally able to conclude the hearing. Elizabeth presented her closing remarks flawlessly, just as I had seen her practice in her office the day prior. Karen's lawyer also had an opportunity to share his closing remarks. I felt disrespected as his closing remarks included a request to have my monthly child support payment amount increased and for Amarius to remain in Karen's custody.

The last person to speak was the judge. I was nervous because I thought a decision was going to be made right then and there. My heart was racing because I just knew the judge was about to announce the fate of Amarius and the results of our custody battle. All the hard work was about to either pay off or we were about to fall short of our goal. Little did I know, I was in for a curveball. Instead of announcing a decision, the judge provided his closing remarks.

3   All right. Mr. Wedlow and Ms.   , the Court's
4 going to take this and look at it and give you some decision
5 in the very near future. It's not going to make a decision
6 today on your case. It appears this is a temporary hearing,
7 so it would be a temporary order and we'll see where we
8 go from there.
9   The Court is going to encourage you to work
10 together so as that this child can be, during the meantime,
11 have an opportunity to talk with his father, see his father if
12 he's here on a local basis at this point.
13   There's no room for either one of you to be
14 voicing any sort of bad names towards each other and
15 making any sort of gestures about the other party. There's
16 no room in that. You shouldn't be doing that. The Court's
17 going to direct that that not take place.
18   But during the meantime, the Court will take it
19 under consideration and give you some decision in the
20 very near future. All right.
21   MR.   : Thank you.
22   MS. BRANCH: Thank you, Your Honor.

The judge's closing statement was very anticlimactic for me. I expected a more conclusive answer, and I was highly disappointed when we didn't get one. What did he mean he would get us an answer soon? I expressed my concerns to Elizabeth after the hearing, but her response helped me feel more optimistic about how the hearing went. Elizabeth explained to me that his ending remarks were a good thing. 'He could have said no to you getting custody right then and there, but he didn't, which meant he had to think about it," Elizabeth explained informatively. Although Elizabeth reassured me that not getting a decision immediately after the hearing was a good thing, it didn't feel that way.

We went back to JaRissa's house after the hearing and I vented to her for hours about how it all unfolded. The next day, I returned to Las Vegas with Kayla and the kids. Apparently, a judge's "soon" is completely different than my "soon" because we literally waited weeks for him to announce the results of the hearing. Up until the judge's announcement, my family and close supporters were calling me daily wanting to know the results of the hearing. I grew frustrated because the more people inquired, the more impatient I got. People who I didn't even talk to on a regular basis were reaching out to me. I couldn't tell if they were being nosey or genuinely being supportive. I didn't understand what could possibly take so long for the judge to announce such a huge decision that would affect our future. I had no choice but to continue with my daily routine.

Resuming my normal work schedule helped me take my mind off of the hearing. The afternoon of January 25, 2016 was a beautiful day. Nothing seemed special about that day up until about lunch time. I had a busy day conducting my normal flying duties, so I was pretty occupied. In my line of work, you aren't allowed to have your cell phone in certain areas of the building. On that particular day, I left my cell phone in the break area while I was flying. I needed to use the restroom, so I took a break from flying and went out to the break area to use the restroom. After I finished using the restroom, I decided to check my cell phone to see if anyone had tried contacting me while I was flying. I picked up my phone and noticed I had a missed call from Elizabeth! This was completely out of the ordinary because Elizabeth hardly called me. Honestly, I tried not to call her too often historically because she charged $200 per hour and those phone call minutes can add up quickly.

Before I returned her call, I decided to walk outside because if I didn't get the news I was hoping for, I was going to verbally let off some steam and I didn't want to disturb anyone's break time. I immediately called her back after I got outside the building because I figured it was pertaining to the results of my case. I was nervous as I dialed her number and was praying to God that she wasn't about to bear some bad news. Elizabeth answered the phone immediately, "We got an order! Amarius is coming to live with you!" She began reading the final order to me but all I could hear was Charlie Brown noises because I had already heard what I was listening for. A feeling of extreme relief and justice came over me suddenly. Before I knew it, I broke down in tears. I was in complete awe that the judge heard my cry and decided to give me a chance to be a father to my son. It was surreal how the same judge that encouraged me to get a second job during the child support modification hearing decided that I deserve to have custody of my son. If I had to describe the feeling I experienced after hearing the news, it was similar to the scene in the Lion King after Simba had just defeated Scar and regained control of Pride Rock. I remember yelling out a loud cry of joy and the people that were outside walking around started looking at me weird, but I didn't care.

Elizabeth explained that the judge was going to allow Amarius to complete the rest of the school year in Georgia and after the school year was over, he would come to live with me for a year. After the year was over, we would return to court to determine if he would remain with me or go back into Karen's custody. Elizabeth also informed me that she would send me a copy of the final order to my email immediately. After regaining my composure, I gave a very sentimental thank you to Elizabeth for her help, ended the conversation, and immediately called Kayla. When I informed Kayla of the good news, she immediately started screaming to the top of her lungs out of pure joy and I could literally hear her running around the house and jumping on and off the furniture. You would have thought we had just hit the lottery. After she calmed down a little, she started asking a million questions. Some of them I didn't have the answer to and the questions I had the answer to were given to her in a tremoring voice in between deep breaths and sniffles. I remember Kayla asking me, "Wait a minute, are you crying?!" "No, of course not," I responded deceitfully. "Yes, you are! Stop lying," Kayla said challengingly. We both burst out laughing. Kayla asked because she doesn't see me cry often and needed confirmation; we both knew I wouldn't be able to hide it from her.

To put it into perspective for you; this final order one-pager cost me over $7K after retainer fees, plane flights, and 8 hours' worth of lawyer fees at a $200 per hour rate during the final hearing that lasted all day.

IN THE SUPERIOR COURT OF BULLOCH COUNTY
STATE OF GEORGIA

NICHOLAS J. WEDLOW,

    Petitioner,

vs.

    Respondent.

§
§
§
§
§
§
§
§
§
§

FILED
BULLOCH COUNTY
CLERK'S OFFICE

2016 JAN 15 PM 3: 51

CIVIL ACTION NO. SU15DR303W
CLERK OF COURT

TEMPORARY ORDER

The above matter came before the Court for a temporary hearing on January 4, 2016. Both parties were notified and both parties were present. Having considered the parties' argument, the record in this case and the law, the Court finds and concludes as follows:

-1-

Petitioner and Respondent shall have joint legal custody of the minor child, Amarius Payton Wedlow, born 2004, and temporary physical custody of the child shall be transferred to the Petitioner, Nicholas Wedlow, at the end of the current school term regardless of participation in extracurricular activities, including baseball. The child shall remain in the custody of the father for one school year. At the end of the 2016-2017 school year the child shall be returned to Georgia, and both parties will attend a final hearing in this matter. At the hearing the father testified that he lives in a one bedroom apartment with his wife and two other children. The Father is ordered to acquire larger living arrangements to ensure there is enough room for the minor child to live in the father's household.

-2-

Respondent shall be entitled to visitation with the minor child for Thanksgiving break and for one-half of the child's Christmas break from school.

-3-

Further, the Court hereby orders that any child support being paid on behalf of the minor child will stop upon transfer of custody. The mother will not be responsible for paying any child support to the father during this period of transferred custody; however, the mother will be responsible for paying the costs of her visitation with the child.

SO ORDERED, this _____ day of January, 2015.

WILLIAM E. WOODRUM
Chief Judge, Superior Court of Bulloch County
Ogeechee Judicial Circuit

CHAPTER 15

THE QUIET BEFORE THE STORM

"He adopted a role called being a father so that his child would have something mythical and infinitely important: a protector."
—Tom Wolfe

ord travels fast; the news of me winning custody swept the city of Statesboro immediately. A Black man winning custody of a biracial child was too much for some people to fathom in small-own Georgia. The close family members who at one point told me to give up had to eat their words and express how proud of me they were for staying persistent! Winning this uphill battle made all the determination and preparation worth it to me! This was my "I told you so" moment to all the naysayers. Finally, the court was able to see that I was the victim in this situation and my son would be better off living with me. Karen and her family didn't take the news so well though. The rumor through the grapevine was that when she heard that I had won custody, she fell on the floor crying, kicking, and screaming. Although we spent a great deal of time rejoicing, the job wasn't done, and we still had so much work to do.

The final order stated that I would be able to get primary physical custody of Amarius upon completion of the school year. The school year of the Bulloch County School system ended in May. This timeframe gave me several months to prepare for the transfer of custody. The first thing I needed to accomplish was to acquire bigger living arrangements to accommodate Amarius once he moved out to Las Vegas. I still had to pay child support up until that time so the remainder of the line of credit came in handy. Kayla and I began searching for a bigger house immediately. We were referred to a realtor by a close friend who helped us begin the process. Rental property homes in our area were flying off of the market as soon as they were posted. The first couple of houses we were interested in were taken before we could even finish viewing the property initially. We grew frustrated because houses in our price range were pretty scarce.

One day, I was preparing to leave for work, Kayla had a property viewing scheduled around the time I was departing and I was pretty disappointed that I wouldn't be able to go. I trusted that she would be able to secure us a good home even if I wasn't available. Although I was worried, everything worked out perfectly. I left the house and headed for work. A few minutes later, I got a call from the mission commander on shift informing me that the Area of Responsibility we flew our aircraft in had terrible weather and I didn't need to come in to work that day. I immediately turned around, called Kayla, and informed her that I would be able to meet her at the property she was about to view because she had already left the house. We arrived at the property around the same time as the realtor did. The realtor informed us that the property was just posted onto the market earlier that morning and there were no applications on the house yet.

The outside of the home was beautiful. It was located in a gorgeous neighborhood and a prime location that would provide me a short commute to my job. As soon as we walked into the house, I saw the living room area and immediately said to the realtor, "We'll take it, where do I sign?!" The layout was so phenomenal I didn't even need to view the rest of the house. I was also trying to hurry up and complete the rental application so that we could secure the property before someone else did. We completed the application, paid the deposit, and within a few hours, we were approved for the home. It was very rewarding to transition from a 400 square foot studio apartment, to a one-bedroom apartment, and then to a 4-bedroom, 1900-square foot, two-story house. "Moving on up" like the Jeffersons was an understatement.

After securing bigger living arrangements, we had other preparations to make before the transfer of custody. We had a bigger house to furnish, we needed to purchase a wardrobe for Amarius (to include sports equipment), and airfare (for my travel to Georgia to retrieve Amarius, and his flight to Nevada). Throughout the process of transitioning into a bigger home, the drama with Karen began to peak. The confrontational interactions through the phone began immediately after the news broke about me winning custody. She began to make threats and say things like, "I'm appealing the judges' decision" and "he's not coming." These threats worried us because we were financially drained from court hearings and we had just entered a 1-year lease for a 4-bedroom house.

My new attorney is appealing the decision of our temporary order. So far two courts have approved the appeal and the decision of the final court will be made in 30 days. Just a heads up.

No need for a heads up I'm well aware of how relentless you are to make sure I don't get adequate time in my sons life

Those are not my intentions. Some disturbing new evidence come to light and it changes things.

●●○○○ AT&T 🛜   5:41 PM   ⚹ 36% 🔋▸

< Messages   [ ]   Details

> Because it's an emergency appeal and your attorney doesn't have to be notified because y'all have no say so in the appeal.

What's the emergency [ ]? The simple fact that you don't want to lose him?

> You'll see.

And how do you have money for an appeal but you haven't paid me my $344?

> You'll see.

 Text Message   Send

I tried not to let her appeal threats phase me and just kept on preparing for the transition at the end of his school year, however, I was extremely worried. I immediately reached out to Elizabeth to check the validity of Karen's threats. Elizabeth informed me that her lawyer drafted an appeal but never filed it because Karen still owed him money from the custody modification. This was a sigh of relief because I was discomforted by the idea of potentially having to go back to court and the judges' decision getting overturned.

During that transitional period, my phone calls with Amarius were few and far in between if at all. The first time I spoke with him after notification of the hearing results, it was a very heated conversation. Karen's temper was flaring, and it influenced the way Amarius engaged with me over the phone. Karen took it upon herself to vent about our past relationship in an attempt to convince everyone that I didn't deserve custody. "You abandoned us!" Amarius snarled over the phone. "You can't take me from my mom!" he added disrespectfully. I couldn't believe how he was addressing me over the phone. I knew that this was a very emotional time for him. I decided to let him slide and not lose my temper because I was aware that he was comforted by the distance between us. He knew I was far away in Las Vegas so I couldn't hold him accountable immediately for speaking to me that way. I was also aware that Karen convinced him that he didn't have to come live with me and brainwashed him into thinking the transfer of custody was never going to happen. The most disturbing part of the conversation was hearing Karen egg him on in the background encouraging his disrespectful behavior.

Despite all of the rejection I was receiving from Karen and Amarius, I remained optimistic and continued to plan travel arrangements to Georgia to complete the transfer of custody. I booked airfare for both of us well in advance. As suspected, Karen wasn't cooperative with planning for me to pick him up despite my frequent and detailed communication via phone calls and text. I had to stay focused and not let her lack of communication deter me and get me off course. I needed to confirm that Karen received the travel itinerary I developed for my upcoming trip so that she could position Amarius where he needed to be to ease the transition. Since she wasn't being responsive, I decided to email her the itinerary in addition to sending her a copy-certified mail to ensure that she got it.

31 March 2016

I, _Nicholas J. Wedlow_, am writing this letter to inform of upcoming travel arrangements for our son Amarius Wedlow. These travel arrangements are pertaining to a recent custody modification hearing that was held on January 4, 2016 in the Superior Court of Bulloch County, State of Georgia, Civil Action number SU15DR303W. During this custody hearing, I was the Petitioner and was the Respondent. After both parties were heard temporary physical custody was ordered to be transferred to me at the end of Amarius' current school term and he shall remain with me for one year. The Bulloch County School year for 2015-2016 ends on May 27, 2016. Below is information detailing the airfare I have purchased for Amarius.

AMARIUS WEDLOW   Add Rapid Rewards Number   Add/Edit

Travel Date	Flight Segments		Flight Summary
MAY 28 SAT	07:40 PM	Depart Atlanta, GA (ATL) on Southwest Airlines	Flight #199 Southwest	Saturday, May 28, 2016
	09:20 PM	Arrive in Las Vegas, NV (LAS)		Travel Time 4 h 40 m (Nonstop)

I will physically be in Georgia to facilitate transfer of physical custody of Amarius prior to his departure date. I will be picking Amarius up from 's current residence:

109 Harvey Dr Apt 96
Statesboro, GA 30458

promptly at 9:00am on May 28, 2016 in order to gather him and

his possessions and ensure adequate travel time from Statesboro,

GA to Atlanta, GA which is approximately a 3.5 hour drive.

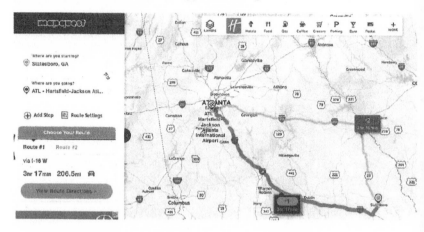

The intent of this letter is to provide this information to

well in advance which will enable her ample time to

prepare for transfer of physical custody of Amarius in

accordance with the times and dates listed above. Any

possessions too bulky to take on an airplane that Amarius wishes

to be bring with him for his stay should be brought to my

attention prior to May 28, 2016 so that I can coordinate

shipping them via mail.

Kind Regards,

Nicholas J. Wedlow

State of _Nevada_
County of _Clark_
Appeared and Signed before me on this
_31_ day of _March, 16_ by
Nicholas J. Wedlow
Jaswinder Kaur
Notary

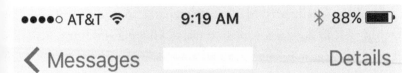

●●●●○ AT&T 🛜   9:19 AM   🅱 88% 🔋

❮ Messages   **Details**

Today 9:07 AM

10271 Headrick Drive
Las Vegas, NV 89166

MARIUS WEDLOW	Add Rapid Rewards Number	🅰 Add/Edit	
Travel Date	Flight Segments		Flight Summary
MAY 28 SAT	07:40 PM Depart Atlanta, GA (ATL) on Southwest Airlines	Flight Southwest #199	Saturday, May 28, 2016
	09:20 PM Arrive in Las Vegas, NV (LAS)		Travel Time 4 h 40 m (Nonstop)

Beginning April 15th this will be my new address ... Also I plan to physically be there around the last week of May to pick up Mari and his possessions and fly back with him on May 28th

If he goes he won't be taking anything with him. If he has to go you can purchase your own belongings for him.

   Text Message   **Send**

May 2016 finally arrived, and all preparations were in place. The only thing left to do was for me to travel to Georgia and bring Amarius back to Las Vegas. Excited was an understatement! Our lives were about to change for the better and we couldn't wait to finish the job! Life without having to pay child support was a dream that was about to come true, and Kayla and I wanted to take full advantage of it. We were also aware that increasing our family size would create new and higher living expenses. This would be the perfect time for Kayla to begin working, but we had one issue—how would we afford childcare long enough for Kayla to start bringing home paychecks? Solution; my mother! We reached out to my mom and propositioned her for help. An all-expenses paid trip to Las Vegas for a few months to spend time with her grandchildren while Kayla began working was an offer she couldn't refuse. My mother was delighted to provide assistance to us for a second time, especially since I had just won custody and was making positive strides in life.

I purchased a one-way flight for my mother to return to Las Vegas with me and Amarius after the custody transfer took place. I planned to fly into Georgia several days before Amarius's school release for the summer to take care of some administrative errands that would assist in a smooth custody transition. I needed to retrieve copies of his medical records so that I could provide them to the primary care provider he would be seen by in Las Vegas. Obtaining his medical and school records was a huge hassle. When I initially reached out to his doctor's office over the phone and spoke with a representative, I was informed that Karen had instructed them not to provide me with copies of his medical records! Once again, I was floored by the audacity of Karen to believe that she had the power to prevent me from retrieving my son's records when I was the sponsor for his medical benefits and had a court order proving joint custody. I found it very odd that she would try to keep his medical records from me. I wasn't sure if she was just trying to make things difficult for me or if she actually had something to hide?

Weeks leading up to the end of his school year, Karen wasn't answering any of my calls or responding to my texts. I thought that a udge getting involved and changing custody would scare Karen into compliance. Boy was I fooled. I needed confirmation that Amarius would be packed up and ready to travel to Las Vegas once school ended but Karen was making it difficult with her lack of communication. Obviously, the behavior was fishy to me, so I decided to reach out to Elizabeth again to see if there was anything we could do legally. Elizabeth instructed me to petition the court for an emergency hearing.

IN THE SUPERIOR COURT OF BULLOCH COUNTY
STATE OF GEORGIA

NICHOLAS J. WEDLOW,	*	
	*	Civil Action No. SU15DR303W
Petitioner,	*	
	*	
v.	*	
	*	
,	*	
	*	
Respondent.	*	

CLARK COUNTY
STATE OF NEVADA

AFFIDAVIT OF NICHOLAS J. WEDLOW

Personally appeared before the undersigned officer duly authorized to administer oaths,

NICHOLAS J. WEDLOW, who after being first duly sworn, deposes and says:

1. Last month on April 15th my family and I moved from a one bedroom apartment into a beautiful home that includes: 1900 square feet, four bedrooms, three bathrooms, and a two car garage. The home is located in a really nice neighborhood where Amarius will have his own room.

2. keeps insisting that she has filed an appeal that she will win and the Appellate Court will have a decision by mid May. has stated that she has new evidence she is presenting in the appeal and that since it's an emergency there is no requirement for me to be notified. My lawyer has assured me that cannot legally file an appeal without providing me notice and new evidence cannot be presented in the Appellate Court so her allegations don't make sense.

3. The main concern I have is the emotional harm she is inflicting on Amarius by lying to him about an appeal. She has told Amarius that he doesn't have to come live with me anymore and she also has discussed her plans to file an appeal with him. This behavior is devastating to Amarius because it further involves him in the litigation, aggravating the emotional tug of war that Amarius is already experiencing throughout this transitional period where, temporary physical custody is about to be transferred. I am very worried about my son's emotional and mental health since he has told me over the phone that his mother told him she is going to fix this in court and that he doesn't have to move to Las Vegas with me. The way Amarius spoke so confidently about his mother telling him that he wasn't coming to live with his dad convinces me that he believes what she is telling him.

4.   has had a period of nearly five months since January to be honest with Amarius about what is happening but she has not taken advantage of the time he has had to come to terms with the temporary order and now its down to a matter of a few weeks for him to adjust. The sooner he knows the truth the better off he will be so that he can make the necessary emotional adjustments to come live with his father for a while. Her dishonesty is causing him to suffer serious emotional harm and it will become more severe if he isn't told the truth soon. I am afraid that if she continues to lie to Amarius it will devastate him and disrupt his emotional stability. He may even end up extremely angry over all of this. I am very worried about the mental, phsychological, and emotional impact her lies may have on him.

5. The Bulloch County Schools are scheduled to complete the 2015-2016 school year this month, with May 27th being the last day of school for the current term. I have arranged to

be in Georgia to escort Amarius to the airport where I have scheduled a flight for us to

return to Las Vegas on May 28, 2016. I have provided a copy of Amarius' travel itinerary to

via text message and email.

6. I don't know what else to do at this point except to ask the Court for help. I am afraid of the

emotional damage that is being inflicted on my son and I do not want to say anything to him

that further confuses him and pulls him into this conflict between his mother and I.

FURTHER, AFFIANT SAYETH NOT.

This the __12__ day of _____May_____, 2016.

Nicholas J. wedlow (Print Name)

SWORN TO before me this

__12__ day of __May__, 2016.

Notary Public
Jaswinder Kaur

Notary Public - State Of Nevada
COUNTY OF CLARK
JASWINDER KAUR
My Appointment Expires
Feb 8, 2020
No. 16-1425-1

173

IN THE SUPERIOR COURT OF BULLOCH COUNTY
STATE OF GEORGIA

NICHOLAS J. WEDLOW,

    Petitioner,

v.

    ,

    Respondent.

* * * * * * * *

Civil Action No. SU15DR903W 2016 MAY 12 P 3: 32

Heather Banks McNeal
CLERK OF COURT

MOTION FOR EMERGENCY HEARING

COMES NOW Petitioner, Nicholas J. Wedlow, by and through his undersigned counsel, and files this Motion for Emergency Hearing showing the Court as follows:

1.

This Petition for Change of Custody came before the Court for a temporary hearing on January 4, 2016.

2.

Following the hearing, which both parties attended along with their respective counsel, Elizabeth A. Branch, for Petitioner and,   , for Respondent, the Court issued a Temporary Order (hereinafter "Order") which transferred temporary physical custody of the parties minor child, to wit: AMARIUS PAYTON WEDLOW, born 2004, currently age 11, to the Petitioner Father at the end of current term for Bulloch County, Georgia schools. [See Temporary Order, attached hereto as Exhibit 1].

3.

The Order further provided that the child would remain in the custody of the Petitioner Father for one school year, at which time the child would be returned to Georgia from the Petitioner's home in the State of Nevada and both parties would attend a final hearing in the matter. [Order, attached as Exhibit 1]

4.

Petitioner was ordered to obtain larger living arrangements to ensure there would be enough room for the minor child to live in the Petitioner's home. [Order, attached as Exhibit 1]

5.

Petitioner has obtained a larger home sufficient to accommodate the child as ordered. [See photos of Petitioner's new residence, attached as Exhibit 2]

6.

The Petitioner Father was ordered to continue paying child support to Respondent through the month of May, at which time child support would be abated pending the Court's final order.

7.

The Petitioner has paid child support through the month of May, including the payment for the month of May.

8.

The last day of school in Bulloch County, Georgia is May 27, 2016, and Petitioner has purchased a flight for the minor child to travel from Atlanta to Las Vegas, Nevada on May 28, 2016. [See Calendar for Bulloch County Schools, attached as Exhibit 3; See Southwest Airlines Flight Confirmation for Amarius Wedlow, attached as Exhibit 4]

9.

Petitioner notified Respondent on March 31, 2016 of his purchase of the flights for the child on May 28, 2016 so she would have ample time to prepare the child for the transfer, and he told her he would be physically present in Georgia to facilitate the transfer and would personally pick up the child from her home on May 28, 2016 at 9:00 a.m. Petitioner also asked Respondent to give him advance notice of any possessions the child wanted to bring that could not be transferred by plane so Petitioner could arrange for these items to be shipped by mail. On April 9, 2016 Petitioner sent Respondent an additional email notification of his intent to pick up the child and fly him to Nevada on May 28, 2016. [See letter and email, attached as Exhibit 5]

10.

Respondent apparently requested and was granted a certificate of immediate review of the Order but no timely application for appeal was filed. To Petitioner's knowledge no appeal or application for appeal was ever filed in any court. [See communications between   and Branch regarding possible appeal, attached as Exhibit 6]

11.

Nonetheless the Respondent insists that an Appeal has been filed, that "two courts have approved the appeal and the decision of the final court will be made in 30 days." [See text message from Respondent, attached as Exhibit 7]

12.

Respondent claims that her appeal is based on "new evidence' and alleges since it's an emergency appeal no notice to the Petitioner or his attorney was required "because y'all have no say so in the matter." [See text messages from Respondent, attached as Exhibit 8]

13.

Respondent says, "If he goes he won't be taking anything with him." [See text message from Respondent, attached as Exhibit 9]

14.

The Respondent has told the child and is continuing to tell the child that the Order is being appealed so he will not have to go with his Father at the end of the school year. [See Affidavit of Petitioner, attached as Exhibit 10]

15.

The Respondent has made it very clear that she does not intend to comply with the Order.

16.

Petitioner had hoped that Respondent just needed some time to accept the inevitable and that she would ultimately tell the child the truth and comply with the Order but she does not show any signs of accepting this Court's Order, and she is still telling the child that the Order has been appealed and is about to be overturned by the appellate court.

17.

The last day of school in Bulloch County is May 27, 2016; there are now only 15 days before the child must be ready to travel to with his Father to Atlanta and then on a plane to Nevada.

18.

There was plenty of time to prepare the child for the custody exchange ordered in January to take place at the end of the school year but, instead of using the six month interval to prepare the child for the exchange the Respondent has lied to him, telling him that the Order has been appealed when it has not and leading him to believe that he will not have to comply with the Order.

19.

Respondent's refusal to tell the child the truth is causing severe emotional harm to the child, and Respondent's lies to the child are setting the child up to suffer even more severe emotional harm.

20.

The severe emotional harm inflicted on the minor child by Respondent's continued lies is an emergency circumstance.

21.

Because of the emergency circumstances the Petitioner respectfully requests that the Court

schedule an emergency hearing to be held within ten days, if possible, to protect the child from further

harm.

Respectfully submitted this 12th day of May, 2016.

BRANCH LAW FIRM

ELIZABETH A. BRANCH
GA Bar No. 076033
ATTORNEY FOR PETITIONER

124 Savannah Avenue, Suite 2B
Statesboro, GA 30459
(912) 871-5968

Re: Wedlow Appeal

Tue 2/9/2016 9:24 AM

To:Elizabeth Branch <eliza301south@hotmail.com>;

I haven't filed anything yet. I actually need to file a notice of appeal instead of an application, so I have some time left. I'm waiting to be paid before I do it...

On Tue, Feb 9, 2016 at 9:22 AM, Elizabeth Branch <eliza301south@hotmail.com> wrote:

I have not been served with anything regarding this appeal. Where are you with filing your application for appeal? I will be representing Nick in this appeal and I need to be served with everything you file in the Court below and in the Court of Appeals.

Thanks,

Elizabeth

Elizabeth A. Branch
BRANCH LAW FIRM
124 Savannah Avenue, Suite 2B
Statesboro, GA 30458

912-871-5968
912-682-1374

eliza301south@hotmail.com

Unfortunately, my request for an emergency hearing wasn't granted. A court date was never scheduled for an emergency hearing and I had to keep pushing forward without further assistance from the court. I flew into Georgia several days before Amarius's school release. My first stop was to his pediatrician's office to retrieve his medical records. It was ridiculous to me how I literally had to visit the doctors' office in person, show them my court order, and after a bunch of back and forth, they finally coughed up the records.

I was still not satisfied with not seeing or hearing from Amarius for quite some time. Now that I was in Georgia, the odds were in my favor. I didn't have to go through Karen at this point to see or talk to him. I strategically waited until he went to school and made a surprise visit during school hours. I had a great relationship with Mrs. Minick who was the vice principal at the time, and I met her in the office. I explained the reason I was there and requested that she let me speak with him. Amarius was at recess and she had the front office clerk call him to the office over the intercom.

Mrs. Minick allowed me to wait in her office for him to arrive. Amarius entered the office a few moments later and when he saw me, his face immediately got pale as if he had seen a ghost. I caught him completely off guard because he wasn't expecting to see me. "Hey Dad," Amarius greeted me with surprise. "Hey Mari, what's up?" I responded. "I've been trying to call you," I injected. "Oh, you have?" he responded questionably. "Yeah, your mom didn't tell you I've been trying to call?" I questioned concerningly. "No, she hasn't," Amarius said informatively. "Oh ok, well did you know that you're supposed to leave with me to go to Las Vegas in a few days?" I asked intrusively. "Yeah, I know," he responded.

After I found out that Amarius was aware of the custody exchange that was about to take place, I felt temporarily relieved. I decided to change the subject and begin a more positive conversation. I gave him a hug, told him I loved and missed him, and began to discuss what he's been up to recently. I could tell that he was happy to see me, but he was also surprised because he wasn't expecting me to just pop up at his chool. He asked me to come back to his classroom with him and hang out for the remainder of the school day, so I gladly did. It was a great feeling for him to not be ashamed of me while we went to his classroom around all of his friends. As I sat in the classroom talking to Amarius, I heard one kid whisper to another, "Payton has a Black dad?" Hearing this made me chuckle. I spent the rest of the school day watching a movie with him and his classmates and having casual conversation. It was a joyful experience to finally be spending some time with him.

The day came to an end and his grandfather Billy was scheduled to pick him up from school that day. Amarius asked me to walk him out to the passenger pick up area where his grandfather would arrive to take him home from school. As his grandfather pulled up to the school, I walked Amarius over to his little blue truck. Billy saw me with Amarius and the look on his face was similar to expressions of surprise and confusion. I cordially greeted his grandfather and he politely spoke back. I was surprised by how inviting he seemed even though I know he was silently questioning why I was there. Amarius asked Billy if he could spend the rest of the day with me. Billy hesitantly informed Amarius that he would ask Karen if she was okay with it and get back to me. It was awesome to see how receptive Amarius was to spending time with me, especially when he tried to get his granddad's permission to hang out with me for the rest of the day. After I left his school, I was eager to find out if Karen would reach out to me and assist Amarius with his request to spend the day with me. Unfortunately, I didn't hear from her at all that day, or the next few days for that matter.

CHAPTER 16

ALL HELL
BREAKS LOOSE

"Sometimes, the poorest man leaves his
children the richest inheritance."
—*Ruth E. Renkel*

*M*ay 27, 2015 arrived, and it was the day prior to the big day. It was the last day of school for Amarius and per the temporary order, custody was supposed to be transferred to me. I couldn't have been more excited. I was also pretty nervous because Karen still wasn't answering the phone, returning my calls, or responding to my text messages. I had faith but I was prepared for the worst. I had emailed Karen my proposed itinerary and also sent it certified mail, so I knew she was aware of the time and place I was going to pick him up. In my itinerary, I decided to pick him up on May 28 which was the day following the last day of school. My intentions were to allow Amarius to pack up and say his goodbyes to his family after the last day—trying to be nice. I had suspicions about her throwing me a curveball when I was supposed to pick him up, so I showed up at his school again on the last day about thirty minutes before school got released. I went to the front office and upon my arrival, I was informed that Karen had already taken Amarius home on an early dismissal. This was very alarming! Who picks their kid up early on the last day of school when the school day is already a half day on the last day? School got released around 12:30 pm and he had already been picked up?!

To me, this was a clear indication that Karen was trying to prevent me from picking him up early and she beat me to the punch! I immediately tried to text and call again but to no avail. I decided to go to her house to see if they were at home. The place was completely empty, the lights were turned off, and her vehicle was nowhere to be found in the parking lot. I knocked several times and waited about fifteen minutes before I decided to leave. I was pissed! I thought to myself, *Is she really trying this bullsh*t again?! Okay, cool, I know exactly what to do.*

I dialed the sheriff's office, explained my situation to them, and requested that they conduct a welfare check on Amarius. I had a hunch that Karen was hiding out at her parents' house in the country, so I provided their address to the officer over the phone. I was fortunate that the officer who was going to conduct the welfare check called me back a few minutes later requesting more information. His name was Officer Sims; he was very polite and cordial when I initially spoke with him on the phone. He seemed as if he was eager to assist and I felt like he was going to help me bring the situation to a resolution. I informed him that I had a temporary order signed by a judge and he requested to see it. I met him at a gas station a few minutes from Karen's parents' house and showed him the order. He informed me that all he could do was ensure that Amarius was alive and safe, but he couldn't help me enforce the order. I informed him that I was aware that he could only check on the health and welfare of Amarius and I was okay with that.

Officer Sims proceeded to Karen's parents' house to conduct the welfare check on Amarius. About thirty minutes later, Officer Sims called me back and informed me that he had located Amarius at the address I provided him, and he was alive and safe. I thanked him for his help; but my blood was boiling at this point. Karen knew I was in town, she knew I was there to get custody, and she was dodging me. I was fed up with Karen's bullsh*t. I decided to take matters into my own hands. I knew it wasn't going to go well, and it was a terrible idea, but my mom and I decided to pull up to Karen's parents' house.

We were alone and unafraid. I was filled with rage; but it was a controlled rage. I knew not to do anything stupid, but I was appalled by their audacity and I wanted them to know I wasn't about to just let them walk all over me. They had some explaining to do! There was an awkward silence as we drove the short transit to Billy's house. All I could think about were the shotguns I had seen in Billy's bedroom when Karen used to sneak me into their house back in high school whenever we played hooky. I was terrified of how this was going to turn out, but I was driven by anger and I was tired of them not respecting my position in Amarius's life. I was prepared for whatever may have happened. I knew it was a strong possibility that something could go wrong, and I could potentially get shot, but I didn't care. I was unarmed; the only thing I had on me was the court order.

Approximately 15 minutes after the welfare check was accomplished, we pulled up onto Billy's front lawn. I walked up to the door and knocked sternly. I could hear my own heartbeat as I waited, anticipating a war. Christine came to the door, saw it was me, didn't speak, and immediately went to get Billy before she opened the door. Billy came to the door, opened it, and stepped towards me as if seeing him coming towards me would make me move out of his way. I stood my ground. We stood there, face to face for a few moments like two bulls ready to lock horns. I calmly asked him where Amarius was. Billy could see in my eyes that I was ready for whatever he wanted it to turn into. I didn't want things to get physical but if he took it there, I wanted all the smoke!

Billy responded defensively, "It isn't any of your business where he's at!" "Actually, it is my business! I'm supposed to get custody today and Karen isn't answering the phone. Can you please call her and get her to comply with the court order?" I responded as calmly as I could. "I'm not calling anyone, take her to court!" Billy said in a smart-aleck way. At this point, I could feel steam forcefully flowing out of my ears. I didn't get out of character though, I remained composed. "Listen, Billy here is the court order," I offered. Billy reached for the order. I snatched it away. "You can't hold it, but I'll let you read it, I don't trust you. This is my only copy, and you might try to tear it up." I said as I took control of the situation.

Billy read the court order silently to himself and his facial expression led me to believe that it was his first time seeing it. If Karen was honest with her parents about the details of the court order, why did they seem so caught off guard by it now? "See Billy," I said as I pointed at the order. "It says right here that custody is supposed to be transferred to me upon the completion of this school year! Today is the last day of school, and school just ended, so where is my son?!" I demanded. "Well, you ain't getting him! You're just a sperm donor, you ain't never did anything for Payton!" Billy yelled out as he tried to convince me that I've been a deadbeat dad.

"Well, the judge doesn't seem to think so," I wittily responded to Billy.

While Billy and I were exchanging words, I felt my mother standing near, observing. Christine had migrated near my mother and began a conversation with her. I couldn't hear what she was speaking to my mother about, but I could hear the nasty things she would randomly yell at me while Billy and I were conversing.

"You're chicken sh*t!" Christine yells out at me.

"That judge was sleep, he was blind!" Christine added to her uninformed outbursts.

I was aware that Billy didn't care for me all these years, but I was completely shocked by Christine getting out of character. I had always seen her act in such a sweet and loving manner up until this moment. The craziest part was that in between her outburst, she would try to smile, laugh, and have a cordial conversation with my mother. All the while my mother was looking at her in disbelief because she had never seen this side of her either. How did Christine have the nerve to say disrespectful things to me in front of my mother and not expect it to affect the relationship she had with my mom? I could read my mom's body language and could tell she felt super disrespected after seeing their true colors. By the grace of God, I was able to maintain my self-control even though I felt like lashing out!

As we stood there exchanging words, I noticed Christine had disappeared into the house. I grew increasingly frustrated because nothing was being accomplished. Billy was growing impatient with my persistence and things were escalating. I grew concerned about the safety of my mom and I didn't think we would be able to come to a resolution. I decided to take the high road, deescalate the situation, and I instructed my mom to get into the car. I stopped responding to Billy and began walking to the car. As I approached the car, I could hear Billy saying, "No, where are you going? Don't leave!" I ignored him, got into the car, cranked it up, and left. I began to accept defeat as I drove off. I couldn't believe what had just happened and was unsure how I would resolve the matter. A few moments later, my phone rang. It was Officer Sims again. This time, he wasn't so polite.

"Mr. Wedlow you better leave their residence right now before I arrest you for trespassing!" Officer Sims yelled through the phone. It immediately became apparent that Christine had disappeared into the house to call the police. I informed Officer Sims that I had already left their residence. Officer Sims angrily informed me that it was a civil matter and that I needed to take it to court. Before he could finish his sentence, I hung up the phone. I thought to myself, *I literally have a court order in my hand granting me custody of my child and they're telling me to take Karen back to court because she won't give him to me?!*

If that scenario isn't an example of White privilege, then I don't know what is. It blew my mind how Officer Sims was so ready to arrest me for trespassing, but he wasn't at all concerned with Karen's blatant act of kidnapping. I let Officer Sims read the temporary order prior to him going to Billy's house and he was in support of my concern. It didn't make sense to me how as soon as he completed the welfare check his entire demeanor towards me changed. I can only assume that while conducting the welfare check, Officer Sims discovered that Karen and her family were Caucasian. Put the shoe on the other foot. If I, a Black male, were to keep my son from his Caucasian mother and the police were called, would they have taken me to jail? All I could think about is the first contempt hearing Karen and I attended when the judge asked me if I was aware that I could go to jail for not transferring custody.

The ultimate slap in the face was the narrative in the police report. I literally let Deputy Sims read the court-order before he conducted the welfare check, and he wrote: "Karen believed that my custody wasn't supposed to start until the beginning of 2016-2017 school year." Typical Karen ideology to interpret the court incorrectly and convince authorities to have empathy for her disagreement with the judge's decision. Additionally, Deputy Sims included irrelevant information in the police report from the welfare check. He mentioned that I hung up the phone on him out of anger. Why was this relevant to the welfare check? After Officer Sims conducted the welfare check he called me and let me know where Amarius was located and that he was safe. During that informatory phone call, he cordially assured me that although he had located Amarius for me, there was nothing he could do to assist in the transfer of custody.

Christine called the police while I was conversing with Billy, which prompted Officer Sims to call me for a second time. During the second phone call from Officer Sims, his demeanor had changed and he was threatening to take me to jail for trespassing. After hearing the change in tone by Officer Sims, as he aggressively yelled at and addressed me, I got upset and hung up the phone for several reasons. For one, I had already left their residence before he called, and second, I was upset because he was willing to take me to jail for trespassing but not willing to hold Karen accountable for disobeying a judge's order. I hung up because I no longer needed his services and I didn't appreciate the way he switched from being a helpful deputy to threatening to take me to jail when I was just trying to follow the judge's order. My understanding is that when Christine called the police on me, it should have been considered a separate incident and the legal results from her phone call should not have been merged together with the welfare check incident. Why were details from the second phone call I received from Officer Sims included in the police report for the welfare check after it had already been completed?

GA	GA0160000		BULLOCH COUNTY SHERIFFS OFFICE INCIDENT REPORT		Case #	2016-05-09974

Public copy

EVENT

INCIDENT TYPE	COUNTS	INCIDENT CODE	PREMISE TYPE
UNASSIGNED1451 - CUSTODY DISPUTE	1	7399	6 RESIDENCE
UNASSIGNED1452 - CIVIL MATTER	1	9999	

INCIDENT LOCATION	LOCATION NAME	LOC CODE	WEAPON TYPE
, STATESBORO, GA 30461			4 OTHER

INCIDENT DATE	INCIDENT TIME	TO	DATE	TIME	STRANGER TO STRANGER
05/27/2016	00:00		05/27/2016	17:24	YES NO X UNK

COMPLAINANT	ADDRESS	PHONE NUMBER
WEDLOW, NICHOLAS JERROD	LAS VEGAS, NV 89166	

VICTIM

VICTIMS NAME	RACE	SEX	AGE	RESIDENCE PHONE	BUSINESS PHONE

ADDRESS	CENSUS TRACT	EMPLOYER OR OCCUPATION

STUDENT ? YES X NO IF YES, NAME VICTIM'S SCHOOL

OFFENDER

NAME	RACE	SEX	DATE OF BIRTH	AGE
	W	M		28

WANTED	ADDRESS	CENSUS TRACT	HEIGHT	WEIGHT	HAIR	EYES
	STATESBORO, GA 30461		505	165	BRN	BRO

WARRANT	CHARGES	COUNTS	OFFENSE CODE	OFFENSE / ARREST	JURISDICTION
ARREST					CI = CITY / CO = COUNTY / ST = STATE / OU = OUT OF STATE / UN = UNKNOWN

TOTAL NUMBER ARRESTED	ARREST AT OR NEAR OFFENSE SCENE	DATE OF OFFENSE
0	YES NO UNK	

VEHICLE

	TAG NUMBER	STATE	YEAR	V.I.N.	PLATE ONLY	VIN PLATE ONLY
STOLEN						
RECOVD	YEAR MAKE		MODEL	STYLE	COLOR	
SUSPECTS	MOTOR SIZE (CID)	AUTO MAN. SPD	INSURED BY			
IMPOUND		TRANS.				

WITNESS

NAMES	ADDRESS	PHONE NUMBER
SIMS, WILLIAM	STATESBORO, GA 30458	

PROPERTY

	VEHICLES	CURRENCY, NOTES, ETC.	JEWELRY, PREC. METALS	FURS	PROPERTY RECOVERY INFO ONLY	JURIS. CODES
STOLEN					THEFT/RECOVERY	1 = CITY
RECOVERED						2 = COUNTY
	CLOTHING	OFFICE EQUIP.	TV, RADIO, ETC.	HOUSEHOLD GOODS	DATE OF THEFT	3 = STATE / 4 = OUT OF STATE
STOLEN						5 = UNKNOWN
RECOVERED						
	FIREARMS	CONSUMABLE GOODS	LIVESTOCK	OTHER	TOTAL	
STOLEN						
RECOVERED						

CLEAR ADM

GCIC ENTRY	WARRANT	MISSING PERSONS	VEHICLE	ARTICLE	BOAT	GUN	SECURITIES
	VICTIM WILL PROSECUTE	UNIF. FOLLOW UP	PHOTO TAKEN?	VIDEO\AUDIO	CID NOTIFIED?	FORWARDED TO CID	

REQUIRED DATA FIELDS FOR CLEARANCE REPORT	CLEARED BY ARREST	EXCEPTIONALLY CLEARED	UNFOUNDED	REPORT DATE
				05/27/2016
DATE OF CLEARANCE	ADULT	JUVENILE	CASE ACTIVE INACTIVE X

DRUG

DID INVESTIGATION INDICATE THAT THIS INCIDENT WAS DRUG RELATED? . IF YES, INDICATE THE TYPE OF DRUG(S) USED BY OFFENDER   YES NO X

1-AMPHETAMINE	2-BARBITURATE	3-COCAINE	4-HALLUCINOGEN	5-HEROIN
6-MARIJUANA	7-METHAMPHETAMINE	8-OPIUM	9-SYNTHETIC NARCOTIC	U-UNKNOWN

NARRATIVE

On the above date and time I spoke with Mr. Nicholas Wedlow in the lobby of the BCSO in regards to a custody dispute. Mr. Wedlow stated that per court order he was to gain temporary custody of his son (listed juvenile) for the 2016-2017 school year. Mr. Wedlow stated that the child's mother, Ms.   , has failed to answer his phone calls and has not relinquished the child to the complainant. Mr. Wedlow stated that he lives in Las Vegas and planned on taking his son back to Nevada once custody was granted. Mr. Wedlow requested a report be done for further legal actions.

Deputy William Sims went to the listed location to perform a welfare check on the child. Deputy Sims reported that the child was okay and the child's grandmother was at the house with him. Deputy Sims spoke with Ms. via telephone who stated that she believed that the father's custody was not supposed to begin until the start of the 2016-2017 school year, not the end of the 2015-2016 school year. I called Mr. Wedlow to explain that his son was okay and that Ms.   stated that custody was not supposed to start until the new school year. Mr. Wedlow became angry and hung up the phone.

REPORTING OFFICER	NUMBER	APPROVING OFFICER	NUMBER	ASSIGNED INVESTIGATOR	NUMBER
CAMPBELL, CLINTON TYLER	424	DINELLO, ROBERT CARMEN	17		

CHAPTER 17

THE EXTRACTION

"My father gave me the greatest gift anyone could
give another person: He believed in me."
—Jim Valvano

*A*fter suffering such a disappointing encounter with Billy, Christine, and Officer Sims, my mom and I immediately went to JaRissa's house to regroup. I couldn't believe what had just taken place. It was beyond comprehension how I almost went to jail for trying to follow the temporary order that the judge had ruled as law. I still hadn't retrieved Amarius and we were scheduled to fly to Nevada the next day. I literally didn't know what else to do. I had already gotten the police involved and they weren't able to do anything; in fact, they tried to take me to jail so I didn't feel confident that I could reach back out to them. Karen still wasn't answering the phone and at that point I didn't expect any cooperation from her parents for the foreseeable future. I felt completely defeated. I was so mad that I was just quiet and not talking to anyone. When I did speak to people, I vented to my family members and close supporters. No one had any solutions for me, they could only offer sympathy.

I called Elizabeth and explained to her how I was unsuccessful in the transfer of custody for Amarius. Elizabeth was out of solutions as well. We had done all we could do. She explained to me that since it was Memorial Day weekend, the courts wouldn't open back up until the following Tuesday and there wasn't anything she could do legally until then. This was news that I didn't want to hear! I was planning to fly out the next day and I couldn't afford to wait until the following Tuesday. I had to formulate a plan, and quick!

I reached out to my supervisor in Las Vegas and explained the difficulties I was experiencing. Luckily, they were understanding and granted me more vacation time so that I could remain in Georgia until I was able to resolve my custody transfer issues. That was one of the most frustrating moments of my life. So, there I was, in Georgia trying to retrieve my son and had no idea how I would accomplish my goal since the courts and the police weren't able to assist me. I became extremely desperate. I asked all my family and friends to poll the community for help. I needed someone with some powerful influence in the community to step in and intervene. I knew I had been wronged but somehow, Karen had continued to prevent me from getting custody of Amarius despite a judge granting it to me.

I knew that Mama Deb and her husband Dr. Al Palmer were prominent members of the Statesboro, Georgia community. Dr. Al is an OB-GYN and had delivered a large number of children in Statesboro, including my wife Kayla. I had maintained a great relationship with Mama Deb over the years mainly because I played football with her two sons, Harrison and Brennan in high school. Mama Deb was like a second mother to me. She had been following my custody battle over the years and she was available when I needed to vent to someone. Additionally, on several occasions, she and Dr. Al would meet up with me at a restaurant of my choice for dinner whenever I was in town just to catch up. One of the fondest memories I have with the Palmers is them picking me up from JaRissa's house so that I could attend Chester's funeral with them.

During that desperate time, I knew I could reach out to Mama Deb and vent about my frustrations. She was very attentive and empathetic. Coincidentally, Mama Deb just so happened to know Deputy Noel Brown, who was in charge of civil matters for the Bulloch County Sheriff's Office. I was already familiar with who Noel was because I had seen him in court on several occasions during the numerous hearings I attended for the custody battle. Mama Deb reached out to Noel and explained my inability to get Karen to comply with the court order. She then returned my call, provided me with Noel's contact information, and informed me that he was expecting my call.

I immediately called Noel and explained the circumstances. He was attentive, understanding, and offered to help me resolve the matter. I provided him with a copy of the temporary order, and he agreed with my interpretation of the judge's intentions for the transfer of custody. He asked me for Karen's contact information and assured me that he would reach out to her and get her to comply with the judge's order. About ten minutes later, Noel called me back and provided me with a game plan to transfer custody. He had convinced Karen to cooperate and encouraged her to allow me to retrieve Amarius from her custody. I don't know exactly what he said to her but whatever it was, I was extremely thankful. I assume that he explained to her how she was breaking the law and presented possible consequences if she continued to defy the court order. Noel informed me that the plan he discussed with Karen to transfer custody was for me to meet them at her lawyer's office on Tuesday morning @ 9 o'clock, following Memorial Day weekend. He also instructed me not to go back to their house and try to take matters into my own hands again. I gladly obliged. I was amazed at how quickly he was able to intervene and produce results, after all else had failed. Although I was happy and relieved, I was confused as to why Officer Sims couldn't deliver the same results.

Now that a plan was established for me to retrieve Amarius, I contacted Southwest Airlines to try and reschedule the return flights for Tuesday morning. Since my flight hadn't taken off from the airport yet, Southwest Airlines allowed me to cancel my reservation and use the credits to reschedule the flights. Finally, things were starting to fall into place. My anxiety began to settle. I could rest easy now that I had a plan to pick up my son, my flights were rescheduled, and my leave days were extended. The only thing left to accomplish was to pick up Amarius. The remainder of Memorial Day weekend seemed to pass by at a snail's pace. All I could think about was how close I was to accomplishing the mission. Victory was so near, I could taste it!

Tuesday morning arrived and I woke up feeling 10 feet tall! It was the day that all the hard work was going to pay off! The transfer of custody didn't start off smooth at all but the support I had from the community enabled me to find someone that could talk some sense into Karen. Thank God for the Palmers and Noel. Ma Jen offered to drive me, Amarius, and my mother to the airport after we left Karen's lawyer's office. We packed our bags, said our goodbyes to JaRissa and the kids, and saddled up. On the way to Karen's lawyer's office, I received a call from Noel. "Nick, we're here waiting on you, I want you to pull up in front, park on the other side of the street, and just wait in the car. I will bring him to you." Noel instructed me thoroughly. My heart began racing. A feeling of complete euphoria overcame me. It felt similar to the feeling I experienced as we approached Six Flags theme park when I was a child.

We arrived at her lawyer's office and I parked and waited as instructed. I could now see Karen, Christine, Amarius, and Ericka all huddled up together standing outside her lawyer's office. It was like a scene from a movie. It reminded me of a military family that was saying goodbye to a soldier who was preparing to ship off for war. They were all crying and hugging Amarius simultaneously. It was the saddest group hug I had ever witnessed. Noel saw me pull up... I couldn't hear what was being said but I could tell he was trying to encourage them to break up the huddle and allow Amarius to walk to the car. They weren't responding to him. After a few minutes of them delaying the transfer of custody, I saw Noel reach out for Amarius. He physically had to separate them from each other only intensifying the crying. Immediately after freeing Amarius from their grasp, he walked him over to the vehicle we were in. He helped Amarius climb into the back seat. I was sitting on the driver's seat and I rolled down my window to say thank you to Noel. "Nick, I want you to drive straight to the airport and don't stop," Noel said sternly. "Yes sir!" I replied as I put the vehicle in drive and began to leave. I heard Amarius's cries get louder over my mother's attempts to greet and comfort him.

As I began to drive away, I felt like a Navy SEAL who had just penetrated into enemy territory, saved the life of a prisoner of war, and was taking him to freedom. It seemed like a scene right out of a movie; a happy ending where I had just literally risked my life to save the life of someone I cared about dearly and took them back to the promised land with me. I felt so victorious! Approximately two minutes after driving away from her lawyer's office, Amarius spoke up. "Dad, wait! I accidentally left my phone in my mom's car!" he said frantically. "Mari, do you have any idea how hard it was to get you in this car?! Noel told me to go straight to the airport and not to stop, I'm following his instructions. I'm sorry buddy, but your mom will have to mail it to you." I responded promptly.

Internally, I was happy that he had accidentally left the phone for several reasons. Karen had not allowed me to speak with Amarius on a regular basis when he was in her custody but now all of a sudden, she wanted him to have a phone that she can contact him with directly any time she wanted? Not happening! That seemed like a sense of entitlement to me and I wasn't okay with it. Even if he didn't accidentally leave the phone, I was planning to mail it back to them because I don't feel like a kid his age needs a cell phone. My house, my rules, right? I planned on allowing him to speak to her on my phone regularly, but I was not okay with her thinking she could just call him any time she wanted to. Him having a cell phone wasn't going to be conducive to "Operation Un-brainwash Amarius" that I planned to begin implementing as soon as we arrived in Las Vegas.

The drive to Hartsfield Jackson airport in Atlanta was a three-hour drive. The entire drive, we were reprogramming his mentality and explaining why a judge had to step in and send him to live with his father. He was too young to process why it was happening, but I was confident that over time, he would mature and become receptive to the change. All the while I couldn't help but wonder, *"What would have happened if I didn't have Mama Deb in my circle. Would I have successfully been able to transfer custody without her and her connections?"* Probably not. It dawned on me that Mama Deb had unintentionally allowed me to borrow her White privilege to resolve my transfer of custody difficulties. I am forever indebted to her. I commend her for her ability to care for and help people no matter their race, creed, color, and/or beliefs.

CHAPTER 18

THE TRANSITION

"Dads are most ordinary men turned by love into heroes,
adventurers, story-tellers, and singers of song."
—Pam Brown

After a long day of travel, we finally arrived at our home in Las Vegas. We escorted Amarius to his new bedroom and as soon as he crossed the threshold of the doorway, he broke down crying again. Reality had set in that he was now living with his father and it was too much for him to bear since he hadn't been provided with much time to adjust before the transfer of custody. Throughout the chaos of the transfer it didn't dawn on me that Karen had sent Amarius to me with only one bookbag worth of his belongings. When we unpacked his bag, he only had three pairs of socks, one pair of shorts, two pairs of underwear, and one t-shirt! When she texted me: "If he comes, he won't be taking anything with him," she meant it!

The audacity of Karen not to provide the clothes that my child support had helped accumulate for Amarius over time was neglectful and beyond comprehension. I'm assuming she refrained to provide his clothes in efforts to punish me financially for holding her accountable in court. I also noticed that she didn't provide him with any Adderall that she claimed he needed so badly for his ADHD to help him focus in class. I was a firm believer that all he needed was some structure and discipline. I decided against continuing his Adderall prescription and wanted to try our luck at letting him attend school without taking any medication.

It took quite some time for Amarius to adjust to life with his new family. He didn't understand why he had to come live with me. It was difficult to explain the whys without showing him all of the court orders and the paper trail that led to the custody transfer. This was an eye-opening experience for him because everything I showed him was in direct contradiction of what his mother led him to believe. He was completely unaware that I had been sending child support to Karen, providing health insurance for him, and his mother's police record. It pained me to show him the documentation, but I needed to provide receipts to avoid him viewing me as the big bad wolf any longer. While reviewing his medical records I was curious about his ADHD diagnosis.

I began asking questions about his prescription because I wanted to determine how reliant he was on the medication in preparation for his school enrollment. His medical records stated that his routine dosage required him to take two doses per day. Upon further questioning, he revealed that he wasn't taking the medication as prescribed. Amarius stated that he recalled only taking one dose of the medication every four to five days. Hearing this information raised my suspicions significantly. I continued to review the thick packet of medical records to gain more insight on his prescription history. The records revealed that Karen had routinely requested refills of the medication approximately every thirty days for the past four years. This was very confusing because if Amarius wasn't taking the medication as prescribed, why was it being refilled so frequently by Karen?

Coincidentally, a few days after recognizing the inconsistency between his medical records and the frequency of the dosages he actually took, I received a phone call from his pediatrician in Georgia. "Mr. Wedlow, is Amarius in Las Vegas with you?" the representative from his doctor's office questioned. "Yes, he is, why do you ask?" I responded curiously. "I remember you presenting your court order to us in preparation for an exchange in custody. I wanted to make sure he was with you because Karen just called us and asked to have his prescription refilled." "Oh, really?" I responded. "That's weird because Amarius told me that he wasn't taking the medication very often and she didn't even send his medication with him to Las Vegas." I informed. "Thanks for the information Mr. Wedlow, I am going to file a report with Child Protective services and if she comes in to pick up a refill, I will have her arrested," the representative assured.

I was in complete shock! I didn't know what Karen was doing with Amarius's prescribed medication, but I knew that whatever it was, they were onto her and were about to take action. I also felt taken advantage of because Karen was abusing the medical benefits that I provided for Amarius and taking them for granted.

---

east georgia healthcare center   **Wedlow, Amarius P**

Telephone Encounter

Answered by   Date: 05/26/2016
                                                       Time: 12:14 PM

Caller   Father

Reason   requested for records.

Message   Patient father Nicholas Wedlow- came into my office Wednesday May 25 to get Amarius medical records.
                    He brought the Temporary Order stating child will go live with him in Nevada for one year. Since the mother didn't provide the modified court documents. the M.R. of the child where release to the father. The father address is 10271 Headrick Drive Las Vegas, NV 89166

Wedlow, Amarius PAYTON

Telephone Encounter

Answered by

Date: 06/03/2013
Time: 09:35 AM

Caller   Mother-

Reason   Medications Stolen from Home

Message   Had an exterminator come in this weekend and they stole of of the medication in their home Including the mother and the child's medication.
A police report has been filed, but she can not get a copy for a few days.
She is requesting that her child's Adderall 5mg BID be refilled. It was written on 5/20/2013 and I called Medical Center Pharmacy to verify when it was filled. The Pharmacist said it was filled that day- 5/20/2013.
Mother is prepared to py cash for the medication because she said that her medication was not covered by Tricare either and she had to pay out of pocket for that. Please write a prescription for the Adderral 5mg BID for 6/1/2013 through 6/20/2013- That would be a total of 40 pills.

Mom's number is- 912-531-9640

Action Taken   6/3/2013 9:41:57 AM > Please let me know As soon as possible if you can refill.
Thanks   6/4/2013 9:28:49 AM > prescription given.

Refills   Start Adderall Tablet, 5 MG, Orally, 40, 1 tablet, twice a day, 20 days, Refills=0

Reason for Appointment
1. Medications Stolen from Home

Current Medications
None

ADHD

Treatment
1. Others
Start Adderall Tablet, 5 MG, 1 tablet, Orally, twice a day, 20 days, 40, Refills 0

Wedlow, Amarius P

Telephone Encounter

Answered by

Date: 06/09/2016
Time: 12:15 PM

Caller	mother
Reason	refill
Message	Adderall(Amphetamine-Dextroamphetamine) 20 MG Tablet 1 tablet in the morning, 1 tablet at lunch Twice a day

Action Taken

6/9/2016 12:16:16 PM >   6/9/2016 12:47:33 PM >
Called mother to call back for appt   6/14/2016 2:40:15 PM > after speaking with the father-Nicholas. child had been with father since June 1 in Las Vegas. per father mother did not send medication nor mention child being on Adderall.. child told father he took med only once in a while. he didn't take ever day. After discussion with Dr.] ... .. she wanted this reported to DHR, a case made against the mother and her arrested. there is another child in the home. Talk to Dr. '   - child needs to be evaluated by Dr. in Las Vegas to see if he needs med and if medication is in his system. Nickolas called back with Dr. on Nellis Air Force Base.   ; Dr.   and I contacted the Dr.] however she has left the base, so her patients are being split. Dr.   spoke to the Nurse on Call. patients needs re-evaluation for ADHD. Left message with Nurse to have Dr. record call Dr.   back.

Patient: Wedlow, Amarius P   DOB: '   Provider: 06/09/2016

Note generated by eClinicalWorks EMR/PM Software (www.eClinicalWorks.com)

Despite my efforts to help Amarius gain some understanding, he still struggled to conform—initially. To expedite his transition into life in Las Vegas, we immediately enrolled him in little league baseball. We were still rebuilding financially from the expensive custody hearing, so we weren't in a position to buy him a new baseball uniform and equipment. Luckily, we had a support group that understood our struggles and they sprang into action to assist. Ma Jen, Mama Deb, and JaRissa came together to help us purchase some cleats, pants, a jersey, a glove, a bat, and a jockstrap for Amarius. Mountain Ridge Little League baseball is a program that was located at a ballpark a few minutes away from our house.

Amarius got selected for a team and instantly started making new friends while participating in a sport that he grew up playing in Georgia. His participation in sports was able to take his mind off of missing his mother. I could see spurts of happiness in him that would surface whenever I took him to do fun activities like baseball, swimming, and recreation at the local YMCA. Amarius also made tons of friends in our neighborhood that would frequently stop by to ask him to go play with them at a nearby park. Amarius slowly began to come out of his shell and embrace life in Las Vegas with his new family; but he still showed signs of resentment whenever we weren't having fun.

We decided to take him to counseling. We researched family counselors in our area and discovered a counselor by the name of Lisa Mallinger through a program called Military One Source. Lisa was amazing! Lisa was able to create a comfortable environment for Amarius to air out his frustrations and concerns. Lisa was very honest and unbiased. She was able to sympathize with Amarius and help ease his transition into his new surroundings. After several counseling sessions, Lisa had determined that he was stable enough mentally and that he no longer needed to attend any future sessions.

Lisa Mallinger, LMFT

Las Vegas, NV 89128

Date: August 22, 2016

RE: Amarius Wedlow

To Whom It May Concern,

I first saw Amarius Wedlow in my office on 07/1/2016. He was brought to therapy by his biological father Nicholas Wedlow for counseling. Amarius's biological parents have been involved in a custody battle for an extended period of time, and his father wanted Amarius seen due to emotional distress. Amarius's chief complaint on his initial visit was " I miss my mom and I want to go home". "I love my dad too I just want to go back home and live with my mom and see my dad in the summer". Symptoms of anxiety, anger, sadness, and depressive symptoms were present in the initial session with Amarius. Feelings of grief and loss were also present. In the therapeutic sessions with Amarius we focused on coping skills, expression of feelings, support and structure and symptom reduction. In addition to making new friends, resuming his favorite sport baseball and transitioning into his new family unit.

I am happy to report that Amarius has transitioned well into his new family unit. On recent visits his feeling of grief have dramatically reduced, he has many friends which he reports liking and getting along well with. He reports looking forward to going to school and meeting new people, and he is excited about playing baseball again. At this point Amarius is stable and symptom free and is no longer in need of therapeutic services. If future challenges should present themselves then he may need further support but as of this date he is functioning well. If you should have any questions or concerns please feel free to contact me at (702) 497-8390.

Kindest Regards,

Lisa Mallinger, LMFT

We enrolled Amarius at Escobedo Middle School, which was near the neighborhood we lived in. After a few short weeks, he adapted to his new school and began to thrive immediately! Amarius attended school without taking any Adderall for an entire quarter and earned straight As. This accomplishment was an affirmation for me that he only needed structure and discipline to thrive academically and I couldn't have been prouder! Academic accolades were not only rewarding for us as a family, but it also positioned me as a parent to be more competitive for the final hearing that we would have to attend after the temporary order.

361-Escobedo, Edmundo Eddie Sr MS
9501 Echelon Point Dr
Las Vegas, NV 89149

MARKS, CITIZENSHIP, WORK HABITS

A Excellent	NM No Mark	O Outstanding
B Above Average	I Incomplete	S Satisfactory
C Average	IP In Progress	N Needs Improvement
D Below Average	RP Repeat Tag	U Unsatisfactory
F Failing	W Withdrew	

STUDENT	Wedlow, Amarius		1241182	GRADE	06	REPORT PERIOD		FROM 08/29/2016	TO 10/27/2016

PRD	COURSE	TEACHER	ACADEMIC MARKS 1ST	2ND	EXAM	FINAL	CREDIT EARNED	CIT	ATTENDANCE ABS	TARDY	COMMENTS
01	English LA 6 Block	DREW, JENIFER M	A					O	0	0	Pleasure to have in class. Excellent Student.
03	Science 6	POLITO, MICHAEL J	A					O	0	0	Participates daily. Excellent Student.
04	Math 6	FRY, SUSAN PAYNE	A					O	0	0	Pleasure to have in class.
05	Beg Art	BRUSS, AMY K	A					S	0	0	
06	Computer Literacy	BENISH, ANDREW W	A					S	0	0	Excellent Student.

If you have questions or concerns regarding your child's progress, please call the counseling office to schedule an appointment.

Quarter 1 Report Card

Kayla Wedlow
Nicholas Wedlow
RE: Amarius Wedlow
10271 HEADRICK DR
LAS VEGAS, NV 89166

CCSD

President's Education Awards Program

presented to

Amarius Wedlow

in recognition of

Outstanding Academic Excellence
2017

U.S. Secretary of Education

President of the United States

Escobedo Middle School

Principal

School

Over time, Amarius began to settle in and become more receptive of his new lifestyle. He developed a great relationship with Keimora and Prestigious. His relationship with Kayla also began to improve once he realized that all the bad things Karen said to him about her weren't true. Amarius was able to see for himself how much Kayla cared for him and they began to embrace each other. My mother was pivotal in helping us transition to our new life with Amarius. She did an awesome job of assisting Kayla with cooking, cleaning, and caring for the children when I was at work and Kayla was on the job search. Once Kayla had landed a job and began supplementing my income, we were able to afford for Keimora and Prestigious to attend preschool and afterschool care.

The temporary order allowed us an entire year for Amarius to get acclimated to living with us. Unfortunately, it went by fast. Throughout the year, we experienced a lot of drama with Karen and her parents. We felt like we were walking on eggshells the entire year and wanted to document everything so that we could prep for the final hearing.

Amarius would exercise routine telephonic visitations with his Georgia family. It was frustrating to have to deal with Karen and her parents' opinionated views about how we were raising him. They criticized us about the clothes we brought for him, activities we did together, calling him by his first name Amarius, how often he could talk on the phone, visitations, etc. They critiqued everything! We realized even more so that the differences between how Black families and Caucasian families raise their children were points of contention for our custody battle. I couldn't fathom why Billy and Christine felt so entitled to the decisions being made for Amarius despite the court agreement being between me and Karen. I remembered the conversation Billy and I had when I would reach out to him for help early on in Amarius's life after experiencing difficulties with Karen's co-parenting style. He would tell me to "Leave the grandparents out of it." So why didn't he take his own advice now that I had custody?

The time frame for the year-long temporary order came to an end and we needed to begin preparing for the final hearing. I had kept Mama Deb updated on the progress we had made with Amarius throughout the first year he lived with us. Mama Deb was aware that we were preparing for the final hearing and wanted to help set us up for success. She provided me with the name and contact information of a lawyer she knew, Leslie Cushner, who was making a name for herself in the community. I trusted Mama Deb's judgement based on the influence she had in the community and we decided to reach out to Leslie for a consultation.

Within the first few minutes of speaking with Leslie, I knew that I needed to retain her! She was so professional, knowledgeable, and accommodating. Leslie was very thorough during our consultation which made me very confident in her abilities. Unfortunately, her retainer fee for a custody hearing was $5K. Although I was hesitant to pay that kind of money, I knew the results would correlate with the price. You get what you pay for, right? I relied on my line of credit once again to retain Leslie and it was one of the best decisions I've made during my custody battle.

As we began to prepare for the final hearing, we crossed all T's and dotted all of our I's. Leslie had two legal assistants named Katie Hardewig and Billy Brinson who were vital in the preparation for the upcoming final hearing. I was very confident in the progress that we had made with Amarius over the year he lived with us and couldn't wait to present our case to the judge. I was on a mission to prove that the judge made the right decision when he transferred custody of Amarius to me. Everything was riding on the results of the final hearing! We had grown accustomed to life with Amarius and we had reached a point where we couldn't picture life without him.

Prior to the final hearing, my legal team received word that Karen had recently gotten herself into more legal trouble with the police. We knew right then and there that it was checkmate as far as the custody battle went. Although we rejoiced after hearing the news, we felt sorry for Amarius because he really loves his mom and had to witness her demise. Without going into too much detail about Karen's most recent run-in with the law; she informed me that her infractions required her to serve some time in a residential substance abuse treatment center for drug-related purposes. After conducting some research, I discovered that Adderall's chemical structure and side effects are very similar to methamphetamine's.

Once again, I flew to Georgia to attend the final hearing during the summer of 2017. We arrived in court and I finally got the opportunity to meet Leslie in person. She was a breath of fresh air. Her personality was vibrant, and she even had a sense of humor that eased my anxiety over being in the courtroom. Karen's legal team knew that the odds were against her and prior to the hearing, her lawyer requested to negotiate the terms in hopes to come to an agreement. After about fifteen minutes of discussion, Leslie returned and informed me that Karen had agreed to letting me retain primary physical custody of Amarius! Victory was ours! Although I had anticipated a similar result, it still felt surreal that the custody battle was finally at a conclusion. Once an agreement was reached, we had to present the terms to the judge and put it on record. As we sat and waited to present the terms to the judge, I was impressed with Leslie's promptness with drafting the documentation as she opened her MacBook in the courtroom and made revisions to the final agreement on the spot. We were also able to address Karen's failure to repay the $344 that she had disregarded for over a year from a previous contempt hearing. The judge swore us in shortly after Leslie completed the final product and we put the following agreement on record.

IN THE SUPERIOR COURT OF BULLOCH COUNTY
STATE OF GEORGIA

NICHOLAS J. WEDLOW,	§
	§
Plaintiff,	§
	§
v.	§ Civil Action No. SU15DR303M
	§
,	§
	§
	§
Defendant.	§

CONSENT FINAL ORDER AND PARENTING PLAN

This matter having come before the Court on the Plaintiff's Petition for Change of Custody and Modification of Child Support and Defendant's Counterclaim, and it appearing that the parties have reached an agreement on all issues between them, the Court hereby orders on a final basis as follows:

1.

Custody and Visitation

The parties shall share joint legal custody of the child of the minor parties, namely AMARIUS PAYTON WEDLOW, born 2004, with the Father being designated as primary physical custodian and the Mother being entitled to visitation with the child as outlined herein below. The Father shall have the tie-breaking authority with all issues regarding the health and well-being of the child, including those issues involving healthcare, education, religion, and extracurricular activities.

For the summer of 2017, the Mother shall be entitled to supervised visitation with the minor child from noon on June 20th, 2017 until July 20th, 2017. The parties shall meet at the Bulloch County Sheriff's Department on June 20th, 2017 for the Mother to receive the child. The Mother shall arrange for the child to fly back to the airport closest to the Father's home on or before July 20th, 2017. The Mother shall be supervised by her parents at all times during this visitation.

Beyond the summer of 2017, the Mother shall not be entitled to any visitation with the minor child until such time as she completes a clinical drug and alcohol evaluation and complies with any recommended treatment. Before the Mother may have visitation with the minor child, she shall supply the Father with the results of her drug and alcohol evaluation as well as documentation showing that she complied with any recommended treatment. Further, the Mother shall take at least a ten-panel hair follicle drug test and supply the Father with the results of that test before she will be entitled to any visitation with the minor child.

Once the Mother has completed the requirements described above, the Mother shall have visitation with the minor child as agreed upon by the parties. In the event they are unable to agree, the Mother shall have visitation in accordance with the schedule outlined herein below. However, the Father shall be entitled to request that the Mother take at least a ten-panel hair follicle drug test prior to any visitation period. The Mother testing positive for any drug use in that test shall result in the Father being entitled to cancel that visitation period. Provided that the Mother provides clean drug test results to the Father in accordance with this paragraph, the Mother shall be entitled to the following visitation:

a) Thanksgiving: In all even-numbered years, the Mother shall have the child for his entire Thanksgiving break from school, provided that the child is returned to the Father's home by at least 6:00 p.m. the evening before school resumes. In all odd-numbered years, the Father shall have the child for the entire Thanksgiving break from school.

b) Christmas/New Year's: In all-even numbered years, the Mother shall have the child from the day after school is released for Christmas break until December

26th. The child shall be returned to the Father's home no later than 6:00 p.m. on December 26th. The Father shall then have the child from December 26th until school resumes. In all odd-numbered years, the Father shall have the child from the time school is released until December 26th. The Mother shall then have the child from December 26th until the day before school resumes. The Mother shall ensure that the child is returned to the home of the Father no later than 6:00 p.m. the evening before school resumes.

c) Summer: In all years, the Mother shall be entitled to have the child from June 23rd until July 31st. The Mother shall ensure that the child is returned to the home of the Father on or before 6:00p.m. on July 31st.

d) Spring Break: In all years, the Mother shall have the child for the entire spring break holiday from the day after school is released until the day before school resumes. The Mother shall ensure that the child is returned to the home of the Father no later than 6:00 p.m. the evening before school resumes.

e) In addition to the parenting time schedule outlined above, the Mother shall be entitled to travel to the place where the Father lives and visit with the child for any reasonable period at her own expense. Additionally, the Father shall be entitled to travel to the place where the Mother lives and visit with the child during the summer for any reasonable period at his own expense. The parties shall fully cooperate to ensure that the child gets quality time with both parents and shall work together to accomplish a parenting schedule that is in the best interests of the child. Any transportation costs that arise from the visitation described in this paragraph are the sole responsibility of the visiting parent and are not subject to be reimbursed via child support deductions as described in paragraph (3) herein below.

2.

Other Stipulations as to Custody and Visitation

a) In the event either changes his or her residence, notification of that change will be given to the other party. The notification shall be given, in writing, at least thirty (30) days prior to the anticipated change of residence and shall include the full address and telephone number of the new residence.

b) The parent not in physical custody of the minor child at any given time shall be entitled to have phone contact (including, Skype, Facetime, or similar technology) with the child two (2) times per week provided that said times of telephone contact does not interfere with the child's schedule. Additionally, the grandparents of the child shall be entitled to have phone contact with the child at least one (1) time per week when the child is not in their child's custody. Neither parent shall monitor, supervise, or record the child's phone conversations with the other parent nor allow others to do so.

c) Neither party shall consume alcohol to excess while in physical custody of the minor child nor allow others to do so. Neither party shall consume any illegal drugs while in the physical custody of the minor child nor allow others to do so. Neither party shall use prescription drugs other than exactly as prescribed while in the physical custody of the child nor allow others to do so. Neither party shall use profanity in any conversation with one another or in the child's presence and neither party shall verbally abuse or harass the other.

208

d) The parents shall not hassle over visitation of the child. This undermines the parents' relationship with the child and burdens the child with the guilt of the responsibility for such hassles. It is beneficial that the child experience affectionate care from both parents. The visitation privileges exist primarily for the child and not the parent.

e) For all visitation periods, the parties shall honor the school schedule of the child and the child will not miss school unless otherwise agreed by the parties.

f) Neither party shall have any unrelated overnight guests not related by blood or marriage with whom they are involved in a meretricious relationship while the child is in his or her custody unless the parties agree otherwise.

g) The Mother shall be solely responsible for all transportation costs associated with the child's visitation schedule. The Mother shall book all flights necessary for the child to visit her at least two weeks prior to the anticipated travel date. Failure to do so shall result in the Mother's forfeiture of that visitation period. The Mother shall forward the Father all such flight information immediately upon her booking it. In the event that the Mother fails to strictly comply with this paragraph, including providing the Father with flight information for both arrival and departure at least two weeks in advance of the child's anticipated arrival, the Mother shall forfeit any such visitation period and the Father shall have no obligation to make arrangements for the child to visit with the Mother for that particular visitation period.

h) Failure of the Mother to return the child to the Father on or before the scheduled end of her visitation period shall result in her automatic forfeiture of the next scheduled visitation period.

i)   Neither party shall drive with the child without a valid driver's license and shall not allow others to do so.

j)   Neither parent shall say or do anything to diminish the child's love or affection for the other parent nor allow others to do so. Neither party shall speak negatively about the other party (or any family member of the other party) in the presence of the child nor allow others to do so. Neither party shall use the child to pass messages to the other party nor allow others to do so. Each party shall speak positively about the other in the presence of the child and do everything within his or her ability to encourage the child's love and affection for the other parent.

3.

Child Support

The Mother shall pay the Father TWO HUNDRED AND THREE AND 00/100 DOLLARS ($203.00) per month for the support of the minor child in accordance with the Child Support Worksheets attached hereto as Exhibit "A" and incorporated herein. Said support payments shall be made directly to the Father and shall be due on the first day of each month beginning immediately.

The Mother shall be entitled to deduct one half (1/2) of any airfare expenses actually incurred by her for the child's visitation periods from her monthly child support obligation up to FIVE HUNDRED DOLLARS ($500.00) per visitation period. The Mother shall not be entitled to this deduction unless she is current on all child support obligations as of the date the flight is booked and complies with all notice requirements outlined in the sections regarding custody and visitation hereinabove. The Mother shall provide receipts or other documentation of airfare actually incurred by her immediately upon her booking of such arrangements. Failure to promptly provide such documentation to the Father shall result in her forfeiture of her right to deduct one half (1/2) of such expenses from her child support.

Said support obligations shall not cease until the child graduates from high school or reaches the age of eighteen (18), whichever occurs last. The Father's obligation to pay child support shall be construed as support pursuant to 11 U.S.C. Section 523; shall not be dischargeable in any bankruptcy proceeding; and any collection action of the same shall not be stayed by 11 U.S.C. Section 362.

4.

Medical and Hospitalization

The Father shall continue to be responsible for providing medical insurance for the child. The parties shall be equally responsible for all medical, drug, hospital, clinic, dental, orthodontic, psychiatric, psychological, counseling, and vision care charges incurred on behalf of the child and not covered by said insurance, including any deductible amounts on covered claims, and including any co-insurance payments due. The incurring party will be responsible for sending all medical bills to the other party which will be required to be paid by him/her, and he/she shall promptly remit payment of one-half (½) the total amount of the bill(s) to the incurring party, but no later than thirty (30) days from his/her receipt of same. Once the non-incurring party has remitted his/her one-half (½) share to the incurring party, the full amount shall be the responsibility of the incurring party.

5.

Tax Matters

For 2016 and each every tax year thereafter, the Father shall be entitled to claim the child for all tax purposes. The Mother shall complete an IRS Form 8332 or any other forms necessary to ensure that the Father is able to do so.

IN THE SUPERIOR COURT OF BULLOCH COUNTY
STATE OF GEORGIA

NICHOLAS J. WEDLOW,	§	
	§	
Plaintiff,	§	
	§	
v.	§	Civil Action No. SU15DR303M
	§	
,	§	
	§	
Defendant.	§	

SIGNATURE PAGE FOR CONSENT FINAL ORDER AND PARENTING PLAN

SO ORDERED this **23** day of June, 2017.

_____
Judge Michael Muldrew
Superior Court of Bulloch County
Ogeechee Judicial Circuit

Prepared and presented by:
Leslie H. Cushner
12 Siebald Street
P.O. Box 327
Statesboro, Georgia 30459
(912)764-9055
lcushner@statesborolawgroup.com
Attorney for the Father

Reviewed and approved by:

Attorney for Mother

212

IN THE SUPERIOR COURT OF BULLOCH COUNTY
STATE OF GEORGIA

NICHOLAS J. WEDLOW,　　　　§
　　　　　　　　　　　　　　§
　　　　Plaintiff,　　　　　　§
　　　　　　　　　　　　　　§
v.　　　　　　　　　　　　　§　　　**Civil Action No. SU15DR264M**
　　　　　　　　　　　　　　§
　　　　　　　　　'，　　　　§
　　　　　　　　　　　　　　§
　　　　Defendant.　　　　　　§

CONSENT ORDER ON PLAINTIFF'S MOTION FOR CONTEMPT

This matter having come before the Court on the Plaintiff's Motion for Contempt, and it appearing that the parties have reached an agreement, the Court hereby orders on as follows:

1.

In an Order of the court dated August 27, 2015, Defendant Mother was ordered to pay Plaintiff Father THREE HUNDRED AND FORTY FOUR AND 00/100 DOLLARS ($344.00). To date, the Defendant Mother has failed to make such payment and is in contempt of the Court's previously entered order. The Mother shall purge herself of this contempt by making payments to the Father as follows: 1) The Mother shall pay ONE HUNDRED AND SEVENTY TWO DOLLARS AND 00/100 DOLLARS ($172.00) to the Father within thirty (30) days of June 19th, 2017; 2) The Mother shall pay an additional ONE HUNDRED AND SEVENTY TWO AND 00/100 DOLLARS ($172.00) within sixty days of June 19th, 2017.

2.

In the event the Mother fails to comply with the repayment requirements contained in paragraph one (1) hereinabove, the Father shall be entitled to schedule a show cause hearing requiring the Mother to appear before the Court to explain why she should not be ordered to the Bulloch County Jail until such time as payment is made.

213

IN THE SUPERIOR COURT OF BULLOCH COUNTY
STATE OF GEORGIA

NICHOLAS J. WEDLOW, §
  §
         Plaintiff, §
  §
v. § **Civil Action No. SU15DR264M**
  §
  §
  §
         Defendant. §

CONSENT ORDER ON PLAINTIFF'S MOTION FOR CONTEMPT

SO ORDERED this _22_ day of June, 2017.

Judge Michael Muldrew
Superior Court of Bulloch County
Ogeechee Judicial Circuit

Prepared and presented by: Reviewed and approved by:
Leslie H. Cushner
12 Siebald Street
P.O. Box 327
Statesboro, Georgia 30459
(912)764-9055   Attorney for Mother
lcushner@statesborolawgroup.com
Attorney for the Father

CHAPTER 19

PRESENT-DAY LIFE

"To the world, you are a dad. To our family, you are the world."
—Unknown

*B*eing victorious during the final hearing allowed me and Kayla to focus our efforts on family prosperity. We finally crossed the finish line with the custody battle, and it removed 90% of the stress we had been battling for years! Amarius was finally mature enough to understand that the best place for him to live was with us. My persistence on wanting to be a part of his life made a huge impact on him. He started being open about his appreciation for not giving up on him. Our bond has strengthened immensely, and we've been able to build the father-son relationship that I've always wanted.

Although we won the custody battle fair and square, not everything is unicorns and fairies. The tension between Billy, Christine, and myself still exists. I try my best to be cordial with them out of respect for Amarius, but I'll never forget the way they treated me that day I went to their house to get Amarius. There have also been instances where they've spoken with Amarius on the phone and said things to him that I don't approve of. Amarius has discussed the content of their conversations with me on several occasions because it bothers him to hear his grandparents speak negatively about me. Karen has also expressed her opinions on decisions that I've made in Amarius's life that she doesn't agree with.

I understand that this custody battle hasn't been ideal for Karen and her family, but I am no longer interested in entertaining drama.

My focus is to help Amarius transition from a boy to a man and we don't have time to bicker. If I were younger, I would have handled their gripes and complaints aggressively by yelling and being confrontational. I've learned how to express myself more professionally and so far, it's been very effective. I've written letters to Karen, Billy, and Christine to address issues cordially and respectfully and since then I haven't experienced any negativity on their behalf. I chose to write letters because it allows me to express myself without being interrupted and/ or having to talk over anyone.

Dear   ,

      I hope all is well with you guys. I am writing this letter in hopes that it will allow us to get on the same page. Historically, I have internalized my thoughts and feelings about how you guys interact with Amarius as his grand-parents but I've reached a point where I can no longer remain passive and I feel that I must intervene and establish some protocol for the future. I want to first acknowledge that I understand that you guys were heavily involved with Amarius upbringing for the first 11 years of his life. Additionally, I want to thank you for loving and caring for him over the years. I am also aware that in some cases your involvement as a parental figure in Amarius' life was due to the shortcomings of   and you guys stepped in to supplement her when necessary so that it wouldn't effect Amarius' well-being. Again, I thank you for coming to   's aid and assisting her with raising Amarius. I am aware that your extensive involvement in Amarius' life throughout his childhood is a causal factor in the beautiful relationship that you guys have with him and your wish is to continue building upon that foundation. I understand that   has not been an advocate for my involvement as a father in Amarius' life over the years and I'm afraid that   's lack of communication to you guys about my involvement in his life has skewed your beliefs about whether or not I am capable and or deserving of having custody. I want to clarify that since his conception I have never shied away from my responsibilities as his father. In the beginning I was only 17 when he was born and still a child myself, but I quickly rose to the occasion and owned up to my responsibilities. Please do not associate my early absences in his life with avoiding my responsibilities as his father, I was simply establishing myself as a man so that I can provide for him; unfortunately, that required me to live out of state. Once I was established in the Air Force I was capable of caring for Amarius by myself but at the time .... was a fit parent and there was no need for me to pursue custody. Although I wasn't physically co-located with Amarius, I was still heavily involved with his life by providing child support, medical/dental insurance, clothing, etc. For some time,   and I were able to co-parent peacefully and I was able to exercise the visitations that were awarded to me through our court order. After I got married, that's when I began experiencing difficulties with   not complying with our court ordered agreement. On numerous occasions I remember reaching out to you guys for assistance with getting   to cooperate with our court order. Unfortunately, my requests fell on death ears and I remember L.   telling me to "leave the grandparents out of it" and "lawyer up". I decided to take action legally because I felt like I was being wronged as his father. It was very frustrating and seemed unfair to me during that time because I was required to send child support and medical/dental insurance but wasn't allowed to exercise my phone calls and visitations with him regularly per our court order. Fast-forwarding to now, I have done everything legally required to be involved in my son's life the way I was deserving of all along but it was a very grueling, painful, and expensive process. You may be wondering what the point of this letter is and I am about to sum up its purpose. The reason for this letter is to establish some rules of engagement for how your interaction with Amarius will be in the future in regard to visitations. We have a court order established and I wish to follow that court order to a T since that is the way you guys required me to pursue my involvement in Amarius' life. To clarify, the court order is between   and I, so the physical visitations are designed for her to exercise and not the grandparents. The only visitations I am required to give you guys are telephonically; we have and will continue to provide those for you. Amarius' only request regarding your telephonic visitations are for you guys to initiate those phone calls more often because he is a child and should not be held solely responsible for your telephonic visitation. Most of the time he is focused on his academics, athletics, and household chores so he doesn't always remember to call you guys with his busy schedule. Him and I both will gladly answer the phone for you guys or return your phone calls at our earliest convenience if we miss any of your calls. Furthermore,　　　 has several stipulations to meet before she is granted a visitation with Amarius. See below:

Beyond the summer of 2017, the Mother shall not be entitled to any visitation with the minor child until such time as she completes a clinical drug and alcohol evaluation and complies with any recommended treatment. Before the Mother may have visitation with the minor child, she shall supply the Father with the results of her drug and alcohol evaluation as well as documentation showing that she complied with any recommended treatment. Further, the Mother shall take at least a ten-panel hair follicle drug test and supply the Father with the results of that test before she will be entitled to any visitation with the minor child.

Once the Mother has completed the requirements described above, the Mother shall have visitation with the minor child as agreed upon by the parties. In the event they are unable to agree, the Mother shall have visitation in accordance with the schedule outlined herein below. However, the Father shall be entitled to request that the Mother take at least a ten-panel hair follicle drug test prior to any visitation period. The Mother testing positive for any drug use in that test shall result in the Father being entitled to cancel that visitation period. Provided that the Mother provides clean drug test results to the Father in accordance with this paragraph, the Mother shall be entitled to the following visitation:

Once the above stipulations are met (per our most recent court order), I am more than willing to coordinate a visitation with .... From there it will be up to　　　 to coordinate with you guys if she wants you all to spend some time with him.

Now I'll get into the "why" of this letter...

Amarius spent the first 11 years of his life with and or around you guys prior to me getting custody. He has only been living with us for roughly 3 years which is very minimal compared to 11. My family and I missed out on the majority of his childhood and now that I have custody, I intend on making as many memories as we can with him before he graduates high school and becomes an adult. I hope that you guys understand that the future holidays with him are precious to my family and I.

Numerous times Amarius has approached me after speaking on the phone with you guys and he mentioned several topics that alarmed me. The first one I will address is the fact that you all have tried discussing holiday visitations with him which put him in an awkward position because he didn't know how to respond. The primary reason he doesn't know how to respond to your attempts at getting him to coordinate a visitation is because he isn't an adult. If you all want to discuss a visitation with him, you should be contacting me or my wife and not Amarius. Amarius isn't an adult and does not make his own decisions, especially involving visitations that are not outlined in our court order. Secondly, Amarius has expressed to me how _ _ _ _ has made negative comments about me to him over the phone. One specific comment that _ _ _ _ _ made to Amarius about me is when he said that "I think your father is less of a man if he doesn't allow you to come visit". This comment is very bothersome to me and I find it disrespectful that   would make a negative comment about me to my son.   , you are entitled to your own opinion about me; but if you have anything negative to say about me, say it to me and not to my son. While we are on the topic of negativity, I would appreciate it if you refrained from making negative comments about my family members to Amarius as well. Amarius mentioned that around the time   went to jail he was speaking to   on the phone and he said that "Everyone goes to jail at some point, you remember when your Aunt Claire and Uncle Henry went to jail?" I   , my brother and sister's business has nothing to do with I   going to jail. Amarius doesn't spend a lot of time around my brother and sister so he isn't aware of the trials and tribulations that they go through. Since he isn't around them often, their troubled past has no influence on Amarius in any way shape or form. When you discussed my family's criminal history with my son, it made it seem like you were trying to tarnish his perception of my side of his family. I just find it odd that during that conversation you failed to include how your son I   has also been to jail before.   has spent more time with Amarius than both my brother and sister have combined. You are entitled to your own opinion about my family members, but if you have anything negative to say about them don't voice it to my son.

Another issue I would like to bring to your attention is the fact that somehow pictures of Amarius that I posted on my social media were sent to I   in jail. I would have appreciated it if you guys would have asked for my consent before just taking my pictures and sending them to   . It really bothered my wife when I   told Amarius that I was in one of the pictures that I _ _ _ _ _ sent her.

Lastly, over the years I   has been very confrontational with me. I have tried my best to remain respectful because after all he is my elder and he is also my son's grandparent. My last interaction with   was when I came to your house with my court order on hand in hopes to locate Amarius and bring him home with me after winning primary physical custody. Although   has apologized for how nasty you guys treated me that day, it is still very fresh to me and a moment that I will never forget. It baffles me how you guys enabled   to keep my son away from me pre and post custody battle. Although there is no way to prove it, I truly believe that if I were not successful in this custody battle you guys would still be confrontational and give me a hard time when it comes to being involved in my child's life. My apologies if my allowing him to visit you guys this past spring has given you the impression that him visiting would be a common occurrence. Ever since the custody battle, we have taken Amarius to counseling often over the past few years to adjust to the emotional hardships that this situation has placed on him. He progressed to a stable emotional state after his first few counseling sessions. His emotional well-being is stable during time spent with us but shortly after he returns from a visitation with you guys, he displays a noticeable regression emotionally. This is very concerning to me and one of the primary reasons that I recommend that we follow the court order from here on out.

Karen,

Hope you are holding up well. I am reaching out to you to clear the air about a concern of yours that you've recently voiced to Amarius. Specifically, your discomforts with Mari calling Kayla "Mom". I am taking all responsibility for this. This was my decision and not Kayla's. Allow me to explain the "why" behind my reasoning for this.

First and foremost, Amarius knows that you're his biological mother and we don't discourage him from clinging to that reality. Kayla and I don't talk down on you to him or try to formulate a negative image of you in his eyes. Kayla isn't out to replace you as his biological mother, nor do we pretend that you don't exist. We encourage his relationship with you. We are aware that you are the only biological mother that he'll ever have, and we acknowledge that.

It was my decision for Amarius to call Kayla "Mom" for several reasons:

When Mari first moved in with us shortly after the custody battle, we had to come up with a title that he could use to properly address Kayla and we initially decided that "Ms Kay" would suffice. Very soon after he began living with us, he openly displayed a lack of respect for Kayla and she has never said or done anything to him that warrants that type of behavior from him. Immediately after noticing the lack of respect we addressed it. When he tried explaining his lack of respect, he told us horrible things that you said to him about Kayla. He admitted that your opinion and views of Kayla affected the way he received her new role in his life and it initially created friction between them until he was able to see for himself that those things you said about her character weren't true.

Another contributing factor as to why I encouraged him to call her mom was the awkward conversations we would encounter when my younger two children would ask why Mari calls their mother "Ms Kay" and they have to call her "Mom". Also, other families that we interact with would question us as well when they hear him address her as "Ms Kay" and I found myself constantly having to explain the long story about how we went through a custody battle because his biological mother wasn't following the original court order and now he lives with us blah blah blah....It was exhausting.

The factors mentioned above led to me feeling like I needed to figure out a way to speed up Mari's acceptance of the new role that Kayla plays in his life, limit the confusion of my younger two children, and reduce the amount of explaining I would have to do for other people when they inquire about why Kayla is "Ms Kay" to Mari but "Mommy" to Keimora and Prestigious. I decided to have him call Kayla "Mom" so that my family dynamic would be a more cohesive unit and my younger two children would no longer be confused or offended when Mari doesn't have to show the same respect for Kayla as they do. Him calling her Mom is also a defense mechanism to protect my family's private life which keeps people out of our business and doesn't make Mari seem like an outcast.

Kayla is fulfilling a motherly role in Mari's life right now and the title of "Mom" isn't preserved for biological mothers only. I truly believe that any woman fulfilling a motherly role in a child's life should have the privilege of being called "Mom". This is very common in the lives of foster children, a lot of them call their foster parents "Mom" or "Dad" because they are fulfilling that parental role and how they address them isn't intended to identify them as a biological parent whatsoever; it's the "role" that deserves the title not the DNA. The same goes for me. You briefly commented that if the shoe were on the other foot, you would never have Mari call another man "Dad". I'd like to comment on that. If I weren't handling my responsibilities as a dad and you or Kayla were in a relationship with another man that was helping you guys take care of my children and they start calling him dad I wouldn't get upset. I wouldn't have the right to get upset if I weren't handling my responsibilities as a father and another man stepped into my role and provided for my kids in my absence.

I know you're still probably not going to accept this and may continue to disagree but since you're concerned about it, I wanted to explain my reasoning behind this so that we can try to co-parent peacefully in the future.

Amarius's Interview

"A father is neither an anchor to hold us back nor a sail to take us there, but a guiding light whose love shows us the way."
—Unknown

I felt like I have learned responsibility from the situation because I didn't do chores or wasn't being pushed to be the best in Georgia. I had never done anything like washing dishes, folding clothes, washing cars, cutting grass, vacuuming, cleaning, or organizing my room. Hygiene wasn't really a big part of my daily schedule when I was living with my mom. The change of custody taught me life skills and values such as being responsible and having integrity. The hardest thing for me was adjusting to moving in with my parents because I was so used to living with my grandparents and my mom. The distance from my family in Georgia was tough for me to adjust to, and it was a reality check because I didn't realize that I wasn't in the most ideal situation with my mom. I was overeating, and not exercising as much. Keimora and Prestigious were much younger than Ericka so it took some time getting adjusted to living with younger siblings. At the beginning of the year, I thought I was only going to live with my dad for a year because my mom led me to believe that, and I also wanted to go back and live with my mom. It was eye opening when my dad showed me all the court orders and evidence because my mom was always so vague about everything going on and didn't share the details about the situation with me. I felt disappointed in my mom when I found out the truth, but I appreciated my dad's honesty and trustworthiness; it made me feel like they were concerned about my best interest. I didn't even discuss the why with my mom because I was so brainwashed into thinking that my dad was such a bad person. It was to the point where I kicked a hole in the wall when I found out that I had to live with him, and I was crying for three days. I thought my mom was this perfect woman until getting exposed to the truth. Once the year was up, I wanted to stay with my dad but just visit my mom because I was used to living with my dad by then, and realized that it was better for me to be with them. When I saw pictures of myself when I lived with my mom and compared them to pictures of myself after the change of custody, I was shocked at how unhealthy I looked. Looking at those pictures made me feel like I was living a healthier lifestyle compared to when I was with my mom. When it came to entertainment, my parents' execution was better because my mom was usually inconsistent with having me to practice on time and regularly taking me to games. My dad being in the military provided more structure in my life, and I thought the Air Force's RPAs were cool. Structure helped me with behavior and grades in school without taking any ADHD medication.

Lisa Mallinger was very helpful throughout my transition. Having someone neutral to talk to about the situation made me feel good. I also want fathers to pursue custody and take control if their son or daughter is in a bad position because it can help them in ways their child may not understand at first, but later on if you communicate the why it can be an eye opener. It can expose the child to more opportunities. It was different adjusting to living with a Black family because of the different culture and habits. In Georgia, I was Payton but with Dad, I'm Amarius. I was also used to riding dirt bikes every day and it was different adjusting to Las Vegas. I preferred the dirt roads. The Adventure Dome theme park was my favorite thing to do in Las Vegas and my most memorable moment during my 12th birthday. My biological mom isn't a bad mom at all, but she didn't provide me with a lot of structure and gave me too much freedom. It was a cool surprise when my dad pulled up on me at school, but little did I know, my life was about to take a turn for the best.

KAYLA'S INTERVIEW

"Being a daddy's girl is like having permanent
armor for the rest of your life."
—*Marinela Reka*

The whole process of going through the custody battle was a learning experience and was super stressful at times. It seemed like Karen was constantly coming out on top despite being nasty and very confrontational with us. The most memorable moment was when Nick called me and said that we won custody! I was cleaning the kitchen in our apartment when he broke the news and I immediately started crying and thanking God! As soon as I got off the phone, I called my best friend, Candace, who of course started crying too. The worst moment during this whole ordeal was when they raised child support; we had to readjust our lifestyle so that we could afford to pay the child support. I remember when we were cleaning up the apartment preparing to move; I decided to take a pregnancy test that was just laying around instead of throwing it away and the results were positive! Prestigious was our shining light during a very dark time. All in all, Amarius is my child too and I intend to be a part of his life for as long as I live. No one can stop that from happening!

ADDITIONAL RESOURCES

Recommendations and Lessons Learned

*This list is in no particular order, nor is it all encompassing; but if implemented correctly, these tips will definitely get you on the right track! *

1. Don't give up! Stay persistent… but most of all, give a d*mn about your child!

2. Don't let your frustration influence you to make a stupid mistake out of anger. They'll try to use your volatile behavior against you to make it seem like you're a monster in the eyes of the judge (kill her with kindness).

3. Document everything! Communication, child support payments, doctor and dental visits, health insurance (if applicable), travel itineraries, receipts, text, emails, social media communication, etc. You'll need these receipts to help your case!

4. Pursue joint custody, at a minimum! I strongly recommend retaining a lawyer with experience if you can afford one! aboutthechildren. org is a great resource if you're "pro se", meaning you don't have a lawyer and plan to represent yourself. If things are cordial with your child's mother, just waltz in the courtroom and get the judge to stamp the agreement between the two of you. Another great resource is fathersrightsmovement.us

5. Stay out of trouble! Trust me, you don't want to be in court explaining your police record to a judge.

6. Keep a steady income... you're going to need it!

7. Exercise your visitations (telephonically, video, and physically)

8. Don't miss a child support payment! This is low-hanging fruit for spiteful women. They'll use child support money as an excuse for you not to see your child.

9. If your child's mother gets in legal trouble, obtain a record of the infraction, take advantage of the situation, and use it as leverage in court.

10. Have the police conduct a welfare check on your child if you can't get in contact with your kid! Trust me, this technique was an ace of spades in my case and it helped me locate my child on several occasions when his mom wouldn't answer the phone or return my calls.

11. Hold the mother in contempt of court if she violates the order in any way, shape, or form. Create the paper trail and hold her accountable. She'll push her limits if you don't provide consequences for violating the agreement.

12. Maintain a decent credit score! You'll need it if you plan to apply for bank loans or credit cards; not everyone has retainer fees for lawyers just laying around. Banks are your friend throughout this process.

13. Wear professional attire to the courtroom. Don't go into court looking like a slob.

14. Articulate yourself well in court and speak professionally.

15. Prepare with your lawyer prior to court. It pays dividends to practice your responses for the types of questions you expect. The last thing you want is to get asked a question you aren't prepared for and you respond without confidence and fumble your words.

16. Do your research on the school your child will attend, access to medical care, extracurricular activities, etc. The judge will want to know how prepared you are before he or she gives you custody.

17. For the questions you don't expect; pause and think before you respond and be as honest as possible, but don't incriminate yourself and don't let them see you sweat!

18. Talk to your child about what they want and don't keep them in the dark about what's going on. There is a chance they may have to speak to the judge, and you want them to be prepared for it.

19. Use your resources! It's not always about what you know. Sometimes, it's about who you know! Lean on family members who are in the legal field, people who have connections, the internet, etc. It paid dividends in my case to have people in my corner who had connections and genuinely cared about helping me.

20. Surround yourself with successful people and those that want to see you succeed. Close family members encouraged me to give up at one point. Had I listened to them and not followed my heart, I wouldn't be in the position I'm in today!

21. Don't have children before you're in a position to care for them! My son was born when I was in high school and I was not ready to be a father! Luckily, I was able to get my life together quickly and provide for him. Sometimes, people aren't always that lucky.

22. Encourage your children not to have sex until they're married. If they do decide to have sex at a young age, educate them on how to protect themselves and use contraception. I'm sure you don't want your teenager to end up in the situation I was in as a teen parent.

23. Have patience! Custody battles can be a long, grueling, and expensive process, especially for fathers. Stay consistent, it won't happen "overnight" (pun intended). Realize that mothers have an advantage, and you'll have to prove them to be unfit in most cases to get custody. This takes time.

24. If you have more than one child with multiple women don't be selective with which kid gets your most effort. Pursue them and take care of them equally. Don't pay child support and or care for one, and not give the other your financial support or spend time with them. That's not fair.

25. If you can help it, try not to have children with multiple women! Some women can be spiteful and if they don't like your significant other, they're not going to want their child around them.

26. If you get married to another woman, make sure your new spouse is willing to support your pursuit of time with your child. In most cases, your child came before your new love interest, so if they aren't supportive, then it won't be an easy process. If she loves you, then she should support you wanting to see your kid.

27. If your child's mother promotes a negative image of you to the child, do everything you can to prove them wrong!

28. Attend your child's extracurricular activities, banquets, sports events, school accomplishments, etc. It means the world to them!

29. Maintain a good relationship with the mother's family, friends, coworkers, etc. If they know that you are a good dad and are actually trying to be involved in the child's life, the majority of the time, they will help you stay in contact with the child despite the mother trying to shut you out!

30. Send your child gifts in the mail! Examples: Birthday/Christmas cards, money, toys, etc. If the mother won't let you visit them, you can still make your presence felt through gifts and it means the world to the child.

Father's Rights and the Impact of Joint Custody on the Children

The primary or well-known and accepted definition of *parental rights* is the legal allowances or allocations and obligations stipulating what it entails or is required of an individual considered to be a parent. These responsibilities include the decisions about the child and their welfare, for instance, in medical cases. It also entails protecting the child from harm and other issues such as financial or emotional problems. However, when referring to divorce, parental rights increase to include concerns on custody, support of the child, and their needs and visitation rights, amongst others. There have been massive debates where organizations and individuals are rising to the occasion arguing for or against equal rights for both parents to custody of the child or children in divorce cases. However, whether the father has been interested and invested in their child or if they've neglected them is usually taken into account. After that, the only question remains: What are a father's rights to their child upon a divorce or separation?

The Child's Welfare

This debate's key focus is about the child's welfare in a case where the parents separate but more so, it is to assess the legal and societal assumption that mothers have and should have more rights over a child's welfare than the father. Most of the legal systems in the country and around the world have been accused of being biased in thinking and reinforcing a mentality or belief that mothers are the only birth parents to a child. At the same time, the fathers tag along for the process. A vast majority of the fathers today want to remain involved in their children's lives as parents after their divorce has been settled. Undoubtedly, studies have shown that very few want to sever ties with their children, even when they cannot maintain a cordial relationship with their former partners (Gregg, 2013). There have been a notable increasing number of fathers fighting to be named the primary guardian who determines where the children live and who similarly wishes to have a majority of the access.

Fathers' Rights

However, the undeniable truth and reality of today's judicial system is that even though judges more than often arbitrarily favor the traditional structure of a family where the mother is a primary caretaker and the father the sole breadwinner, decisions of who will serve as primary guardian primarily depends on the depth and essence of each spouse's involvement in the children's lives. In turn, what this means is that fathers equally have rights as long as they meet certain criteria. For example, whether they were involved in their child's or children's lives before the divorce. Fathers are entitled to custody, be it full or joint in any divorce, as long as they can prove a previous interest in their children and their activities or lives (Gregg, 2013). Furthermore, where there are no incidences of neglect or abuse, they also have rights to their children for continuity purposes and also for support both psychologically and financially. Despite the norm or the presumption society has that children need their mother; it is equally true that they need their fathers as well.

Children's Rights

Aside from the fathers, there is another party whose rights and welfare should be paramount and supersede the rest, and that is the child. Divorce or separation of parents has, on many occasions, caused damages to the children—sometimes irreversible, particularly in regard to the child's identity and socialization habits and capabilities. A lot of research is going into the effects of divorce and separation on children where a variety of factors have been uncovered as playing pivotal roles in the studies. Children's change and adoption potential were predominantly influenced by the relationship they had with their parents.

In instances where they were close and there were disruptions noted, they became more of underachievers in school and had poor relations or relationships with their peers strained or withered (Fagan & Churchill, 2012). They also became more isolated and adopted introverted tendencies who additionally had low self-concepts, low self-esteem, and confidence. Furthermore, the literature indicates that the core situational and demographic factors with the highest tendency to influence negative results in the children include personal characteristics such as gender and age. There are also family characteristics that pertain to upbringing and socio-economic status that are relationships and financial status of the family.

Appropriate Responses to Conflict

Other issues that have come up consistently throughout the various studies include conflicts within the family before the separation or divorce, which alter a child's attitudes, behavior, and perceptions about family and relationship building or maintenance (Fagan, 2012). Similarly, the custody agreement in itself can cause concerns as if there is no parity or equal understanding. The child may miss out on the relationship or the value of having both parents making them depressed and suicidal in some instances as they may come to believe the fathers or mothers no longer love or care for them, thus their absence. Lastly, the issue of lack of a consistent and reliable or dependable support system from both or either of the parents is lowering their esteem and creating an emotional imbalance in their lives, which altered their socialization as it creates embarrassment for some and self-hatred for others who may feel responsible in some way, or worse, rejected by their families and thus the world as a whole (Department of Justice Canada: Research and Statistics Division, 1997).

The Negative Impact

The effects of divorce and joint custody vary and are mainly negative, inevitably leading the children down a similar or worse path that is destructive and only ends in their loss academically, socially, physically, emotionally, and also religiously as they lose the faith and belief in such structures and systems. However, it is not a lost cause, and there are a variety of methods that can be utilized to curb, eliminate or remedy the effects of the situations leading to divorce and joint custody where it is inevitable. The current rate of divorce is still high but declining, which is a good sign (Baer, 2015).

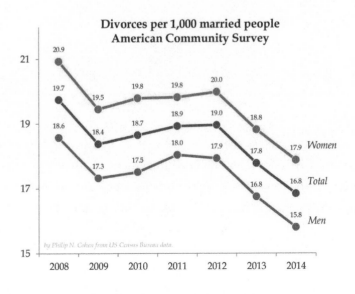

Ensuring A Child's Stability After Divorce

The American community conducted a survey to determine the divorce rates in 2008. It was discovered that divorce rates are decreasing by almost three percent, all dependent on factors like race and ethnicity, education, marital duration, and nativity, amongst others (Baer, 2015). Similar surveys show the significance of having the biological fathers and mothers remain in the lives of the children making joint custody effective and an optimal option as the alternatives do not have positive outcomes on the children. For instance, a past survey on fatherly love amongst biological, stepfathers, and live-in fathers shows there is a major difference in their value addition (Fagan & Churchill, 2012).

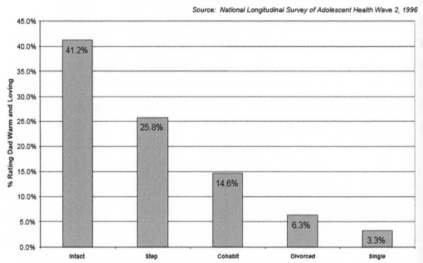

Father Rated Warm and Loving

Source: *National Longitudinal Survey of Adolescent Health Wave 2, 1996*

Therefore, amongst the measures that can be utilized to improve this situation first involves the encouragement of further studies and research into the impact of divorce and custody plans on children. The current information is thin, and thus, neither parents nor counselors are clear on all or the best approach in helping their children adjust to the changes. Similarly, should the ruling be in favor of sole custody, the parent needs to ensure that they are self-sufficient, so the child does not worry or suffer at the loss of continuity in issues such as status they were accustomed (Department of Justice Canada: Research and Statistics Division, 1997). Similarly, the reduced conflict between the separated parents would help relieve the stress and impact as it creates a cordial perception.

Improved Access

Moreover, improved access plans for both of the parents are also useful as it reduces the risks of depression and belief that they have been rejected or pushed aside. Having both parents around as often as possible is good for the transition and also helps maintain the relationship the child has with either and/or both parents. Additionally, a useful technique also entails involving the rest of the family and other parties, for instance, the teachers or a professional psychologist, so that should there be an issue, the child has someone trustworthy to approach and discuss it with (Department of Justice Canada: Research and Statistics Division, 1997). This is critical as sometimes the reactions of the child are negative, leading to destructive behavior such as crime, drug-taking, violence or conflicts, and sometimes a breakdown of moral beliefs and behaviors leading to vices such as early sexual relations. Thus, a support structure becomes critical to their adaptation to the situation in a manner that maintains their balance emotionally and morally.

Establishing Paternity

One of the most crucial steps for fathers seeking children's custody is to establish paternity. In other words, they are supposed to establish that they are the biological father of the children. Unmarried women have the right to sole physical and legal custody of children until their father is identified. It is straightforward to establish the child's mother but determining the child's father is more complicated. Fathers should understand that when the mother acknowledges the child's father, either on the child's birth certificate or through other mechanisms, without other external objections, the child's paternity will not be questioned even though it lacks definitive proof of the father's parentage. When the mother disputes the father's parentage, the father can request a paternity test if he believes to be the father of the child. However, in some cases, the mother may not consent to the test. In such a situation, the father has the right to seek court intervention, where the court may order genetic testing, which tests the DNA of the father and child to find out parentage. When the man petitioning the court is determined to be the biological father of the child after DNA testing, the court will issue a declaration or order declaring him the child's father.

Seeking Custody

Once the court finds out that the man is the child's father, he has the right to seek a child's custody. The father can petition the court to grant joint custody, which allows both parents to spend time with the child. The father also has the right to make crucial decisions regarding the child. However, in almost all cases, the court has the discretion to determine the custody arrangement for the best interests of the child. The father's rights in joint custody can be terminated when the father fails to perform his obligations pursuant to the Court ruling but must be supported by sufficient evidence.

A good example is the court's ruling in State ex rel. Children, Youth, & Families Dep't v. Alfonso M.-E. (Court Listener, 2015), where the trial court terminated the father's rights for failure to maintain weekly contact with the CYFD, give any gift to the child, provide support for the child, and communicate with the child when he was incarcerated. On appeal, the Court of Appeal found that the trial court erred in terminating the father's parental rights since evidence supported the finding that the father was "present before termination and that he expressed a legitimate desire to take responsibility for the child" (Court Listener, 2015). The child's best interests typically determine the father's rights and custody arrangement to be held by the court.

Importance of the Father

Overall, the research has been consistent and unbiased in proposing and emphasizing that fathers are an important part of a child's life and, as such, should have equal rights upon separation or divorce. The research also supports that joint custody is not always successful. Still, nonetheless, it is more efficient and less aggressive in repercussions of identity and socialization compared to sole custody issues when handled correctly.

FAMILY LAW EDUCATION FOR FATHERS

Introduction

According to the U.S. Census Bureau, out of an estimated number of 13.7 million custodial parents, only 17.8% are fathers. The whole world seems to agree that fathers play huge roles in the lives of their children, but when it comes to custody, the pendulum just doesn't swing far enough in our favor. This is why mothers are most likely to obtain primary custody over children than fathers. Paternity rights then subtly degenerate from full access to financial responsibility and streamlined visitation hours, which is a very sad turn of events.

Questions for discussion:

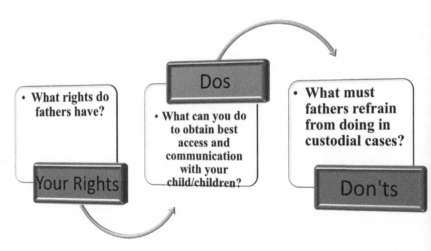

- What rights do fathers have?

Your Rights

Dos

- What can you do to obtain best access and communication with your child/children?

- What must fathers refrain from doing in custodial cases?

Don'ts

Also, how and when can you enforce your rights? These are some of the questions that will be discussed in this section.

What the Statistics Say

The number of visitation hours you will be entitled to as a father depends on the state you reside in, but according to a survey carried out by Custody Xchange in 2018, a father is only likely to receive an average of about 35% of child custody time.

Below is a diagram illustrating the different possibilities and percentage of visitation time that fathers may be entitled to depending on the different states in the United States:

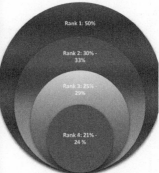

Figure 1

Ranks	States	Percentage
Rank 1	1. Alaska 2. Arizona 3. Colorado 4. Connecticut 5. Delaware 6. Florida 7. Kentucky 8. Maine 9. Massachusetts 10. Minnesota 11. Missouri 12. Nevada 13. New Hampshire 14. New Jersey 15. New Mexico 16. North Dakota 17. Vermont 18. Virginia 19. West Virginia 20. Wisconsin	50%
Rank 2	1. Alabama (33.7%) 2. Texas (33%) 3. Nebraska (32.9%) 4. California (32.8%) 5. Hawaii (31%) 6. New York (30.4%)	30% - 33%

Rank 3	1. Oregon 2. Wyoming 3. Iowa 4. Pennsylvania 5. Arkansas 6. North Carolina 7. Michigan 8. Kansas 9. Utah 10. Maryland 11. Montana 12. Louisiana	25% - 29%
Rank 4	1. Idaho 2. Rhode Island 3. Washington 4. Ohio 5. South Dakota 6. Georgia 7. Illinois 8. Mississippi 9. Oklahoma 10. Tennessee	21% - 24%

However, these statistics and incidences are not entirely due to societal perception. Sometimes, fathers fall short of the expectation of the law inadvertently. **As a father, there are steps you must take and there are factors you must establish in order to increase your chances of winning custodial cases,** be it in court, during negotiations and even outside Court. This Chapter is research-based and specifically compiled to help position dads for more wins in custodial battles.

Preliminaries to Note Before a Custody Battle

There are two factors you must put in mind during early stages because they go a long way to determine your rights and how far they can be stretched regarding custody.

- ☛ **Were you married to your child/children's mother?**
- ☛ **Have you established parentage?**

The answer to the first question may determine if your case will be resolved sooner or with much more stringent criteria.

Children Born Within the Subsistence of Marriage

Please note that if you were legally/officially married to your child/children's mother, you are entitled to paternity privileges and responsibilities AS A RIGHT! What this means is that it is inconsequential whether you are divorcing, going through an annulment, or whether there is a healthy relationship between you and your former spouse, etc. Paternity rights are fundamentally exercisable where spouses have been legally married before, regardless of how long or how short the marriage lasted.

Also note that in 21[1] states of the USA, if you have been married to your child/children's mother before the issues of custody arose, you are entitled to custody of:

- Children conceived or born during the subsistence of the marriage and 300 days after then (they are also presumed as legitimate by the law)

---

[1]   Alabama, California, Colorado, Delaware, Hawaii, Illinois, Kansas, Massachusetts, Minnesota, Missouri, Montana, Nevada, New Jersey, New Mexico, North Dakota, Ohio, Rhode Island, South Carolina, Tennessee, Texas, and Washington.

- Children born before the celebration of marriage if you agreed/indicated interest to allow the child to bear your name and/or to support the child(ren)
- Children you welcome or accept into your home
- All children born within the subsistence of the otherwise void marriage are also yours (if you attempted to marry the child's mother but discovered later that the marriage was invalid).

The above provisions are called the ***Parentage by Estoppel,*** such that you cannot accept the child(ren) and deny them later and as such, you are also entitled to custody as though you were a biological father. To further seal this kind of case, you must have taken positive steps/responsibilities in the exercising of your paternity rights (meaning that you must have cared for the child, and you must have been financially responsible for the child during the marriage).

What is Establishing Parentage?

A father establishes parentage where although he is not the biological father, he has done something in the past that legally gives him the status of a father through which he becomes entitled to all the paternity rights and benefits under the law.

You establish paternity:

1. Where you consent to be enlisted as the father in his/her birth certificate (this is the easiest way to establish paternity, once your name is on your child's birth certificate, you are one step closer to exercising paternity by right).
2. Where you have acknowledged being the father (in writing).
3. Where you are obliged to take care of the child either willingly (supported by written evidence) or by an order of court.
4. If you have lived with the child while he/she was a minor and acknowledged paternity publicly.

When do you have to establish parentage?

Scenario No. 1	Scenario No. 2
Where you were not legally married to your child's mother	**Where you are not the biological father but wish to exercise paternity rights**

In any of the two scenarios above, you have to establish parentage before you can begin any custody moves. Without establishing parentage, you will not be entitled to any paternity rights over that child.

In 42 states[2] of the United States of America, you can establish parentage by taking the following steps:

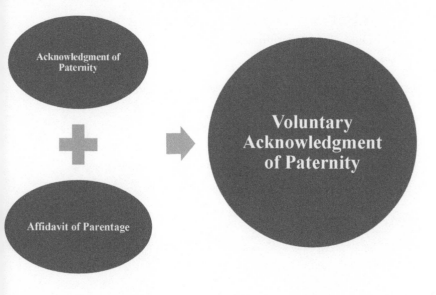

Acknowledgment of Paternity

Affidavit of Parentage

Voluntary Acknowledgment of Paternity

---

[2] Alabama, Alaska, Arkansas, Indiana, California, Colorado, Connecticut, Delaware, Florida, Georgia, Hawaii, Idaho, Illinois, Indiana, Iowa, Kansas, Kentucky, Louisiana, Maine, Maryland, Massachusetts, Michigan, Missouri, Montana, Nebraska, New Mexico, New York, North Dakota, Ohio, Oklahoma, Oregon, Pennsylvania, Rhode Island, South Dakota, Tennessee, Texas, Utah, Virginia, Washington, Wisconsin, and Wyoming

You can carry out voluntary acknowledgment of paternity by filling out the State's Governmental Form, which will be signed by both parents and filed with the Department of Child Support Services Parentage Opportunity Program. When signed and filed, this form bestows upon you the status of "father" and you become entitled to paternity rights as though it were a court order.

To file the form, you will need preliminary information about yourself such as:

- ✓ The names and addresses, social security numbers, and dates of birth of putative father and the child's birth mother.
- ✓ The name and address of any other person who has been adjudged by a court to be the child's father.
- ✓ Information about the child, such as his/her name, and date of birth.
- ✓ Date of registration, etc.

Note: You can rescind your application even after acknowledgement of paternity. Since you are reading this book, I presume rescission is not on the radar. However, if you must rescind, you have to be quick about it because 27 out of the 42 states only provide for rescission within 60 days of your application—after then, you are legally the child's father for life.

Father's Rights in Family Law

So much is said about maternal rights that when it comes to custody matters, fathers start doubting their rights and how far they can exercise them. As a father, you have equal rights as the mother and that is as much factual as it is legal! **However, there are mistakes that may affect how far you can exercise those rights or that may turn the judge**

against you (we will discuss this later in this section). All things being equal, paternity rights include but are not limited to the following:

Right No. 1

Right to have your name on the legal documents: As the father, you have a right to request that your child bear your surname/name. Once you have established paternity, this feature flows naturally and you can apply to the court to have a name change. This application is called **Petition for Name Change.** It doesn't matter if you were present at his/her birth (although this is a much easier way to add your name on his/her birth certificate) or if you have a good relationship with your child's mother.

> In your petition for name change, the court will consider what's best for your child and whether a name change at that stage will be detrimental to the child. For example, if the child is close to adulthood, or if the child already has a business career under his/her former name. Albeit, you have the right to request that your child bear your name.

Right No. 2

Access to Family Medical Reports: As a father, you also have the right to access your child's medical reports and health status. If your child's birth mother is keeping secrets about the child's health, you can demand to know. Once again, this right has nothing to do with the relationship between both parents. You can assert your right in the hospital and demand to see the records.

Furthermore, you can exercise this right by collaborating with your child's birth mother in procuring health care for the child when there's a need. If there is no court order regarding who should bear the cost or make decisions on health care/insurance, it is advisable that you settle it amicably and in the most peaceful way possible.

Right No. 3

Right to visit: As a father, you also have an inherent right to visit and have a relationship with your child(ren). It is this right that serves as a foundation for custody matters. In some cases, we find both parents fighting over who should have the child, and when or how visitations should be made. If you are going through such tussles with your child's birth mother, you should either:

- ✓ **agree on a parenting plan (a time-table for visitation):** If this works, please endeavor to file it in court and obtain a consent order regarding the agreed plan. Doing this ensures that both parties follow the plan and if either party defaults, the other can apply for enforcement or the defaulting partner may be charged for contempt of court order (which is punishable). Either way, registering the plan as a court order ensures that even if the relationship between both parents goes south, the plan will continue to stand.
- ✓ **apply to court for custody:** You can apply to have the matter decided before a court within jurisdiction (where your child resides).

Right to Prevent Relocation:

An extension to your right to visit is the right not to have your child relocated outside the state/jurisdiction. Usually, the court will review the relocation from the light of the best interest of the child, and if such a relocation would severely affect access to the child. The court is well aware that a child needs both parents and any deliberate attempt to deny you access such as relocation to a farther place without your consent will be prevented.

Another angle to this is when your child's birth mother moves him/her to another country entirely. In this case, it becomes a dispute involving international law. Here's how to handle this:

- Institute an action in the original court where custody was determined OR
- Institute an action in the child's home country OR where the child has been a resident, for the past six months (it helps your case if you are based there, too).
- **Speak to a lawyer.**

Summary of this right: your child's birth mother cannot just move the child arbitrarily to another state. You can petition the court if moving affects your visitation rights.

If the child is arbitrarily moved to another country, **The Hague Convention has provisions that support you.** You can apply for your child to be returned to his home country. The USA is a signatory to the Hague Convention, but some other countries aren't. Therefore, you need to speak to a lawyer about this.

Note: If you or the child consent (where he/she has attained majority), there's little to nothing you can do.

Right No. 4

Right to welfare: You have the right to care and provide for your child. Sometimes, the relationship between you and your child's birth mother may have broken down irretrievably and she may desire no contact with you, but she cannot deprive you of the right to care and provide for your child.

If exercising your right to provide for your child becomes an issue, you can apply to the court to have custody determined.

Usually, this right can transform into an obligation where the court orders a specific amount of support that parents should make on a weekly, monthly, or yearly basis.

Benefits of Paternity on a Child

Many times, it isn't about the fathers. It is about the child that we want the best for. The best structure is one where both parents love and care for the child under one roof. But when that is impossible, we must strive to give the best semblance of that structure that we can. Below are some of the benefits of paternity on a child:

a. *Financial support from both parents*

Both parents contribute towards the upkeep, maintenance, and welfare of the child. This ensures that the child receives the best education and life practicable.

b. *Health and insurance coverage from both or either parent*

Sometimes, courts may order that one parent should cover the cost of health while other roles are divested to the other. Paternity ensures that where there is an urgent medical need that requires the pooling of resources; the child won't be stranded.

c. *The right to inherit from both parents*

Furthermore, when you establish paternity, your child earns the right to inherit from both parents.

d. *Emotional support*

Last but not least, establishing paternity gives your child unrivalled emotional support, and a relationship with a fatherly figure. This cannot be underestimated.

A – Z of Custody Rights for Fathers

As earlier stated, the first thing you should do is establish that you are the father. However, it doesn't stop there. You must take steps to indicate genuine interest in being part of your child's life. By doing this, you have started laying the proper foundation to convince a judge to grant you access on clear terms.

Types of Custody

Generally, there are two types of custody:

1. Physical custody
2. Legal custody

Physical custody is the daily custody of the child. The child lives and spends most hours with the parent having physical custody and the parent is granted the opportunity of day-to-day upbringing. Admittedly, there is a very huge chance that physical custody may be granted to the mother of your child, except where you are able to prove to the court that it is either detrimental to have the child stay with his/her mother (emotionally, psychologically, or physically) OR where you can prove that it is in the best interest of the child to have him/her stay with you. In the latter case, you will have to prove that your work schedule and daily routine will be adjusted to provide ample time to care for and nurture the child.

Legal custody on the other hand, is more intangible than physical. You have legal custody where you can decide where the child should live, have his/her education, or what kind of health care services they should maintain, etc. Usually, both parents are granted legal custody of a child.

Best Case Scenario for You: To reach an agreement with your child's birth mother OR to be granted sole custody over your child (both physical and legal custody).

Best Case Scenario for Your Child: Both parents reach an agreement on a parenting plan OR joint custody is granted by the court. (Because a child needs both parents no matter how irreconcilable their differences are.)

Worst Case Scenario for you: Sole custody is granted to your child's mother.

The worst-case scenario above is definitely not admirable. In the next segment on "dos and don'ts for custody cases", we will discuss how to prevent this from happening.

Steps You Can Take to Strengthen Your Case

1. Start being financially involved in the child's life
2. Attend crucial activities such as Parent and Teachers Association/ Meetings.
3. Show up for school activities or sports to support your child

4. Request more time with your child (You can send a text/email asking the mother for additional time with your child; and keep records of the messages. You can tender these as evidence in court).

5. Take deliberate steps to make time for your child amidst work and other activities, and always choose visitation hours that are best for your child and not necessarily at your convenience.

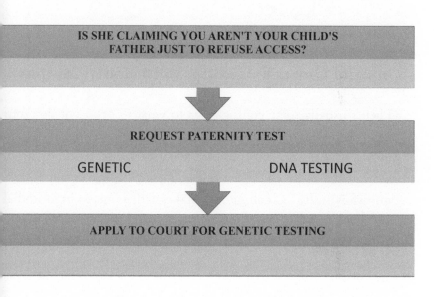

IS SHE CLAIMING YOU AREN'T YOUR CHILD'S
FATHER JUST TO REFUSE ACCESS?

REQUEST PATERNITY TEST

GENETIC   DNA TESTING

APPLY TO COURT FOR GENETIC TESTING

Upon the court's intervention for genetic testing, if the results prove that you are the father, the court order will establish your paternity over that child.

Alternatives to Court Petitions

✓ A mutually-reached agreement

✓ Child custody mediation is available in most states. It involves a mediator—a middle person—who can help both parents decide on a parenting plan that is best suitable regarding their case. This method is inexpensive and faster.

Note: If you are able to reach an agreement with your child's mother on physical custody and a parenting plan, file the agreement in court and obtain a consent order just in case future communication is not amicable. The consent order makes it binding for both of you continually until it is altered by the court.

Do's and Don'ts for Fathers in Custodial Matters

There's usually some confusion as to what to or to not do. Your child's birth mother may already be pressuring you to your limit. All of that negative energy plus pressure from work and expectations all around you can cause you to act out of character. This is why in this section, we will discuss common mistakes fathers make in custodial matters that harm their case and fight against their interest. We'll also discuss some little things you can do that will help you win.

1. **Flexible visiting schedules:** Request flexible visiting schedules that put your child first.
2. **Prove availability:** You have to prove flexibility from your workplace—retrieve a letter from your boss or ask your boss to testify about your **availability** (Especially where you have not been the primary caregiver of your child before).
3. **Do not violate custody and court orders:** Custody and support orders can be modified upon an application to court, so do not be the one to violate it. (Otherwise, you are damaging your case further).
4. **Pay support orders:** Although you still have access, (by right) to visitation even if you haven't paid child support, you should pay. You may be out of a job, but always try to pay something reasonable consistently, no matter how small. This shows you are genuinely interested in the child's welfare.
5. Ask for more time in writing and gather the proof.
6. Do not turn down an opportunity to spend more time with your child.

The goal here is to establish a substantial relationship with your child.

1. Don't do illegal stuff that may affect your case.
2. Do not remain idle; secure a job.
3. Do not take off with the child, regardless of how genuine your ground is (except where real harm is anticipated against the child).
4. Do not violate court orders—this is contempt, and you can be charged for it. (You may even go to jail.)
5. Do not focus on yourself while making decisions that affect the child.
6. Do not withhold visitation or obstruct the flow of visitation.
7. Do not think you can prove your case yourself. Hire a lawyer.
8. Do not talk to the child about the case or ask probing questions. You must leave them out of the custody drama.
9. Do not coach the children on what to say or do at home. Let them live freely.
10. Avoid hateful social media posts about the custody case or things that may hurt the child. Children see these things by incidence or accident, and it doesn't fare well if such evidence reaches the court. You must love the child and allow him/her to groom a relationship with the other parent.

☞ **Advice:** You have the right to petition the court for contempt if your child's birth mother breaches the visiting arrangement but don't do that too often. In order not to appear as the belligerent parent, be as lenient and practicable as possible.

Laws Containing Paternity Rights in the USA

1. Uniform Child Custody Jurisdiction and Enforcement Act of 1997[3]
2. United Nations Ratification on the Rights of the Child 1989
3. New Jersey Statutes Title: 2A Administration of Civil and Criminal Justice; Section 2A:34-12.3: Parent's Education Program
4. O'Donnell-Lamont (2004) of Oregon Supreme Court
5. Texas Family Code
6. Troxel V. Granville (2000) of the US Supreme Court
7. Code of Alabama 30-3-1: Child Custody and Support
8. Family Law of various States

Conclusion

Let's conclude with one move that could never be wrong—speak to a lawyer before you begin. There may be slight variations depending on states, and your lawyer will always know how to best secure your interest.

This concludes this section. If you would like to personally chat, please reach out/contact me via my email at nicholasjwedlow@gmail.com or by visiting my website www.nicholasjwedlow.com

---

[3] Adopted by 49 states except for Massachusetts

More About
the Author

"My father didn't tell me how to live. He
lived and let me watch him do it."
—*Clarence Budington Kelland*

I get questioned by people all the time wanting to know why they call me "Juice". I want to take this time to explain the origin of my call sign.

I'm sure most of you have seen or heard of the movie Top Gun. In this movie, Tom Cruise and Anthony Edwards play the roles of fighter pilots in the United States Navy. In this movie, Tom and Anthony are addressed by their call signs, Maverick and Goose. The United States Air Force has a similar tradition in regard to assigning call signs to aircrew members. Traditionally, aircrew members who have earned the right of passage to receive a call sign must attend a "Naming" ceremony. During the Naming, aircrew members gather together to share food and drinks and share funny stories about the members who are being considered for a call sign. The Air Force tradition is that the story you share about the Namee only has to be 10% truth. You are allowed to embellish the story to increase the humor behind the call sign. Furthermore, members usually receive a name for doing something stupid or a very funny moment they've been a part of. In my case, it was a little different. In fact, my call sign largely has to do with my custody battle.

So, there I was, sitting in the cockpit with my pilot the very next day after finding out that Karen didn't put Amarius on the plane for my summer visitation. I was still fuming and couldn't focus on the mission. My pilot's name was Kareem "Kreamy" Haskett who was a brother from Jersey who had graduated from the University of Georgia. Kreamy was my favorite pilot to fly with and he was a great mentor for me. We spoke about sports, family, and goals when we flew together so I was comfortable sharing my business with him. On this particular night I was so pissed off all I could talk about was how Karen had pissed me off for the last time. I vented to him for several hours about the situation and I'm pretty sure I said some mean things.

Fast forward to the Naming ceremony. A few other guys and I were candidates to be named that night. The goal is to get the Namees drunk prior to being named. We were several shots in by the time it was my turn to be named so I was feeling pretty good. The way it works is several people who have a funny story about the Namee share their story, the suggested name, then everyone votes on the name that you'll receive. You have no influence whatsoever on what call sign you receive. Kreamy volunteered to share the first story and the name he was suggesting for my call sign. Remember only 10% truth. Kreamy goes on to discuss the night I was flying with him and venting about my custody battle. All of a sudden, he tells everyone that I said, "I wanted to kill her!" Everyone burst out laughing. He then ties it all together by mentioning that I was a college football player who wore the number 32 that had a rough relationship with a Caucasian woman. The laughter erupted as everyone started putting two and two together. He then said I think we should call him "Juice".

If you aren't aware, OJ Simpson was a famous football player who had a very controversial murder trial that was televised for allegedly killing Nicole Simpson (a Caucasian woman). OJ's nickname was "Juice". But wait, there's more. Some way or another, Kreamy had gotten ahold of a music video I had filmed before. I used to be into music and at one point I had aspirations to become a hip-hop artist. Kreamy then began playing my music video for everyone to see. After the video concluded he goes on to explain that he thinks my facial features are similar to a mixture between OJ Simpson and Tupac Shakur. Tupac Shakur was a famous hip-hop artist and actor. The icing on the cake was when Kreamy pointed out that Tupac had a starring role in the movie "Juice".

After everyone shared their stories about me, they took a vote and "Juice" won by a landslide. So, there you have it. That is the story behind my callsign. Traditionally, I'm not supposed to share the story behind my call sign unless we are discussing it over a beer; but since it was relevant to my book, I decided to give you privileged access.

Below is the link to the music video that Kreamy shared during my naming ceremony:

https://youtu.be/47vteq7jCDs

… or you can search "Thoro feat Don Rio" on YouTube. The song is titled *"Never Had Sh*t"*

Funny story behind this video… I recorded this video while on active duty. I posted it to my social media account and within 24 hours my supervisor pulled me into the office. My superintendent at the time was Chief Edward Story, aka "Old Swag". Old Swag was a great mentor to me and he typically addressed me as "Young Swag" due to the way I carried myself as a young, fly, ambitious knucklehead. He sat me down in his office and I remember him saying, "I like the video but I need you to remove it from social media because it's not promoting the right image." I was pretty upset because I spent a lot of money during the production of that video and wasn't allowed to promote it. That's when I decided to stop doing music. If I couldn't record and promote the type of music I wanted to make, then I didn't want any part of it. Old Swag, if you're reading this, I appreciate you getting me back on the right track! Besides, I wasn't aware at the time, but I was going to need the money I spent on music for the custody battle I was about to endure.

.

OVERNIGHT FATHER

A secret relationship, hidden pregnancy, and a premature baby that built character and changed the narrative...

NICHOLAS J. WEDLOW

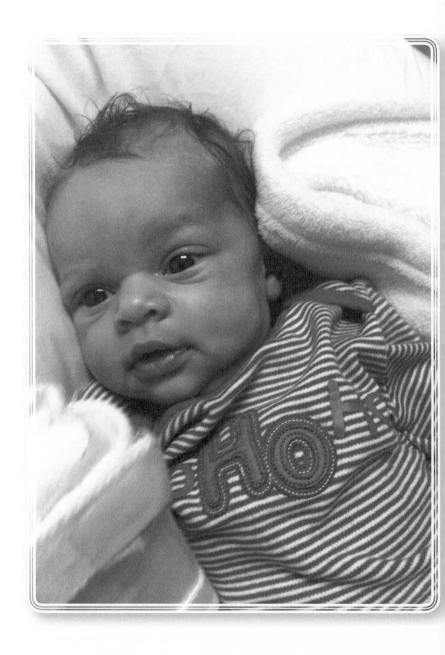

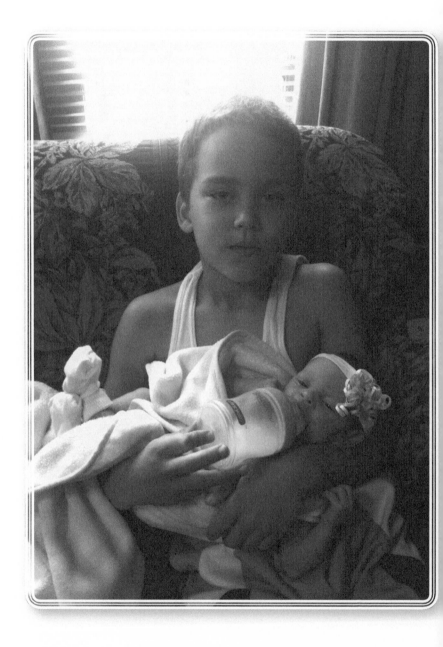

ACKNOWLEDGEMENTS

I want to publicly extend special gratitude to the following:

Kayla Wedlow. Where do I start? You were there to pick me up when I felt helpless. You were my support "group" when no one else seemed to care. You embraced Amarius as if you birthed him and you've continuously been a great mom to all of our children. You stuck around through the good, bad, and the ugly. You encouraged me to share my story with the world. You kept the kids quiet and occupied while I wrote not only this book but also completed a bachelors' degree. You nursed me back to good health when I was sick. The list goes on and on but most of all, I want people to understand that you were there with me every step of the way and a substantial amount of my accomplishments would not have been achieved without support from you! From the ground up! Love you, Chevy ;-)

Connie Alston. Ma! What a strong and admirable woman you are! Thank you for instilling intangible values in me that made me who I am today. You were supportive of everything I did. I can count on one hand how many athletic events you missed throughout my entire life and that is an amazing feat! You made sure I never missed a meal, had a place to sleep, and had opportunities! You stopped what you were doing to assist me even as an adult! I love you unconditionally!

> "There's no way I can pay you back, but the plan is to
> show you that I understand, you are appreciated!"
> —Tupac

Jennifer Blackburn "Ma Jen". Thank you so much for all those wonderful home-cooked meals, the continued support, believing in me, and your witty sense of humor. I really appreciate you flying out to Las Vegas and San Diego to visit for my college graduation and all the other visits you paid us. Kayla and I are thankful to have you as one of our biggest supporters and we love you dearly.

Dr. Al and Debbie Palmer "Mama Deb". You guys are pillars in the medical community of Statesboro, Georgia, in addition to Blue Devil athletics. I can't thank you guys enough for not only supporting me but numerous other students and athletes in our community. Mama Deb, you have played a pivotal role in my life by being available to vent to, referring me to Leslie, and discussing my life's trials and tribulations over dinner at El Sombrero. You are truly a blessing by the way you have pioneered the appropriation of supporting all athletes in the community no matter their race or creed. I consider you guys family and I'm forever indebted. Love you guys!

Shawn T. Blanchard. Shawn, you're one of the best mentors in the game! University of Moguls Publishing company has provided me with a platform, resources, and constant guidance that has guided me through the process of telling my story and I can't thank you enough for the opportunity! For all current and aspiring authors, visit www.universityofmoguls.com to check out the resources Shawn has available to help you publish your own book!

Felishia George Prince, Ed. D. You were a main source of inspiration that motivated me to write my book after seeing you publish *The Class Store*. I remember reaching out to you and curiously asking questions about the process. Your initial support lit a fire inside me. I've always enjoyed seeing your passion as you played the piano and taught choir rehearsal in church. I am proud to call you my cousin and fellow author.

Jeremy. Thank you for all the support, structure, and guidance you provided for me as a child. Falling in love with a woman who has children that aren't your own is a huge undertaking. You owned this responsibility and provided a stable home for me and my siblings. For that, I commend you. Tough love is still a form of love. I don't have any hard feelings toward you for the way you raised us. I only shared my experiences with you as my stepfather in this book to highlight how they shaped me as a parent. Consider this acknowledgement as an olive branch to resolve any contention between us.

Henry Wedlowe "Big Henry". I appreciate your ability to overlook the fact that I was not your biological son. You were the epitome of the phrase "blood couldn't make us any closer". I really enjoyed spending summer visitations with you, and I commend you for providing me with a positive fatherly role-model. I apologize for not keeping in touch with you as often as I should have as I got older, but the truth is that after I found out you weren't my father, I was hurt and confused. I know that isn't an excuse but it's my truth. I have yet to encounter any barbeque ribs that are even close to tasting as good as the ones you made! I hope you are watching over me and proud of the man I've become. Rest in heaven… looking forward to reuniting one day.

JaRissa Brown. Auntie Jaiye aka my bestie! You called it! I remember you telling me that you knew I would get custody before I even filed for a modification of custody. You believed in me when I didn't believe in myself. You aided me when I needed a ride from the airport, a place to stay, a car to drive, food to eat, and a shoulder to lean on! I appreciate your consistent availability when I needed to vent to someone when no one else was available. Sorry you sat outside the courtroom all day waiting to be called in to testify as a witness and it never happened lol. I appreciate you and I love you so much!

Michael Spruill. What up, big homie?! I just wanted to let you know how much I truly appreciated you introducing me to Emily. That referral allowed me to begin the paper trail necessary for me to be where I am today.

Emily Stevens. I remember you told me, "The ones that care never give up!" This was all I needed to hear! Thank you so much for educating me on the process and drafting all the necessary documents to establish legitimation, custody, visitation, and child support. You have become a force in the legal field after all of the fathers you have helped throughout this process and I speak for them all when I say we appreciate you!

Ashley Donaldson "Tank". You're like an older brother to me! You've always been there when I needed to chat or anything whatsoever. Mari and I both look up to you! You have helped ease my struggles with not having a relationship with my biological father and trying to mediate. Also, I credit you for molding me into the running back I was in high school and college. It all started in grandma Della's front yard where we would gather to play football. You placed the pigskin in my hands early on. I latched on and never looked back.

Adrienne and Alysia. You guys have always been tough on me and encouraged me to make something of myself. I only hope that I have amounted to someone that makes you guys proud. Thanks for your unwavering support and guidance throughout this custody battle. I truly believe that without your help, I wouldn't have had the balls to pursue custody! Love you guys!

Elizabeth Branch and Mark Smith. It means so much to me because you guys were the first legal team to recommend that I pursue a change of custody and assisted me with the process. Elizabeth identified early that I had a chance at winning primary physical custody and convinced me to step out on a limb. One of the best decisions I've ever made! I appreciate all the hard work you guys did for me!

If you live near Statesboro, Georgia and want to contact Elizabeth for a family law consultation, please email elizabeth@elizabethbranchlaw.com and tell her I sent you!

Leslie Cushner, Billy Brunson, and Katie Hardewig. When Mama Deb referred me to you guys, I didn't hesitate to reach out and get the ball rolling. During my initial consultation, I knew right then and there that I was in good hands! I appreciate your professionalism and your punctuality which assisted in swiftly bringing my case to a resolution. Thank you so much for assisting me and solidifying a future with my son.

If you live near Statesboro, Georgia and want to contact Leslie for a family law consultation, please email info@cushnerlawandmediation.com and tell her I sent you!

Katrina Brunson-Archie. You were vital to my communication with Amarius during difficult times and I thank you from the bottom of my heart for helping me bridge the gap! You're awesome!

Debra Minick. You coordinated for me to meet with Amarius at your school on several occasions and supported me in my efforts to see my child. I'm ever so thankful for your efforts and assistance with my pursuit!

Chester McBride. A true hero; literally and figuratively, in every sense of the word! A simple deed such as sending me a picture of my son when I wasn't able to see or hear from him consistently meant the world to me, brother! I admired how everything you touched became better. You were such a caring, intelligent, and athletic young king who did everything right. You served your country honorably and I hope you are watching over me and celebrating the victorious conclusion to my custody battle. Rest in heaven, big bro. I wanted to celebrate you in my book so that people continue to speak your name forever!

Sheriff Noel Brown. Your involvement with getting Karen to cooperate during the exchange of custody was the most groundbreaking moment in the entire custody battle. I appreciate your professionalism and your expeditious engagement which enabled me to finally get some well-deserved time with my son. Your swift aid returned some of the faith in the legal system that I had lost along the way. Thank you, Sherriff!

Judge Woodrum. You reviewed the facts of my case and decided to give a father a chance to raise his son. I commend you for your unbiased judgment in this case; your final decision changed our lives for the better. Thank you!

Character reference letter providers. I want to extend my gratitude for sticking your neck out for me and helping me present myself to the judge as a positive role model for Amarius!

Priscilla Romer. Thank you so much for allowing my family to move into your beautiful home which provided enough space for Amarius to come live with us! You were very receptive to our requests and flexible with communication. We appreciate you!

Lisa Mallinger. Lisa, your counseling services were superb and vital to Amarius settling into life with his new family. He felt really comfortable speaking with you which really allowed him to open up to you and begin adjusting. Thank you so much for helping Amarius become receptive to why he had to come live with me! We really enjoyed speaking with you and would refer you to anyone going through similar circumstances.

Go Fund Me contributors. You guys were so organically invested in me spending time with Amarius and I am so thankful and blessed to have people like you in my corner! Without y'all it wouldn't have been possible to afford airfare at the time and together we were able to pull it off. This was one of the most vulnerable moments in my life and instead of judging me you decided to lend a helping hand! It was phenomenal how the community came together to assist a father in need! I can't thank you guys enough!

Last but not least, I'd like to thank **YOU** for reading my story! Without an audience, a story has no life. Thank you for taking the time to learn about my journey as a father. I hope it lived up to your expectations and reached the hands of a father that can use the education provided to assist them with seeing their children!

Contact Info

UNFALTERING F.A.T.H.E.R.S LLC
Families Always Thrive Having Essential Role-Models

nicholasjwedlow.com

📞 **7025692083**

@NicholasJWedlow

@NicholasJWedlow

@njwedlow

Nicholas J. Wedlow

REFERENCES

(Entries with no specified retrieval dates were last successfully accessed on January 4, 2021)

Baer, D. (2015, November 21). *The divorce rate in America is plunging.* Retrieved July 19, 2016, from www.techinsider.io: http://www.techinsider.io/divorce-rate-in-america-is-plunging-2015-11

California Courts. (n.d.). Parentage (Paternity). Retrieved from https://www.courts.ca.gov/selfhelp-parentage.htm

Child Welfare Information Gateway. (n.d.). The Rights of Presumed (Putative) Fathers: Summary of State Laws. Retrieved from https://www.childwelfare.gov/pubPDFs/putativeall.pdf

Child Welfare Information Gateway. (n.d.). The Rights of Unmarried Fathers. Retrieved from www.childwelfare.gov/pubPDFs/putative.pdf

Court Listener. (2015, December 14). State ex rel. CYFD v. Alfonso M.-E., 2016 NMCA 21 Retrieved from https://www.courtlistener.com/opinion/3183669/state-ex-rel-cyfd-v-alfonso-m-e/

CustodyXchange. (2018, June 05). How much Custody Time does dad get in your state? Available at www.custodyxchange.com/maps/dads-custody-time-2018.php Retrieved July 29, 2020

Department of Justice Canada: Research and Statistics Division. (1997). THE EFFECTS OF DIVORCE ON CHILDREN. *Journal of Marriage and Family*, 1-40.

Fagan, P. F., & Churchill, A. (2012). The Effects of Divorce On Children. *Marriage and Religion*, 1-48.

Fagan, P. (2012, November 8). *The Effects of Divorce on Children*. Retrieved July 19, 2016, from worldcongress.org: http://worldcongress.org/wcf2_spkrs/wcf2_fagan.htm

Gregg, N. (2013, March 22). *Father's Rights In Divorce: Myths and Facts*. Retrieved July 19, 2016, from www.huffingtonpost.com: http://www.huffingtonpost.com/natalie-gregg/fathers-rights-in-divorce_b_2903819.html

Justia. (2018 October) Father's Rights. Retrieved from https://www.justia.com/family/child-custody-and-support/child-custody/fathers-rights/

Kiral, B. (2019, January). The Rights and Responsibilities of Parents According to the Views of Teachers. Retrieved from https://www.researchgate.net/publication/330992372_The_Rights_and_Responsibilities_of_Parents_According_to_the_Views_of_Teachers

Stevenson, M., Braver, S., Ellman, I., Votruba, A. (2013 January). Fathers, Divorce, and Child Custody. Retrieved from www.researchgate.net/profile/Sanford_Braver/publication/288260632_Fathers_Divorce_and_Child_Custody/links

Swango, J. (2016, October 03). 7 Shocking Statistics About Fathers' Rights Retrieved from https://www.thefirmformen.com/articles/7-shocking-statistics-fathers-rights/

The Climate Change and Public Health Law Site. (n.d.). The Presumption of Legitimacy. Retrieved from https://biotech.law.lsu.edu/Books/lbb/x650.htm

Wolf, J. (2013 July) Establishing Paternity Voluntarily. Retrieved from https://www.masslegalhelp.org/children-and-families/acknowledging-paternity